RURAL
SOCIAL WELFARE

RURAL SOCIAL WELFARE

Educators and Practitioners

Dennis L. Poole

PRAEGER

PRAEGER SPECIAL STUDIES • PRAEGER SCIENTIFIC

Library of Congress Cataloging in Publication Data

Poole, Dennis L
   Rural social welfare.

   Includes index.
   1. Social service, Rural—Bibliography. I. Title.
Z716.C4P66 [HV67]   016.361'91734   80-28691
ISBN 0-03-059331-X

Published in 1981 by Praeger Publishers
CBS Educational and Professional Publishing
A Division of CBS, Inc.
521 Fifth Avenue, New York, New York 10175 U.S.A.

© 1981 by Praeger Publishers

123456789 145 987654321

Printed in the United States of America

TO MY PARENTS,

WHO HAVE SACRIFICED SO MUCH OF THEIR OWN LIVES

FOR THEIR CHILDREN

FOREWORD

Those who have attempted to conduct research on rural social welfare,
or develop courses on the subject, or organize seminars to explain
current issues in the field have been frustrated as Dr. Dennis L. Poole
was when he began his career as a university faculty member. Materials
on the subject seem plentiful but scattered. For example, works on
rural social welfare only superficially mention key sources in rural
sociology which, in turn, rarely includes references from social work.
Experts on rural health have little to say about the materials developed
in agriculture and agricultural extension which, in turn, tend to
neglect highly relevant historical sources.

Rural social welfare, with its demand for comprehensiveness and inclu-
siveness, now has much of its problem solved because Dr. Poole decided
to do something about it. That something was the development and publication of this annotated bibliography. Now educators, students, researchers, and conference planners have an information source on which
to draw that will lead them, by topics rather than titles or disciplines,
to the major sources currently available.

With this contribution to the literature of rural social welfare, Dr.
Poole has rendered all the rest of that literature more accessible and
usable than it has ever been before. With one complex and intense
effort he has created an information source that is ingeniously organized and better developed than any bibliography available for any other
area of social welfare study.

It is no surprise that Dr. Poole has made this contribution to the field.
He is comprehensive in his approach to social welfare but specialized in
his own way. A native of the Appalachian region and a graduate of the
West Virginia University School of Social Work when its rural emphasis
was at its peak, the author has also studied at one of the least rurally-
oriented insitutions in the U.S.--Massachusetts' Brandeis University.
And he has taught and has conducted research in the Southwest. Dr.
Poole has worked in agriculture and community development as well as
social services so, in his own way, the author has prepared a volume
that reflects his own broad and diverse interests.

Those who care about social welfare in rural areas--students, admini-
strators, educators, practitioners, public officials, and recipients
of services--are all likely to benefit from the industry and creativity
of Dr. Dennis L. Poole.

> LEON H. GINSBERG
> Commissioner
> West Virginia Department of Welfare

CONTENTS

PREFACE

This book is the first comprehensive annotated bibliography for education and practice in rural social welfare since the inception of the field at the turn of the century. Its purpose is to provide educators, practitioners, and students with a knowledge base for theoretical formulations, model-building, research, and effective social welfare practice in rural communities.

An array of literature and training materials can be found in rural social welfare, reflecting the variety of professional practitioners and the diversity of their roles. Practitioners have ranged from caseworkers to community developers; psychiatrists to ministers; regional planners to extension agents. Similarly, their practice modalities have varied from traditional casework and clinical practice to the broader areas of policy formulation, administration, planning, community development, and research.

However, efforts to advance rural social welfare beyond its present state of theoretical knowledge have been severely limited by overlooking the lessons of the past and by neglecting the wealth of knowledge already established in other disciplines. As Emilia Martinez-Brawley has observed, "few are aware of the long and rich history of struggle" in rural social welfare. Furthermore, few have taken advantage of the vast reservoir of useful knowledge that has been developed in such disciplines as sociology, political science, business, public administration, and anthropology. Consequently, the field of rural social welfare has lacked depth in its research, and been plagued with the nagging criticism of re-inventing the proverbial wheel. It is my hope that this book will help us advance beyond this state by providing a knowledge base for our field, and, in effect, promote research and training toward more effective practice in the rural setting.

In writing the book no attempt was made to include all of the literature and training materials ever produced in the broad history of the field. I have taken the position that it is more important that the bibliography be comprehensive in nature; that is, comprehensive enough to reflect both the variety of roles performed by rural professionals and the geographical and cultural diversity of the many rural regions throughout the nation.

A word about the organization of the book. Entries are separated by the general topic and specialization areas that are commonly found in the curricula of schools of social work. The book is divided into ten chapters. Chapters 1 - 5 cover general topics in rural social welfare education and practice: Human Behavior in the Rural Social Environment, Rural Social Research, Rural Social Policy, Rural Human Services, and Planning, Administration and Community Development in Rural Areas. Chapters 6 - 9 provide specialized entries, including Health, Mental Health, Children and Youth, and Aging. Finally, Chapter 10 consists of resources for educators, entitled Curriculum Materials for Social Work Education.

For ease of usage, entries are listed alphabetically by title and num-
bered in consecutive order throughout each chapter. An alphabetical
listing of authors is provided at the end of the book. Users will also
find that several entries appear in more than one chapter, reflecting
unavoidable overlap of content between subject areas.

Most of the entries were identified through library computer searches,
particularly via the Educational Resources Information Center (ERIC),
the National Technical Information Service (NTIS), and Social Sciences
Abstracts. Documents available through ERIC and NTIS can be accessed
through any university or college library, as well as most public
libraries. Some entries were taken from prior bibliographies, with the
kind permission of their authors. These bibliographies include RURAL
WOMEN, by Becky Fowler and Hilda Heady of West Virginia University;
INDUSTRIALIZATION OF RURAL AREAS, by William Linder and the Southern
Rural Development Center; and AN ANNOTATED BIBLIOGRAPHY OF COMMUNITY
RESOURCE DEVELOPMENT MATERIALS, by Mariorana Russell of the University
of Connecticut Cooperative Extension Service. To these authors I am
very indebted.

I am also indebted to many gracious people for the completion of this
book. I thank Francisco Aguirre for his research assistance and help
in preparation of entries. I am deeply appreciative of the unlimited
patience of Donna Smith, who prepared the manuscript and brought a
tedious effort to a pleasant conclusion. Appreciation must also go to
Donald Umlah who, as Director of the Title XX Manpower Development
Project of Arizona State University, provided needed financial support
and patience in the development of this document. I thank Stephen A.
Webster of the NASW Rural Social Work Task Force for his encouragement
and advisement. Finally, I am grateful to Leon Ginsberg, Commissioner
of the West Virginia Department of Welfare, for direction during the
early stages of manuscript preparation and for writing the foreword
of this book.

DENNIS L. POOLE
Tempe, Arizona

FORMAT: SAMPLE ENTRIES

Journal Article

ENTRY
NUMBER ⟶ 57

TITLE ⟶ THE NEW RURALISM: THE POST INDUSTRIAL
AGE IS UPON US

AUTHOR ⟶ Ellis, William N.   VOLUME
                                                               NUMBER
                                                               PAGES
JOURNAL ⟶ The Futurist, 10(4): 202-204. 1975. ⟵ DATE

Chapter in Edited Book

ENTRY
NUMBER ⟶ 80

CHAPTER ⟶ RURAL COMMUNITY CHANGE
TITLE

AUTHOR ⟶ Wilkinson, Kenneth P.

BOOK ⟶ In Rural U.S.A.: Persistence and Change.
                                                               LOCATION
EDITOR ⟶ Thomas R. Ford, ed. Ames: The Iowa
                                                               PAGES
           State University Press, 115-125. 1978. ⟵ DATE

                                                               PUBLISHER

Resource Center Publication*

ENTRY
NUMBER ⟶ 72

TITLE ⟶ THE MIGRANT - A HUMAN PERSPECTIVE

           Washington, D.C.: Department of Housing ⟵ ORIGINAL SOURCE
                                                               RESOURCE CENTER
           and Urban Development. ERIC: ED086412. ⟵ PUBLICATION
                                                               NUMBER

*The user will find that many documents can be purchased in hard copy or
microfiche form through the Educational Resources Information Center (ERIC)
and the National Technical Information Service (NTIS). These can be easily
ordered through most libraries when complete bibliographic information and
publication number (e.g., ED086412 or NTIS/PB 251 676/1ST) are provided.

RURAL
SOCIAL WELFARE

CHAPTER 1

HUMAN BEHAVIOR IN THE RURAL SOCIAL ENVIRONMENT

General Topics

Part A: Individuals, Groups and Families	Part B: The Rural Community Environment
American Indians	Agricultural Mechanization
Anglo Culture	Community Power
Blacks	Defining Rurality
Farmers	Nonmetropolitan Growth
Farm Families	Population Characteristics
Farm Labor	Poverty
Mexican Americans	Religion
Migrants	Rural Community
Rural Women	Rural Life Patterns
Sharecroppers	Rural-Urban Migration

Part A: Individuals, Groups and Families

1
ACCULTURATING THE INDIAN: FEDERAL POLICIES, 1834-1973
Cingolani, William
Social Work, Vol. 18: 24-28. November 1973.

This article discusses the extent to which Indian policies have been
successful in converting the Indian to European culture.

2
ADJUSTMENT TO MODERN SOCIETY BY YOUTHS FROM RURAL REAS: A
LONGITUDINAL ANALYSIS, 1965-1971
Geurin, Virginia, et al.
Fayetteville, Arkansas: University of Arkansas, Agriculture Experiment
Station, Division of Agriculture, Bulletin 280, April 1977.

This report describes the occupational adjustment of a group of Arkansas
males who left a rural area for employment in an urban, technologically
oriented society. Poor correspondence between occupational aspirations
and occupational treatment was found.

3
AFFECT STURCTURE AND ACHIEVEMENT IN A SELECT SAMPLE OF RURAL NEGRO
CHILDREN
Power, Evan R. and William F. Whyte
The Journal of Negro Education, 41(1): 53-56. 1972.

This study examines cognitive and affective relationships among a select
sample of rural black children who were economically deprived.

4
AGRICULTURE NEEDS YOU
Gillies, Jean
Farm Journal, 100: 36-37. August 1976.

Discusses how farming women have helped promote agriculture and its
products. Cites four women's organizations and their activities:
Tennessee Valley Cotton Wives, Colorado Cowbelles, Porkett's and NY
Women for Survival of Agriculture.

5
THE AMERICAN COWBOY IN LIFE AND LEGEND
McDowell, Bart
Washington, D.C.: National Geographic Society, 1972.

The culture of the cowboy in the past and the present is depicted in this
special edition by the National Geographic Society.

6

AMERICAN INDIAN MIGRANT SPATIAL BEHAVIOR AS AN INDICATOR OF ADJUSTMENT
IN CHICAGO
Lazewski, Tony
1976. ERIC: ED124319.

Data derived from interviews with 54 Chicano American Indian migrants
were used to evaluate Indian Urban Adjustment. The analysis was centered
on three measures of spatial behavior of initial and current residential
location, activity spaces, and residential stability.

7

AMERICAN INDIAN MYTHS
Locklear, Herbert H.
Social Work, 3: 72-80. May 1972.

Mistaken beliefs about American Indians have been thriving for years and
are still being perpetuated. The author presents evidence refuting these
myths, explains major problems of the Indian people in adjusting to urban
life, and tells how American Indian Centers are helping them.

8

AMERICAN INDIAN PERSONALITY TYPES AND THEIR SOCIOCULTURAL ROOTS
Spindler, G. D. and L. S. Spindler
Annals of American Academy of Political and Social Science, 311: 147-157.
May 1967.

It appears that American Indians probably exhibit some pivotal and core
features of psychological structure in common, and that these core
features function differently in variant tribal and areal cultures.
The combination of these features in the basic personality structure of
each society appears to exhibit considerable stability through time, and
apparently selectively limits effective choices of new cultural alternatives as long as it continues to function. By reversing the relationship between culture change and psychological structure, one can see that
several distinct types of personality emerge representing various combi-
nations of experience, needs, and results of experience. These types
are cast somewhat differently in the framework of male and female roles
in culture change.

9

AMERICAN INDIAN RELOCATION: PROBLEMS OF DEPENDENCY AND MANAGEMENT IN
THE CITY
Ablon, Joan
Phylon, 24(4): 362-371. 1965.

This paper describes some of the factors involved in the relocation
experience, and analyzes typical Indian attitudes of dependency and
modes of coping with problems of the new urban milieu.

10
AMERICAN INDIAN URBANIZATION
Waddell, Jack O. and O. Michael Watson
Institute Monograph Series Number 4, 1973. ERIC: ED124343.

This monograph contains nine essays on the American Indian in urban
societies, and is an attempt to improve on earlier research. These
essays focus on various aspects of urbanization on different Indian
tribes in the U.S.

11
AMERICAN MOUNTAIN PEOPLE
Washington, D.C.: Prepared by the Special Publications Division,
National Geographic Society, 1973.

This narrative and pictorial account of the lives of American mountain
people from the Appalachians is particularly revealing of their strong
spirit of self-reliance and independence.

12
ASPIRATIONS, WORK ROLES AND DECISION-MAKING PATTERNS OF FARM HUSBANDS
AND WIVES IN WISCONSIN
Wilkening, E. A. and L. K. Bharadwaj
Madison: University of Wisconsin Agricultural Experiment Station
Research Bulletin 266, 1966.

The main focus of this report is upon the characteristics of farm families with respect to their goals, their work and their decision-making
patterns, and upon the comparison of these and other characteristics
between husbands and wives.

13
ATTITUDE AND VALUES IN A RURAL DEVELOPMENT AREA: VAN BUREN COUNTY,
ARKANSAS
Folkman, William S.
Fayetteville: University of Arkansas, Agriculture Experiment Station
Division of Agriculture, Bulletin 650, January 1962.

Chronic low incomes of families in a rural development area were found
to be related to a system of attitudes and values through which individual decisions for action were filtered.

14
BELIEFS AND VALUES IN AMERICAN FARMING
Gulley, J. L.
U.S. Department of Agriculture Economic Research Service ERS-558.
1974.

Topics covered include: ways of change in society, factors shaping agrarian thought, agricultural fundamentalism, technological development,
freedom and independence, institutions and control in farming.

15

THE BLACK MIGRANT: CHANGING ORIGINS, CHANGING CHARACTERISTICS
Miller, A. R.
Washington, D.C.:   Department of Labor, Manpower Administration, 1974.
ERIC: ED126226.

This paper examines the character of black migration, as well as the
significance that migration will play in the future of the black
population.

16

BLACK MIGRATION TO THE SOUTH: PRIMARY AND RETURN MIGRANTS
Johnson, Daniel M., et al.
Columbia: University of Missouri Agricultural Experiment Station,
Department of Health, Education and Welfare, Public Health Service.
1974.   ERIC: ED102237.

The purpose of this paper is to examine the feasibility of differ-
entiating between primary and return migrants within the black migration
counterstream.   The paper focus is on black return migration to the South.

17

BLACKS IN RURAL AREAS: CONSIDERATION FOR SERVICE EFFECTIVENESS
Icard, Larry
In 2nd National Institute on Social Work in Rural Areas Reader.
Edward B. Buxton, ed.
Madison: University of Wisconsin -- Extension Center for Social Service.
68-75.   1978.

In this paper the author makes the argument that since a significant
number of blacks reside in rural areas and since disparities exist between blacks in rural and urban centers, there is a need for professional social work to identify and address skill and knowledge bases
that take into account the idiosyncracies of these people.   Problems,
needs, and cultural aspects of rural blacks are examined in the paper.

18

CHANGE IN FARM TEHCNOLOGY AS RELATED TO FAMILISM, FAMILY DECISION-MAKING
AND FAMILY INTEGRATION
Wilkening, E. A.
American Sociological Review, 19(1):   29-37.   1954.

Based on the assumption that the family and the farm are interdependent,
the author hypothesized that family relationships would affect the
farmer's acceptance of innovations and improvements in farming.   Little
evidence was found to support the hypothesis.   Of higher predictive value
were specific items related to the operation of the farm enterprise, such
as whether the farmer learned most about farming from his father than
from other sources, or the nature of farm arrangements between father and
son.

19

CHANGES IN LABOR FORCE CHARACTERISTICS OF WOMEN IN LOW-INCOME RURAL
AREAS OF THE SOUTH
Terry, Geraldine B. and J. L. Charlton
Fayetteville: University of Arkansas, Agricultural Experiment Station,
Southern Cooperative Series, Bulletin 185, June 1974.

This report describes a study of female labor force participation in
rural low-income areas of the South. Factors included into the description are: migrant trends, female characteristics, work and household status, and occupational distribution.

20

"CHICANOS" AND "ANTI-CHICANOS": SELECTED STATUS INDICATORS OF ETHNIC
IDENTITY POLARIZATION
Miller, Michael V.
Washington, D.C.: U.S. Department of Agriculture, Cooperative State
Research Service. ERIC: ED121501.

The general thesis of this study was that identity polarization tends to
be a reflection of meaningful structural divisions within the Mexican
American population. Social status attributes such as sex, socioeconomic
status, stability of household head's employment, parents' origins, and
migrant farm-labor participation are examined.

21

CHICANOS AND RURAL POVERTY
Briggs, Vernon M., Jr.
Baltimore: The Johns Hopkins Press, 1973. ERIC: ED085142.

The relationship between the rural economy and the general welfare of
Chicanos is demonstrated in this study. The author emphasizes that the
"Chicanos of America are geographically concentrated in the Southwest.
Their high rate of rural poverty has assumed a character that is dis-
tinctly different from the poverty of other regions and other groups.
Any hope for possible resolution of their plight must begin with the
recognition of these differences."

22

COUNTRY WOMEN: THE FEMINISTS OF ALBION RIDGE
Coleman, Kate
Mother Jones, 23-24. April 1978.

Interviews and discusses lifestyle and philosophy of feminist country
woman, owner of farm in Mendocino County, California. Coleman is co-
founder of rural feminist magazine, Country Women.

23
THE COURTS AND THE MIGRANTS
Mahood, R. Wayne and John Hopf
1973. ERIC: ED114232.

The study's objectives were to determine how many migratory farm workers
were charged with criminal offenses, who they were, and how they were
treated in Lay Courts in two counties of New York in 1968 and 1969. A
comparison between migrants and a random sampling of residents in these
same courts were used in the primary analysis.

24
CREATIVITY IN RURAL, URBAN, AND INDIAN CHILDREN
Williams, John D., Johanna Teubner, and Steven D. Harlow
The Journal of Psychology 83: 111-116. 1973.

"Torrance Tests for Creative Thinking" were administered to test the
verbal and figural creativity of five groups: urban-middle income,
urban-lower income, rural children, Indian-lower income children, and
Indian-impoverished children.

25
CULTURAL DIFFERENCES: A MAJOR THEME IN CULTURAL ENRICHMENT
Ballard, Louis W.
The Indian Historian, 2(1): 4-7. 1974.

26
CULTURAL FACTORS IN CASEWORK TREATMENT OF A NAVAJO MENTAL PATIENT
Tyler, I. M. and Sophie Thompson
In Differential Diagnosis and Treatment in Social Work. F. J. Turner, ed.
New York: Macmillan Publishing Co., Inc.: 503-511. 1976.

This article discusses a case in which the importance of the social
worker's understanding of the Navajo language and culture is illustrated.
Information is also given about the Navajo and their mode of living.

27
CUSTER DIED FOR YOUR SINS: AN INDIAN MANIFESTO
Deloria, Vine, Jr.
Toronto, Ontario: MacMillan, 1969.

The author, with wit and insight, presents in a provocative manner the
grievances of today's Indians. He also gives a picture of reservation
life as he relates how the white man has molded and shaped it.

28
THE DESTRUCTION OF AMERICAN INDIAN FAMILIES
Unger, Steven, ed.
New York: Association of American Indian Affairs, 1977. 90 pp.

Unwarranted and unjust governmental interference with Indian family life
is perhaps the most flagrant infringement of the right of Indian tribes
to govern themselves. The essays included in this book examine the Indian
child-welfare crisis, documents the human cost of the crisis, and reports
on innovative programs designed and implemented by Indian tribes.

29
DIFFERENCES IN FAMILY SIZE AND MARRIAGE AGE EXPECTATION AND ASPIRATION
OF ANGLO, MEXICAN AMERICAN AND NATIVE AMERICAN YOUTH IN NEW MEXICO
Edington, Everett and Leonard Hays
Adolescence, 13(51): 393-400. 1978.

Findings of this study in New Mexico included: (a) significant differences existed between ethnic groups in family size expectations and
family size aspirations; (b) significant differences existed between
ethnic groups in age expected and desired for marriage; (c) no difference existed between age groups for expected and aspired age of marriage
or number of children; (d) a proportionately larger number of Native
Americans were not future oriented in aspirations and expectations than
Anglos and Mexican-Americans.

30
DIFFERENCES IN PRESTIGE STANDARDS AND ORIENTATION TO CHANGE IN A
TRADITIONAL AGRICULTURAL SETTING
Fliegel, Frederick
Rural Sociology, 30(3): 279-290. 1965.

This paper reports on data from 142 farm operations in a small farm setting in southern Brazil. The study centers on an index of prestige
standards which differentiate between an orientation to ownership and
consumption of goods and services, and an orientation to giving of time,
resources, and energy. Analysis indicates that prestige orientation
based on giving inhibits the seeking of information about new ideas and
this, in turn, results in non-adoption of modern farm practices.

31
DIFFERENTIAL PERCEPTIONS OF INNOVATIONS AND RATE OF ADOPTION
Kivlin, Joseph E. and Frederick C. Fliegel
Rural Sociology, 32(1): 78-91. 1967.

This study contrasts two samples of respondents with respect to perceived
attributes of innovations to determine the effect of differences in
perceptions on the rate of adoption of farm practices.

32
DISCARDING THE DISTAFF: NEW ROLES FOR RURAL WOMEN
Flora, Cornella B. and Sue Johnson
In Rural U.S.A.: Persistence and Change. Thomas R. Ford, ed.
Ames: The Iowa State University Press: 168-181. 1978.

The basic functions of the rural woman's role, the sources of power and
status, and the future of rural women are discussed.

33
THE DIVISION OF LABOR IN CITY AND FARM FAMILIES
Blood, Robert O., Jr.
Marriage and Family Living, 20(2): 170-175. 1958.

The division of labor in city and farm families was proven significantly
different. Farm women were found to perform a larger share of household

tasks than city wives. Also, more of the farm wives helped their
husbands with their work.

34
EDUCATION, ECONOMIC STATUS AND SOCIAL CLASS AWARENESS OF MEXICAN-AMERICANS
Penalosa, Fernando and Edward C. McDonagh
Phylon, 29(2): 119-126. 1968.

The perception of their own class structure by Mexican-Americans as they
become incorporated into the majority social class system is the subject
of this report. The findings are based on a study of a Mexican-American
population in a rural California community, namely Pomona.

35
EDUCATION FOR SOCIAL WORK PRACTICE WITH AMERICAN FAMILIES:
PART I. INTRODUCTORY TEXT, PART II. INSTRUCTOR'S MANUAL
Brown, Eddie F. and Timothy F. Shaughnessy
Tempe, Arizona: Arizona State University, School of Social Work
American Indian Projects for Community Development, Training and Research.
1977.

The introductory text and instructor's manual serve several purposes in
social work training: (1) provide an introductory knowledge of diverse
lifeways of Southwest Indian tribes to help the practitioner become better
prepared to deal with the social problems of Indian children and families;
(2) develop an understanding of Indian extended families, clan systems,
and tribal social networks and their impact upon tribal members' beliefs
and behavior, (3) relate social work practice concepts to serving Indian
people; (4) provide an account of the unique Federal tribal relationship
and its significance on the lives of Indian people; and (5) provide
information on child/family welfare services available to Indians.

36
EDUCATIONAL NEEDS OF RURAL WOMEN AND GIRLS
Clarenbach, Kathryn R.
Washington, D.C.: National Advisory Council on Women's Educational
Programs, 1977. 71 pp.

Provides thorough review of both federal agencies and national private
sector programs which were directing, or had a potential to direct,
resources toward the education of rural girls and women.

37
THE EMPLOYMENT OF RURAL FARM WIVES
Sweet, James A.
Rural Sociology, 37(4): 553-577. 1972.

Cites reasons for urban women's role in the labor force. Tries to
establish why rural farm wives would work, characteristics of a variety
of individual and areal parameters, sources of income, etc. Uses 1960
census data; finds about 23 percent of rural wives are working. Uses
a multi-variate analysis to determine relationships between employment
rates of rural farm wives and education, family status, characteristics
of area of residence, and husband's occupation.

38
ESKIMOS, CHICANOS, INDIANS
Coles, Robert
Boston: Little, Brown: Vol. 4, Children in Crisis, 1978.

In this volume Coles attempts to describe what it is like growing up not
only poor, but outside the dominant culture in America as children in
the lower castes as well as the lower classes. He argues that the
children of Eskimos, Chicanos and Indians, even more than other poor
children, are discouraged from independence and assertiveness; they learn
to hold back their thoughts, not to take issue with outsiders or to
make their individual presence felt.

39
ETHNICITY AND THE RECOVERY OF REGIONAL IDENTITY IN APPALACHIA
Whisnant, David E.
Soundings, 56: 124-138. Spring 1973.

The author examines a movement by Appalachian people in rejecting the
melting pot ideology and turning to their historical and cultural roots
as a source of pride, strength and political identity.

40
FACTORS IN DECISION-MAKING IN FARMING PROBLEMS
Tully, Joan, E. A. Wilkening, and H. A. Presser
Human Relations, 17(4): 295-320. 1964.

The purpose of this study was to determine how ideas about farming are
communicated and what social, economic, and attitudinal factors influence change in farming practices. The data suggest that non-adaptors
put more value on ease and convenience than on increasing production
and economic return and vice-versa.

41
FAMILIES BEHIND THE AFDC STEREOTYPE
Grendering, Margaret P.
Journal of Extension, 14: 8-15. January-February 1976.

This article demonstrates that the majority of AFDC recipients in both
urban and rural areas do not fit the public's stereotype. Implications
and future directions for extension programs are also discussed.

42
FAMILIES UNDER STRESS: AN INTERETHNIC COMPARISON OF DISABILITY AMONG
SELECTED METROPOLITAN AND NONMETROPOLITAN FAMILIES
Jackson, Sheryl R. and William P. Kuvlesky
Washington, D.C.: U.S. Department of Agriculture, Cooperative State
Research Service, 1973. ERIC: ED086383.

The purpose of this paper was to explore the extent to which differentials in occurrence and degree of disability existed among selected families of different ethnic types. The study revealed that individual and
family disability were influenced more by ethnicity than place of residence.

43
FAMILY AND COMMUNITY ACTIVITIES OF RURAL NONFARM FAMILIES WITH CHILDREN
Bollman, Stephen R., Virginia M. Moxley, and Nancy C. Elliott
Journal of Leisure Research 7(1): 53-62. 1975.

Six factors--resource level, stage of family lifecycle, presence of a
pre-school child, family size, geographic mobility, and employment
status of the mother--were analyzed in terms of their effect on nonwork
activities of families with children.

44
FAMILY INTEGRATION AND RELATED FACTORS IN A RURAL FRINGE POPULATION
Sebald, Hans and Wade H. Andrews
Marriage and Family Life 24(4): 347-351. 1962.

This article deals with the specific problem of the relationship between
the degree of family integration among non-farm families living in the
rural fringe and their level of community satisfaction, social participation, formal education, rural background, length of fringe residence,
age and size of family. Generally speaking, the question asked was:
How does degree of family integration in the fringe family vary with
these seven other variables?

45
FAMILY MOBILITY IN OUR DYNAMIC SOCIETY
Iowa State University Center for Agricultural and Economic Development,
Ames: The Iowa State University Press, 1965.

Family adjustment to change and transition in agriculture is discussed
from an interdisciplinary perspective in this text.

46
FAMILY NORMS, SOCIAL POSITION AND THE VALUE OF CHANGE
Johnson, Cyrus M. and Alan C. Kerckhoff
Social Forces 43(2): 149-156. 1964.

This study focuses on variations in family norms. Nuclear family norms,
rather than modified extended family norms, were more likely found among
men with high levels of education, better jobs, higher incomes and with
less rural experience and more geographic mobility during their lives.

47
FAMILY ROLE DIFFERENTIATION AND TECHNOLOGICAL CHANGE IN FARMING
Straus, Murray A.
Rural Sociology 25(2): 219-228. 1960.

The relation of the wife's characteristics to the husband's occupational
performance is examined. The technological competence of a farmer was
found to be associated with an "integrative-supportive" wife role.

48
FARM LABOR
Fuller, Varden and Bert Mason
In the Annals of the American Academy of Political and Social Science 429.
F. Clemente, ed.: 63-80. January 1977.

Estimates of farm occupations for 1974 imply that the nation's agriculture
is dominantly a self-employment industry. Farm labor in the U.S. lacks
market structure and is seldom a chosen lifetime occupation. Recent
developments in federal policies indicate that farm workers are likely
to receive federal protection equal to nonagricultural workers.

49
FARM WORKERS IN RURAL AMERICA, 1971-1972: PARTS 1-5. HEARINGS BEFORE
THE SUB-COMMITTEE ON MIGRATORY LABOR OF THE COMMITTEE ON LABOR AND
PUBLIC WELFARE. U.S. SENATE 92ND CONGRESS, 1ST AND 2ND SESSIONS,
THROUGHOUT 1971 AND 1972.
Washington, D.C.: Congress of the U.S. Senate Committee on Labor and
Public Welfare. ERIC: ED118327.

This series of hearings covered many topics, a few of which were:
general problem areas affecting the rural poor, particularly the migrant
laborer and his family; the policies and efforts of federal agencies
responsible for providing rural programs; the syndication of farmlands
by conglomerates; and the quality of rural life.

50
FARMING OUT THE HOME: WOMEN AND AGRIBUSINESS
Hacker, Sally
Second Wave 5: 38-49. Spring/Summer 1977.

Documents changes in women's lives resulting from the shift from family
farm to agribusiness. Author narrates experience of attending Agribusiness classes at an Iowa community college. Substantiates the fact
that Agribusiness exploits women. Explores problems of women migrant
workers, whose maternal and infant mortality rates are 100% higher than
the national average.

51
FORGOTTEN AMERICANS: THE MIGRANT AND INDIAN POOR
Bauman, John F.
Current History 64(382): 264-267+. 1973.

The problems of Indian and migrant peoples in adjusting to technological
changes in agriculture and other industries have made it extremely difficult for them to escape conditions of poverty.

52
GEOGRAPHICAL PERSPECTIVES ON NATIVE AMERICANS: TOPICS AND RESOURCES
McDonald, Jerry N. and Tony Lazewski, eds.
Publication No. 1, 1976. ERIC: ED124313.

This publication is a collection of 10 papers designed to constitute
basic lecture topics for a college level course concerned with Native

American human geography and to serve as a guide to published materials and primary data documentary sources on Native Americans. The papers emphasize human geography.

53
HARD TRAVELING: MIGRANT FARM WORKERS
Dunbar, Tony and Linda Kravitz
Cambridge, Mass: Ballinger Publishing Company. 1976.

Discussion of the plight of migrant laborers and their families.

54
A HISTORY OF THE INDIANS OF THE UNITED STATES
Debo, Angie
Norman: University of Oklahoma Press, 1970.

A book which confines itself to the history of Indians in what is now the United States, beginning with the Indians on their homeland and progressing through the twists and turns of federal Indian policy to the present. Factoral and informative, with a comprehensive biblio-graphy. Well-indexed.

55
HUMAN PROBLEMS IN AN INDIAN CULTURE
Dyer, D. T.
The Family Coordinator 18(4): 322-325. 1969.

This article discusses the organization of a class in which reservation Indians attended in North Dakota. The emphasis of the class was on human resources.

56
THE IMMIGRANT CONTRIBUTIONS TO AMERICAN HISTORY
Saloutos, Theodore
Agricultural History 50: 45-67. Jan. 1976.

Discusses the female immigrant's role in agriculture. Poor women, often from Eastern European countries, usually helped in the field along side the men.

57
THE IMPACT OF THE WHITE MAN ON INDIANS
Josephy, Alvin M., Jr.
The Indian Historian 1(3); 7-10. 1968.

58
INDIANS, ESKIMOS AND ALEUTS OF ALASKA; INDIANS OF ARIZONA; INDIANS OF CALIFORNIA; INDIANS OF THE DAKOTAS; INDIANS OF THE GULF COAST; INDIANS OF MONTANA AND WYOMING; INDIANS OF NEW MEXICO; INDIANS OF NORTH CAROLINA; INDIANS OF THE NORTHWEST; INDIANS OF OKLAHOMA; INDIANS OF THE CENTRAL PLAINS; INDIANS OF THE GREAT LAKES; INDIANS OF THE LOWER PLATEAU; AND INDIANS OF THE EASTERN SEABOARD
Washington, D.C.: U.S. Government Printing Office, 20402 (15¢ ea.)

A series of booklets describing the culture and history of these tribes.

59

INFLUENCE OF FAMILY DISABILITY ON SOCIAL ORIENTATIONS OF HOMEMAKERS
AMONG DIFFERENT ETHNIC POPULATIONS: SOUTHERN BLACK, WESTERN MEXICAN
FARM MIGRANT AND EASTERN WHITE RURAL FAMILIES
Jackson, Sheryl R. and William P. Kuvlesky
Washington, D.C.: U.S. Department of Agriculture, Cooperative State
Research Service, 1973. ERIC: ED085168.

The research explored whether or not the occurrence and degree of family
disability introduced a distinguishable patterned set of social life
among homemakers and, if so, to what extent the problems are general to
different populations. Disability was defined as the inability to assume
expected roles.

60

INFORMATION SOURCE AND NEED HIERARCHIES OF AN ADULT POPULATION IN FIVE
MICHIGAN COUNTIES
Reiger, Jon H. and Robert C. Anderson
Adult Education Journal, 18(3): 155-175. 1968.

A 1965 survey of five rural counties in Michigan was used to analyze
hierarchial patterns of information needs and information sources by
residence (urban and rural), education, age and sex.

61

JOINT DECISION-MAKING IN FARM FAMILIES AS A FUNCTION OF STATUS AND ROLE
Wilkening, E. A.
American Sociological Review, 23(2): 187-192. 1958.

The roles of husband and wife in decision-making were found to be
determined more by their perceived needs of farm and household than by
culturally determined patterns.

62

LABOR FORCE CHARACTERISTICS OF NON-METROPOLITAN WOMEN
O'Leary, Jeanne M.
Associates of the National Agricultural Library, New Series, 2(2): 22-27.
1977.

Rate for labor force participation is lower than in urban areas. Recommends increased federal attention to the growing importance of the
participation of rural women in the labor force.

63

LEADERSHIP AND RESISTANCE TO CHANGE: A CASE FROM AN UNDERDEVELOPED AREA
Fathi, Asghar
Rural Sociology, 30(2): 204-212. 1965.

This paper makes a distinction between "opinion leadership" and traditional leadership in the process of directed change in underdeveloped
areas. Using the case study method, an attempt is made to demonstrate
that each of the two types of leadership is suited to a specific
situation.

64

LINKAGE OF MEXICO AND THE UNITED STATES. STUDY BASED ON MODIFIED
PROBABILITY SAMPLES OF RURAL MICHIGAN, THE U.S. GENERAL PUBLIC, SPANISH-
SPEAKING LATINOS OF THE SOUTHWESTERN UNITED STATES, URBAN MEXICO, AND
RURAL MEXICO
East Lansing: Michigan State University. Agricultural Experiment
Station, AES-R-BULL--14, 1976. 90 pp. ERIC: ED075124.

This study was based on modified probability samples of rural Michigan,
the U.S. general public, Spanish-speaking Latinos of the southwestern
United States, urban Mexico, and rural Mexico. Hypotheses concerning
the potential collaboration of citizens of the U.S. and Mexico were
tested. The findings are discussed under the following chapter titles:
"Factors of Knowledge and Mass Communication"; "Actual Behavioral
Linkages"; "Attitudes Toward the Across the Border Linkages with that
Country"; "Desire for Linkage and Collaboration" and "The Meaning of
the Linkage-Contrast of Mexico and the United States."

65

LOCUS OF CONTROL DIFFERENCES BETWEEN RURAL AMERICAN INDIAN AND WHITE
CHILDREN
Tyler, John D. and David N. Holsinger
The Journal of Social Psychology, 95: 149-155. 1975.

The data of the study support the hypothesis that culturally disadvantaged
children are more externally controlled than white children.

66

A LONGITUDINAL STUDY OF THE ECONOMIC ABSORPTION AND CULTURAL INTEGRATION
OF MEXICAN AMERICAN AND NEGRO IMMIGRANTS TO RACINE, WISCONSIN
Shannon, Lyle W., et al.
1974. ERIC: ED099449.

This study, which began in 1958, focuses on the social and economic status
of Mexican-American and Negro immigrants. The researchers concluded that
the socioeconomic status of Mexican-American and Negro immigrants was a
matter of concern to the entire community rather than an adjustment
problem of the residents of the Barrio, and a problem related to the
organization of individuals.

67

THE MEXICAN AMERICAN MIGRANT WORKER - CULTURE AND POWERLESSNESS
Galarza, Ernesto
Integrated Education, 9(2): 17-21. 1971. ERIC: EJ035552.

Short excerpts from the author's testimony before the subcommittee on
migratory labor of the Senate Committee on Labor and Public Welfare on
July 28, 1969.

68

MEXICAN AMERICANS, CHICANOS, AND OTHERS: ETHNIC SELF-IDENTIFICATION AND
SELECTED SOCIAL ATTRIBUTES OF RURAL TEXAS YOUTH
Miller, Michael V.
Rural Sociology 41(2): 234-247. 1976. ERIC: EJ150541.

This paper explores ethnic self-identification among youths residing in
a relatively homogenous area of south Texas, tests the generalizability
of past findings and examines several factors not considered in previous
research.

69

MEXICAN WOMEN ADAPT TO MIGRATION
Melville, Margarita B.
International Migration Review 12(2): 225-235. 1978. ERIC: EJ186212.

This study focuses on recent Mexican female migrants to the city of
Houston. It determines the strategies used by these migrants to cope
with the stress of migration.

70

MIGRANT AGRICULTURAL WORKERS IN AMERICA'S NORTHEAST
Friedland, William H. and Dorothy Nelkin
1971. ERIC: ED085157.

The study explores the migrant labor system as it operates in northeastern United States. It is concerned with how the system affects life
in migrant labor crews, the details of daily routine, and the problems
and adjustments made by the people to the circumstances in which they
live.

71

MIGRANT FARM WORKERS IN NORTHWESTERN OHIO
Howell, James D. et al.
1971. ERIC: ED065228.

The basis for this study was the employee and employer aspects of the
Mexican-American migrant farm workers. Sociological profile data, wage
earnings of migrants, migrant opinion about housing and employment,
educational progress of migrant children, and growers' views about the
role of migrant laborers.

72

THE MIGRANT - A HUMAN PERSPECTIVE
Washington, D.C.: Department of Housing and Urban Development.
ERIC: ED086412.

This report inventories and analyzes the housing needs of the region's
migrant population. Attention is given to education, training, health,
social services, and recreation.

73

MIGRANT WORKERS (A BIBLIOGRAPHY OF ABSTRACTS)
Kenton, Edith
Springfield, Va.: National Technical Information Service, July 1979.
86 pp.

Needs and problems of the migrant worker are reviewed. Aspects include
medical and health care, housing, employment, education needs and the
interaction of the migrant and the community. This updated bibliography
contains 78 abstracts.

74

MIGRANT WORKERS (A BIBLIOGRAPHY WITH ABSTRACTS)
Young, Mary E.
Springfield, Va.: National Technical Information Service, April 1978.
74 pp. NTIS/PB-277 813/2ST.

Needs and problems of the migrant worker are reviewed. Aspects include
medical and health care, housing, employment, education needs and the
interaction of the migrant and the community. This updated bibliography
contains 60 abstracts.

75

THE PLIGHT OF WOMEN IN UPSTATE NEW YORK
Syracuse, New York: Syracuse University School of Social Work and
Maxwell Non-Violent Studies. 1976.

Conference proceedings from April 2, 1976. Changes needed to help women
of rural America include revitalization of the areas themselves; health
care; transportation; housing; an agricultural cooperative extension
model for services/programs; and research specifically on the subject of
rural women. Traditional sex roles ascribed to rural women must be
modified.

76

PLURAL SOCIETY IN THE SOUTHWEST
Spicer, Edward M. and Raymond H. Thompson, eds.
Albuquerque: University of New Mexico Press, 1972.

This text is an excellent collection of readings for understanding the
three basic cultural identities in the Southwest: the Indian, the
Mexican, and the Anglo-American (including Mormons). The problems and
prospects of pluralism and pluralist policies/programs are also
examined.

77

A POVERTY CASE: THE ANALGESIC SUBCULTURE OF THE SOUTHERN APPALACHIANS
Ball, Richard
American Sociological Review, 33(6): 885-895. 1968.

The author argues that social planners often fail to understand and deal
with the folk subcultures of Southern Appalachians because they have
nonrational responses to situations, rather than the rationalistic ones
of social planners.

78
POVERTY, RURAL POVERTY AND MINORITY GROUPS LIVING IN RURAL POVERTY, AN
ANNOTATED BIBLIOGRAPHY
Institute for Rural America in Association with Spindletop Research,
June 1969.

This bibliography contains generally representative entries for each of
a number of topics under three headings: Poverty in the United States;
Rural Poverty; and Minority Groups Living in Rural Poverty.

79
POWER STRUCTURE AND DECISION-MAKING IN A MEXICAN BORDER CITY
Klapp, Orrin E. and Vincent L. Padget
The American Journal of Sociology 65(4): 400-406. 1960.

A reputational study of the local power structure of Tijuana shows the
elite to be composed mainly of businessmen, though no single group runs
things; local government is weak; and the major power sources are outside the community.

80
PREDICTION OF MULTI-PRACTICE ADOPTION BEHAVIOR FROM SOME PSYCHOLOGICAL
VARIABLES
Chattopadlyay, S. N. and Udai Pareek
Rural Sociology 32(3): 324-333. 1967.

Adoption behavior is a resultant of several sets of independent variables,
and the activities of change agents. In this study of farmers in a
north Indian village, an attempt was made to locate some psychological
variables that account for a large amount of variance in multi-practice
adoption behavior.

81
PREDICTIONS OF THE FARM WIFE'S INVOLVEMENT IN GENERAL MANAGEMENT AND
ADOPTION DECISIONS
Sawer, Barbara J.
Rural Sociology 38(4): 412-426. 1973.

The wife's farm information-seeking activity, her involvement in farm
tasks, and situational variables including family size, income, and farm
size were found to be associated with the extent of the wife's involvement in farm decision-making leading to the adoption of agricultural
innovations.

82
PROFILE OF MEXICAN-AMERICAN WOMEN
Cotera, Martha
Austin, Texas: National Education Laboratory Publishers, Publication
No. EC-037, 1976.

The Mexican-American woman, frequently described by stereotype or myth,
is here described as a human being. Using information from newspapers,
her own writings, lesser known publications, and research, the author

gives the history of the Chicano as a background for her profile of the contemporary woman. As migrant worker, family member, and activist the Mexican-American woman has not been given the attention she deserves. This book describes some of the problems and achievements in education, housing, employment, and other areas.

83
RACE, LABOR REPRESSION, AND CAPITALIST AGRICULTURE: NOTES FROM SOUTH TEXAS, 1920-1930.
Montejano, David
Institute for the Study of Social Change, Working Papers Series #102
ERIC: ED165929.

A historical analysis of racism and racial exploitation in "Imperial Texas" between 1900-1910 and 1920-1930. Emphasis is placed on the system of "Labor Repressive Control" which was used to keep Mexicans in the fields. Various conditions which resulted in the ultimate failures of labor controls are examined and discussed.

84
THE RATE OF TECHNOLOGICAL CHANGE AMONG LOCALITY GROUPS
Coughenour, C. Milton
The American Journal of Sociology, 69(4): 325-339. 1964.

The rate of diffusion for innovations in farming in an area is found to vary among communities and other types of sociogeographic areas. Data obtained from Kentucky farmers demonstrated these variations.

85
RECENT FERTILITY CHANGE AMONG HIGH FERTILITY MINORITIES IN THE UNITED STATES
Sweet, James A.
Madison: University of Wisconsin, Institute for Research on Poverty, November 1975. 44 pp. ERIC: ED120291.

Trends and differentials in fertility for three high fertility minority populations--southern rural blacks, Spanish surnamed, and American Indians--are examined for the intervals between 1957-60 and 1967-70. Fertility levels and patterns of differentials within these three minority populations are also compared with those of the urban white majority populations.

86
RELIGION IN A RURAL COMMUNITY OF THE SOUTH
Alexander, Frank
American Sociological Review, 6(2): 241-251. 1941.

The analysis of religion presented here is one aspect of a broad cultural study of Ruralville, an open-country community in southwestern Tennessee. With the exception of one black family, the population of Ruralville is entirely white. This study leads the author to believe that the complex described is fairly common to many rural communities of the area.

87
RETURN OF THE WETBACK
Portes, Alejandro
Society 11(3): 40-49. 1974. ERIC: EJ097188.

Examines both the wetback and legal migration from Mexico in the years
following the termination of the Bracero program in 1964.

88
THE ROLE OF COMMUNICATION AND ATTITUDES IN SMALL FARM PROGRAMS
Southern Rural Development Center
Mississippi State, Mississippi: Rural Development Series No. 4.
SRDC, Box 5406, 39762 ($1.00).

The author discusses how lack of access to resources, limited access to
information, and farmer values and attitudes affect the small farmers
and the adoption of new farm practices.

89
RURAL BLACKS--A VANISHING POPULATION
Jones, Lewis W. and Everett S. Lee
Atlanta, Georgia: W.E.B. Dubois Institute for the Study of the American
Black. October 1974. 17 pp. ERIC: ED126219.

Examines the high rate of out-migration of black populations from rural
areas, particularly the South.

90
RURAL ETHNIC MINORITIES: ADAPTIVE RESPONSE TO INEQUALITY
Durant, Thomas J., Jr. and Clark S. Knowlton
In Rural U.S.A.: Persistence and Change. Thomas R. Ford, ed.
Ames: The Iowa State University Press, 145-167. 1978.

In this article the author reviews briefly conditions of deprivation and
inequality of the three largest ethnic minorities in rural America -
Blacks, Mexican-American, and Native Americans.

91
RURAL AND URBAN ATTITUDES TOWARD WELFARE
Osgood, Mary H.
Social Work 22(1): 41-47. 1977.

Suggested that more negative attitudes toward welfare found among rural
populations may account for rural/urban differences in the number of
persons receiving welfare benefits.

92
RURAL-URBAN DIFFERENCES IN ATTITUDES AND BEHAVIOR IN THE UNITED STATES
Glenn, Norval and Lester Hill
In the Annals of the American Academy of Political and Social Sciences.
Vol. 429: 36-50. F. Clemente, ed. 1977.

This study discusses the importance of rural-urban distinction, and of
the community-size variable on attitudes and behavior. City residents

with rural backgrounds tend to retain rural attitudes and behavior
characteristics, size of community and origin being a stronger pre-
dictor of some attitudes than size of community of current residence.

93
RURAL VALUES AND CONCENSUS (SIC)
England, J. Lynn, et al.
New York, N.Y.: Annual Meeting of the Rural Sociological Meeting,
August, 1976. 25 pp. ERIC: ED128137.

Sample populations from 15 Intermountain West communities were surveyed
to examine value differences between rural and non-rural communities.
The values examined were: intellectualism, kindness, social skills,
loyality, academic achievement, physical development, value of status,
honesty, value of religion, self control, creativity, and independence.
Differences and similarities between rural and non-rural communities
were found on the 12 value dimensions.

94
RURAL WOMEN: AN ANNOTATED BIBLIOGRAPHY 1976-1979
Fowler, Becky
Rural Community Development Learning Center
Morgantown, West Virginia: West Virginia University, School of Social
Work, May 1979.

95
RURAL WOMEN--IGNORED BUT NO LONGER SILENT
Christian Science Monitor 9: February 1979. 26 pp.

Cites interesting statistics on rural women. Problems faced by rural
women are: financial inequality, lack of educational benefits and
feelings of isolation. Lack of resources in rural areas further intensifies these problems. Cites coalition, Rural American Women, Inc.,
whose purpose is to help give rural women a voice in expressing and
articulating their ideas.

96
RURAL WOMEN WORKERS IN THE 20TH CENTURY: AN ANNOTATED BIBLIOGRAPHY
Moser, Colette and Deborah Johnson
East Lansing, Michigan: Michigan State University, Center for Rural
Manpower and Public Affairs, Department of Agricultural Economics,
Paper No. 15, August 1973. 61 pp.

Excellent resource. Concerned with farm and non-farm related issues.

97
A SEARCH FOR A SUCCESSFUL AGRICULTURAL MIGRANT: AN ACCOUNT OF FIVE FRUIT
HARVESTS ON THE WEST COAST OF THE UNITED STATES
Mintz, Warren
Washington, D.C.: Department of Labor, Manpower Administration, Office
of Research and Development, 1971. ERIC: ED081942.

The study is focused on four major themes: (1) a search for a population of successful migrants and the ways this population sustains the life of migrancy; (2) the continuing development in the agricultural economy of the large-scale agribusiness and the impact on employment opportunities of migrants; (3) a description of the work of the fruit picker; and (4) employer-employee relationships.

98
SEEING WITH A NATIVE EYE: ESSAYS ON NATIVE AMERICAN RELIGION
Capps, Walter H., ed.
New York, N.Y.: Harper and Row Publishers, 1976.

This book is a collection of essays which look into the religious horizons of Native American people. Its proposal is straightforward - simply that Native American religion needs to be reckoned with.

99
SELF-CONCEPTIONS OF MIGRANTS AND SETTLED MEXICAN AMERICANS
Gecas, Viktor
Social Science Quarterly, 54(3): 579-595. 1973. ERIC: EJ095345.

A study of the self-conceptions of migrants and settled Mexican Americans reveals a significant difference in their self-evaluation: migrants have a more positive and more favorable view of themselves than settled Mexican Americans.

100
SELF IMAGE OF THE AMERICAN INDIAN: A PRELIMINARY STUDY
Bromberg, Walter and Sarah H. Hutchison
The International Journal of Social Psychiatry, 20: 39-44. Spring/ Summer 1974.

By studying drawings, the authors found clues to the self-image and psychology of the American Indian.

101
SELF-IMAGE: HOW DO THE POOR SEE THEMSELVES?
Sailor, Patricia and Wilma Crumley
Journal of Home Economics, 67(3): 4-8. 1975.

Professionals working with welfare families sometimes speak, write, and act as if all poor families share the same outlook and the same characteristics. This paper reports findings from a study which addressed the question of the reaction of the poor to materials written for their use.

102
SETTLING OUT AND SETTLING IN
Provinzano, James
1974. ERIC: ED138412.

This study focuses on 27 Mexican American migrant farmworkers who left farmwork in south Texas to settle in Wisconsin. The analysis was centered on the socioeconomic characteristics and adaptation of the emigrants to an Anglo sociocultural context.

103
SEX STRATIFICATION IN COMMUNITY POLITICS AND DECISION MAKING
Stuart, Nina G.
Illinois Agricultural Economics Staff Paper, 1977. 15 pp.

Paper argues that institutional barriers exist which effectively exclude
women from entry into community politics and decision making and that
the exclusion may result from women's socialization into their "proper"
roles with consequent self-elimination from high status positions, as
well as through barriers that are external to the person.

104
THE SILENT LANGUAGE
Hall, Edward T.
Greenwich, Conn.: Fawcett Premier Books, 1959.

This text is an excellent source for workers in new or culturally
different settings. The author discusses the components of culture and
offers suggestions on how to deal with cross cultural differences.

105
SOCIAL ASPECTS OF FARM OWENERSHIP AND TENANCY IN THE ARKANSAS COASTAL
REGION
Charlton, J. L.
Fayetteville, Arkansas: University of Arkansas, College of Agriculture,
Bulletin 545, June 1954.

This study evaluated the tenancy system in the Coastal Plain of Arkansas.
In addition to income, the evaluation included such considerations as
security of tenure, level of family living, social participation,
association among families, and education and occupational advancement
of the children of farm operators.

106
SOCIAL INTERACTION PATTERNS AND RELATIVE URBAN SUCCESS: THE DENVER
NAVAJO
Snyder, Peter F.
Urban Anthropology, 2(1): 1-24. 1973. ERIC: EJ075443.

This examination of the social factors of urban adaptation of Navajo
Indian migrants to Denver, Colorado--based on reference-membership group
theory--attempts to isolate primary groups within the Navajo urban en-
clave and investigates the relationship of group membership to adaptation.

107
SOCIAL AND LABOR ADJUSTMENT OF RURAL BLACK AMERICANS IN THE MISSISSIPPI
DELTA: CASE STUDY OF MADISON, ARKANSAS
Grimstead, Mary Jo, Bernal Green and J. Martin Redfern
Washington, D.C.: U.S. Department of Agriculture, Economic Research
Service, AER 274, 1974.

Studies the socioeconomic factors affecting employability of the rural
poor, primarily blacks. As a group, it was found that blacks were more

willing to work, to move, or to commute to find employment than their
white counterparts. Lack of transportation was the major deterrent to
employment; 48 percent of all households reported they had no means of
getting to work, although major industries were located within 5 to 25
miles of the community. Develops and tests models and scales designed
to measure the various aspects of behavioral and attitudinal patterns
as influenced by socioeconomic characteristics.

108
THE SOCIOCULTURAL SETTING OF INDIAN LIFE
McNickle, D'arcy
American Journal of Psychiatry 125(2): 115-132. 1968.

It is commonly assumed that the American Indian is faced with 'inevitable'
assimilation, either voluntary or involuntary, into the majority culture.
As this author points out, however, the Indian has managed to find alternatives in the past when, in his relations with the white man, he has
faced seemingly inevitable choices. Illustrations from recent workshops
for Indian students are used to demonstrate that, despite many problems,
it may be possible for the young Indian to use skills acquired from the
majority culture in support of his traditional society.

109
SOME CHARACTERISTICS OF FARM OPERATORS SOUGHT AS SOURCES OF FARM
INFORMATION IN A MISSOURI COMMUNITY
Lionberger, Herbert F.
Rural Sociology 18(4): 327-338. 1953.

Farm operators sought as sources of farm information were found to have
larger farms, higher incomes, greater technological competence, and
greater involvement in community organizations.

110
SOME THOUGHTS ON THE FORMATION OF PERSONALITY DISORDER: STUDY OF AN
INDIAN BOARDING SCHOOL POPULATION
Krush, Thaddeus P. et al.
American Journal of Psychiatry 122: 868-876. February 1966.

The authors contend that Indian boarding schools promote "psycho-social
nomadism" and shifting value systems which lead to confusion and disorganization of the Indian child's personality.

111
SOURCES AND CONSEQUENCES OF AGRARIAN VALUES IN AMERICAN SOCIETY
Buttel, F. H. and W. L. Flinn
Rural Sociology 40(2): 134-151. 1975.

Possible origins and consequences of holding agrarian values in the
contemporary United States are examined. The general hypothesis that
holding agrarian values is likely to lead to anomie and discontent with
the American social order is supported, more strongly among urban residents than with rural residents.

112
STABILITY OF STATUS ORIENTATIONS AMONG YOUNG WHITE, RURAL WOMEN FROM
THREE SOUTHERN STATES
Falk, W. W. and N. J. Salter
Journal of Vocational Behavior, 12: 20-32. February 1978.

Based on a panel study of 138 women from Georgia, South Carolina and
Texas. Looked at social origin variables and their effects on career
and self orientations. Mother's educational background had greater
effect on orientation than father's. Other factors were early aspirations and expectations. Six percent of women projected traditional
career aspirations.

113
A STATISTICAL PORTRAIT OF WOMEN IN THE U.S.
Schneider, Paula J.
U.S. Department of Commerce: Bureau of the Census, Special Studies
Services, #58, April 1976. 23 pp.

References made to rural farm and non-farm women. Specific reports on
employment status, employment, distribution of females according to race
and number of children. In 1970, 25.8% of women in the U.S. were classified as rural.

114
STRATIFICATION AND RISK-TAKING: A THEORY TESTED ON AGRICULTURAL
INNOVATION
Cancian, Frank
American Sociological Review 32(6): 912-926. 1967.

This paper examines the relationships between the adoption of agricultural
practices and farmer wealth.

115
THE STRUCTURE OF ADAPTIVE SENTIMENTS IN A LOWER CLASS RELIGIOUS GROUP
IN APPALACHIA
Kaplan, Berton H.
Journal of Social Issues 21(1): 126-141. 1965.

The author finds that this group of people searches for identity through
membership in a fundamentalist religion which is against material
possessions, thereby helping to maintain poverty in the area.

116
STRUCTURING INFLUENCE OF SOCIAL GROUPS ON FARM INFORMATION-SEEKING
RELATIONSHIPS WITH AGRICULTURAL ELITES AND NONELITES IN TWO MISSOURI
COMMUNITIES
Lionberger, Herbert F. and Gary D. Copus
Rural Sociology 37(1): 73-85. 1972.

This study is concerned with the manner in which social cliques structure
interpersonal communication with agricultural elites and nonelites in two
Missouri communities - one comparatively stable from the standpoint of

prevailing agricultural enterprises and the other rapidly changing under economic pressure.

117
A STUDY OF NEW MEXICO MIGRANT AGRICULTURAL WORKERS
Borrego, John G. et al.
1971. ERIC: ED055697.

This report presents the kinds of problems faced by migrant agricultural workers, farmers, and by agencies offering services to these migrants in New Mexico. Various problems and concerns are explored in an attempt to bring about an awareness.

118
A STUDY OF RIESMAN'S INNER-OUTER DIRECTEDNESS AMONG FARMERS
Barban, Arnold M. et al.
Rural Sociology 35(2): 232-243. 1970.

The basic purpose of this study was to investigate Riesman's theory of social character as it applies to a farm population. In addition, two other sociopsychological variables - innovation proneness and adoption leadership - were examined among the sampled population.

119
A STUDY OF RURAL LANDOWNERSHIP, CONTROL PROBLEMS AND ATTITUDES OF BLACKS
TOWARD RURAL LAND
McGee, Leo and Robert Boone
Nashville: Tennessee State University, 1976.

This study was undertaken to yield factual information on the status and trends of black landownership in Tennessee, provides information in regard to the institutional practices associated with transfers, and determines the attitudes held by blacks toward rural land in Tennessee.

120
A STUDY OF SELECTED SOCIO-ECONOMIC CHARACTERISTICS OF ETHNIC MINORITIES
BASED ON THE 1970 CENSUS
Arlington, Virginia: R. J. Associates. July 1974. 114 pp.
ERIC: ED107426.

The analysis consisted of natural and local data focusing on such population characteristics as family structure, education, employment, income, poverty, housing, sanitation, and health.

121
TERRITORIAL BOUNDARIES OF RURAL POVERTY: PROFILES OF EXPLOITATION
Reul, Myrtle R.
East Lansing: Michigan State University, Center for Rural Manpower and Public Affairs and the Cooperative Extension Service, 1974.

This book examines rural poverty in various parts of the country with particular emphasis mainly on one segment of the rural poor--namely migrant farm laborers. A major contribution of the book is the development of a framework for understanding psycho-social-cultural commonalities and differences of the rural poor--whether they be American Indians, Appalachian and Southern whites, Southern Blacks, or Chicanos.

122
THESE COUPLES HAVE TAKEN AN EXTRA STEP
Brunoehler, Ron and Gary Vincent
Successful Farming, 76: 26-27. November 1978.

Article on several husband-wife management teams from all over the U.S. Couples from Memphis, Missouri; Jamestown, Indiana; Lancaster, Wisconsin; and Watseka, Illinois.

123
TODAY'S FARMER: TOUGH, COMPETENT AND FEMALE
Freeman, J. T.
Redbook, 152-154. May 1976.

Reports increasing numbers of farm manager women are helping to change the traditional farm woman's image. Interviews an Iowa cow-calf manager and Wisconsin dairy farmer and discusses their experience.

124
THE TOKEN MINORITY: AN ATTITUDINAL COMPARISON OF BLACK, ORIENTAL AND ANGLO RURAL YOUTH UTILIZING A MATCHED SET ANALYSES
Cockerham, William C., Peter B. Imrey, and Sidney J. Kronus
Sociological Methods and Research, 6(4): 493-513. 1978.

This paper examines the attitudes of a "token" number of black and Oriental youth who live in a rural and predominantly anglo setting.

125
TRADITIONALISM IN THE FARM FAMILY AND TECHNOLOGICAL CHANGE
Fliegel, Frederick
Rural Sociology, 27: 70-76. 1962.

This study demonstrates that family characteristics which reflect a traditional orientation toward credit and dependence on family labor may serve as an obstacle to technological change.

126
UP FROM THE FARM
DiPerna, Paula
Working Woman. 36-42. February 1979.

Currently women occupy jobs at every level of agricultural production and their numbers are increasing. Agricultural schools are also experiencing tremendous growth of female students. Discusses women's traditional farm jobs and compares them with today's woman farmer. Critiques several farm women's organizations, farm lobbies and a few women's personal experiences. Resource list includes important agencies concerning farm women.

127
URBAN-RURAL BACKGROUND AND FORMAL GROUP MEMBERSHIP
Jitodai, Ted
Rural Sociology, 30(1): 75-82. 1965.

Past research indicates that rural people who migrate to urban areas have
lower membership rates than others in urban voluntary associations. The
major purpose of the study is to re-examine the importance which urban-
rural backgrounds have on membership in voluntary associations when
simultaneous controls are employed for variables that are jointly associated with migration and with membership in voluntary associations.

128
VALUE, BELIEF, AND NORMATIVE SYSTEMS
Larson, Olaf
In Rural U.S.A.: Persistence and Change. Thomas R. Ford, ed.
Ames: The Iowa State University Press, 91-112. 1978.

This paper examines the value systems and beliefs of rural people in
contemporary American society, compares them with those held by non-
rural residents, and discusses changes in rural values which are underway.

129
THE VALUE OF THE PRODUCTION TIME OF FARM WIVES: IOWA, NORTH CAROLINA
AND OKLAHOMA
Huffman, Wallace E.
American Journal of Agricultural Economics, 58: 836-841. December 1976.

Assesses production of farm wives engaged in farm work.

130
VARIETIES OF SOUTHERN WOMEN
Florin, John W.
Southern Exposure, 4(4): 95-97.

Many Southern women can be characterized as rural, low income and with
high fertility rates. Women, more than men, experience poverty, with
fewer alternatives.

131
VIEWS HELD OF INNOVATOR AND INFLUENCE REFERENTS AS SOURCES OF FARM
INFORMATION IN A MISSOURI COMMUNITY
Lionberger, Herbert and Joe Francis
Rural Sociology, 34(2): 197-211. 1969.

This study is directed to the conceptualization of views held of farm
information sources, and to assessing the differential manner in which
farmers in a south Missouri community viewed personal innovator and
influence referents as sources of farm information.

132
WE STOOD BY OUR MEN BUT WE STOOD UP FOR OURSELVES, TOO.
Brody, Charlotte
UMWA Journal, 87: 12-15. March 1976.

Documents women's efforts during strikes, in organizing of coal unions,
schools for children and Black Lung Benefits.

133
WHEN A WOMAN RUNS THE FARM
Gilles, Jean
Farm Journal, 102: December 1978. 37 pp.

Only 4% of agricultural bosses are women. Summarizes the experiences of
five women bosses from around the U.S. Advice to farm women: get
involved with farm business to prepare for unforeseen illness or death
of husband; when help is needed, get the best available; and, most
importantly, believe in yourself and your abilities.

134
WHITE AND MINORITY SMALL FARM OPERATORS IN THE SOUTH
Lewis. James A.
Washington, D.C.: U.S. Department of Agriculture, Economic Research
Service Agricultural Economic Report 353, 1976.

This study describes the status of white and minority small farm operators
in the South. The report identifies, compares, and contrasts resources
and characteristics of farm operators by race and economic class of
farm.

135
WHITE WORKER-MINORITY CLIENT
Mizio, Emelicia
Social Work 17(3): 82-86. 1972.

The social work profession must increase its efforts to eliminate the
blocks to effective interaction between the white worker and minority
client if its professed goal of serving all clients effectively is to
be taken seriously.

136
WHY MIGRANT WOMEN MAKE THEIR HUSBANDS TAMALES
Williams, Brett
1975. ERIC: ED145333.

Stereotypes of migrant women are focused upon in this study of three life
histories of migrant women. These life histories reveal that stark
poverty and limited upward mobility results in individuals finding
greatest security in gathering and binding kin. Women are critical
liaisons, among kin, working to insure their lifelong involvement in
one another's travels and concerns. Marriage is a special case of
such kin-work, and the complexity of this relationship is explored.

137
WOMEN IN THE AGRICULTURAL SETTLEMENT OF THE NORTHERN PLAINS
Hargreaves, Mary W. M.
Agricultural History, 50: 179-189. January 1976.

Discusses the different experience of Plains women compared to their
urban counterparts. Women were queens, children were angels. Women,
like rivers, were few and they gained in importance proportionally.
First four states to grant women the vote were Plains states: Wyoming,
Colorado, Utah and Idaho. In 1900's rural women continued jobs that
their urban counterparts quit as a result of household conveniences.
Historical and interesting.

138
WOMEN IN AMERICAN AGRICULTURE: A SELECT BIBLIOGRAPHY
Fera, Darla
Washington, D.C.: U.S. Govt. Printing Office, U.S. Department of
Agriculture, Economic Research Service and National Agricultural Library.
Library List No. 10, 1977.

139
WOMEN FARMERS
Kellogg, M. A. and E. Sciolino
Newsweek, 88: 86. November 8, 1976.

Approximately 74,000 women own or manage farms in the U.S. Many are
widow farmers. Seventeen percent of farm workers (paid) are women.
Women's enrollment in agricultural schools has increased 90% since 1973.

140
WOMEN IN RURAL AMERICA
Washington, D.C.: Rural America, Inc. December 1977. 7 pp. (50¢).

Discusses special problems facing rural women in such areas as employment, education, health and legal status.

141
WOMEN IN THE RURAL LABOR FORCE
O'Leary, Jeanne M.
In Rural Development Perspectives.
Washington, D.C.: U.S. Department of Agriculture, Economic Development
Division, RDP1, 25-26. November 1978.

Examines changes in the participation of women in the rural labor force
between 1940 and 1970.

142
WOMEN IN THE SOUTH - A BIBLIOGRAPHY
Southern Exposure 4(4): 98.

Comprehensive bibliography. Good resource.

143
WOMEN UNLIMITED
Lafayette, Indiana: Purdue University, 1976. 35 pp.

Discusses program designed to facilitate an understanding of the changing roles of women in today's society and to assist women in discovering
within themselves the capacity for growth and personal development.
Offers a model for seminars to develop women's potentials. (Includes
slide set.)

144
WOMEN OF THE WEST
Gray, Dorothy K.
Milbrae, California: Les Femmes, 1976. 180 pp.

See Chapter IX, "Women on the Cattle Frontier", pp. 109-120, and Chapter
XI, "Women of the Farm Frontier", pp. 135-146. Discussion of several
prominent women included in each category.

145
WOMEN AND WORK IN APPALACHIA: THE WAGING WAR
Lilly, Leslie
Human Services in the Rural Environment, 1(1): 40-44. 1979.

The role of women in Appalachian work and the problems encountered
through discrimination are discussed in this article.

146
WORKING WITH LOW-INCOME RURAL FAMILIES
Phifer, Bryan
Washington, D.C.: U.S. Department of Agriculture, Federal Extension
Service ESC-557, 1964.

This publication deals with raising family living standards, youth
development, increasing income through improved management and production
practices, and increasing income through improved marketing.

Part B: The Rural Community Environment

1

AGRICULTURAL MECHANIZATION AND SOCIAL CHANGE IN RURAL LOUISIANA
Bertrand, A. L.
Baton Rouge: Louisiana State University Agricultural and Mechanical
College, Agricultural Experiment Station, Bulletin 458. June 1951.

One of the most important contributions of this unusual study was to
examine how many socio-economic changes in agricultural areas of
Louisiana were attributed to the adoption of mechanical power on farms.
The following social changes were reported: decreases in the rural
populations; a loosening of the ties on individual members of the rural
family; a loss of many of the rural family's functions to other
social institutions; a decline in the influence of the rural church; a
decrease in mutual aid practices; an increase in leisure time; an
increase in social participation; and improved town-country relations.

2

AGRICULTURAL TECHNOLOGY AND THE DISTRIBUTION OF WELFARE GAINS
Bieri, Jurg, Alain de Janvry, and Andrew Schmitz
American Journal of Agricultural Economics 54(5): 801-808. 1972.

This article is a discussion of economic theory applied to the distribution of income and welfare gains accruing from technological advances in
agriculture.

3

THE AMERICAN COMMUNITY: A MULTIDISCIPLINARY BIBLIOGRAPHY
Monticello, Illinois: Council of Planning Librarians, Box 229.
September 1970. 56 pp. ERIC: ED101428.

This is an extensive bibliography of publications dealing with the
quest for community in the United States.

4

AMERICAN RURAL LIFE
Lindstrom, David E.
New York: The Ronald Press Company, 1948.

This textbook in sociology examines all dimensions of rural life in the
United States. Many of the ideas presented in the text are outmoded;
nevertheless, a rich body of information within it is still relevant
today.

5
APPALACHIA ON OUR MIND
Shapiro, Henry D.
Chapel Hill: The University of North Carolina Press, 1978.

The author examines the origins and consequences of the idea of
Appalachia as a region. As noted, the idea "is a history of America and
of the American consciousness, for its concern is with the attempts of
Americans to understand the nature and meaning of their civilization,
and to develop modes of action which to them seem consonant with this
understanding."

6
APPALACHIA IN THE SIXTIES, DECADE OF REAWAKENING
Walls, David S. and John B. Stephenson, eds.
Lexington: The University of Kentucky Press, 1972.

This book is a selection of articles about what happened in Southern
Appalachia in the 1960's. The book is divided into three sections: the
early sixties, the quality of life, and the lessons in fighting poverty,
and where do we go from here. Issues, such as the "Pork Barrel" war on
poverty, the politics of coal, migration, grass roots organizing, and
the role of the Appalachian Regional Commission, are discussed.

7
APPALACHIA IN TRANSITION
Glenn, Max E., ed.
St. Louis: The Bethany Press, 1970.

This collection of articles focuses on the problems of rural poverty in
Appalachia. Particularly useful are the discussions in the community as
a factor in Appalachian Development and religion's contribution to
community in Appalachia.

8
AS YOU SOW
Goldschmidt, Walter
New York: Harcourt, Brace, 1947.

This book is a study on the effects of farm scale on two communities in
the Central Valley of California. It was found that as corporate farms
supplanted smaller family farms, rural community life deteriorated.

9
THE CAUSES OF RURAL TO URBAN MIGRATION AMONG THE POOR, FINAL REPORT
Hamilton, William L., et al.
Washington, D.C.: Office of Economic Opportunity, March 1970. 392 pp.
ERIC: ED149943.

Focusing on individual decisions, the study examined why the rural poor
migrated to urban areas. Southeastern blacks, Appalachian whites, and
Southwestern Spanish Americans were interviewed in two "destination"
cities and eight "origin" counties in the Southeast, Appalachian, and
Southwest migrant streams.

10

CHANGE IN RURAL AMERICA: CAUSES, CONSEQUENCES, AND ALTERNATIVES
Rodefeld, Richard et al.
St. Louis, Missouri: The C. V. Mosby Co., 1978.

This volume is the most comprehensive collection of articles available on
twentieth century changes in the rural sector of the U.S. Changes that
occurred in the following six areas are examined: agricultural technology, farm organizational and occupational structure, transportation,
community, urban population distribution and rural economic base.

11

THE CHANGING AMERICAN FARM
Breimyer, Harold F.
In The Annals of the American Academy of Political and Social Science,
429: 12-22. F. Clemente, ed. January 1977.

This study discusses the changes of the traditional family farm due to
external and internal factors. Alternate kinds of farming are discussed,
and policies, in the past, are seen as ambivalent.

12

THE CHANGING NATURE OF RURAL RELIGIOUS INSTITUTIONS
Photiadis, John and Joseph J. Simoni
Paper presented at the Fourth World Congress of Rural Sociology,
Torun, Poland, August 1976. 23 pp. ERIC: ED133101.

Much of this study examines the contributions to societal integration of
the flexible and diversified religious institutions of rural Appalachia.
It was found that religious pluralism in Appalachia has functioned to
alleviate the anxieties of the socially maladjusted whose needs are not
met by other established social institutions, and also has displayed the
flexibility needed to function as a status maintenance and stabilization
vehicle for those who have done well in society.

13

CHANGING SOCIAL CHARACTERISTICS OF RURAL POPULATIONS
Demerath, N. J.
In Social Work in Rural Areas: Preparation and Practice,
R. K. Green and S. A. Webster, eds.
Knoxville: The University of Tennessee, School of Social Work, 18-23.
1978.

This paper examines some of the social changes in rural America and
briefly discusses the role of social workers in rural development.

14

COMMUNITIES LEFT BEHIND: ALTERNATIVES FOR DEVELOPMENT
North Central Center for Rural Development
Ames: The Iowa State University Press, 1974.

The story of declining small towns and the options open to them in their
fight for survival. The book covers three major areas of decline--

population, economic, and social--their symptoms, causes, effects, and possible alternatives.

15

COMMUNITY PREPARATION FOR ECONOMIC DEVELOPMENT IN ARIZONA--POWER STRUCTURE ANALYSIS
Mangin, Frank
Norman: University of Oklahoma, Industrial Development Institute, Thesis Manuscript. 1973.

Author states that effective development hinges on local power structure as well as on economic factors. Thesis is that not all communities desire or are capable of growth. Supports this with observed attitudinal patterns in 29 Arizona communities.

16

COMMUNITY PROBLEMS IN RURAL-URBAN FRINGE AREAS: IMPLICATIONS FOR ACTION PROGRAMS
Heasley, Daryl K., D. H. Tuttle and R. C. Bealer
University Park: The Pennsylvania State University.
Agricultural and Home Economics Extension Service, Leaflet 270 (undated).

A survey of a rural-urban fringe community north of Pittsburgh reveals some of the "growing pains" of the area. Problems for action programs are briefly discussed and guidelines for adjustment are presented.

17

A COMPARATIVE STUDY OF THE ROLE OF VALUES IN SOCIAL ACTION IN TWO SOUTHWESTERN COMMUNITIES
Vogt, Evon and Thomas O'Dea
American Sociological Review, 18: 645-654. 1953.

It is the central hypothesis of the values study project that value-orientations play an important part in the shaping of social institutions and in influencing the forms of observed social action. Upon a comparison of the Mormon community of Rimrock with the Texas community of Homestead, it is felt that differences in response to situations are central to these communities.

18

CONTEMPORARY RURAL AMERICA: PERSISTENCE AND CHANGE
Ford, Thomas R.
In Rural U.S.A.: Persistence and Change, Thomas R. Ford, ed., 3-18.
Ames: The Iowa State University Press, 1978.

The author presents an overview of rural characteristics, social and economic behavior, values, beliefs, and attitudes associated with community which continue to persist despite recent transformations in American society.

19

CONTRIBUTIONS OF RECENT METRO/NONMETRO MIGRANTS TO THE NONMETRO
POPULATION AND LABOR FORCE
Bowles, Gladys K.
Agricultural Economics Research 30(4): 1978. ERIC: ED162809.

An assessment of contributions of metro/nonmetro migrants to the population and labor force of nonmetro localities. The data base for this
assessment was the March 1975 population survey of the Bureau of the
Census. Major findings indicated that: (1) metro/nonmetro migrants
replaced those moving in the opposite direction; (2) migrants did not
have a negative impact (related to occupation, industry, and income)
on nonmetro populations; and (3) geographic gain/loss in regional
exchange is discussed.

20

COUNTRY AND CITY WOMEN - STILL DIFFERENT?
Hale, Dorinda
Sojourner 3(10): 5, 21. 1978.

Author interviews several members of an extended family in rural Vermont.
Main difference between rural-urban women is that the rural woman
often lacks non-traditional role models and experiences feelings of
isolation.

21

THE DECLINE AND FALL OF THE SMALL TOWN
Simon, William and John H. Gagnon
Transaction 4(5): 42-51. 1967.

Three southern Illinois towns are examined in terms of how different
traditions and different political structures led to three different
ways of adjusting to similar crises. However, the authors recognize
that in spite of these differences, the community holds one key aspect
in common--a deep-seated resistance to social change of any real
significance.

22

DETERMINANTS OF GENOCIDE FEAR IN A RURAL TEXAS COMMUNITY: A RESEARCH
NOTE
Farrell, Walter C., Jr. and Marvin P. Dawkins
American Journal of Public Health 69(6): 605-607. 1979.

This article explores the relative importance of social background
factors as predictors of genocide fear among blacks in a rural Texas
community.

23
DIFFUSION AND FARMING ADVICE: A TEST OF SOME CURRENT NOTIONS
Polgar, Steven, Howard Dunphy and Bruce Cox
Social Forces 42(1): 104-111. 1963.

This study demonstrates that social scientists should recognize that
acceptance of innovations by farmers may differ depending on the type
of innovation and location of the community.

24
DOES MOTHER NATURE REALLY SELL MARGARINE? THE UNCERTAIN RURAL FUTURE
Schwartz, Peter
ERIC: ED167324 (undated).

Examines two possible, but contrasting directions in which U.S. society
and its agricultural system can go: 1) a "modernization trend" characterized by scientification of human knowledge, secularization of human
values, industrialization of human activity, and economic rationality;
or 2) greater insistence on self-determination, greater emphasis on the
quality of life, a movement toward "appropriate technology", greater
acceptance of an ecological ethic, and a widespread search for trans-
cendental meanings.

25
ECCLES NO. 6: WORKING THE SEAM IN A WEST VIRGINIA COAL MINE
Leamer, Lawrence
Harpers 243(1459): 100-110. 1971.

The author presents a narrative account of the miners of Eccles No. 6 in
West Virginia. A description of the miners and the mine is presented.

26
THE ECOLOGY OF SOCIAL TRADITIONALISM IN RURAL HINTERLAND
Willits, F. K., R. C. Bealer and D. M. Crider
Rural Sociology 39(3): 334-349. 1974.

The utility of metropolitan and urban dominance constructs for dealing
with patterning of non-economic and non-demographic factors in Hinterland areas is explored by examining attitudes toward selected aspects
of traditional morality.

27
THE ECONOMIC AND SOCIAL CONDITION OF NONMETROPOLITAN AMERICA IN THE 1970'S
Washington, D.C.: U.S. Department of Agriculture, Committee Print,
94th Congress, 1st Session, May 30, 1975. Economic Research Service,
Economic Development Division. ERIC: ED113099.

Topics discussed in this document are: population settlement patterns,
employment, income, education, health resources, local governments, and
housing.

28

THE ECONOMIC AND SOCIAL CONDITIONS OF RURAL AMERICA IN THE 1970'S.
PART 2: IMPACT OF DEPARTMENT OF HEALTH, EDUCATION, AND WELFARE PROGRAMS
ON NONMETROPOLITAN AREAS, FISCAL 1970.
Washington, D.C.: Department of Health, Education, and Welfare.
September 1971, 101 pp. ERIC: ED056799.

The report was prepared by DHEW for Senate hearings on a Bill to Revitalize Rural and Economically Distressed Areas. The report contains (1) an
analysis of DHEW programs which were included in Title IX of the USDA's
rural report to Congress; (2) a summary of criteria used in determining
the development, location, and construction of DHEW facilities and
services; (3) a list of all programs having potential for encouraging
distribution of future industrial growth and expansion more evenly
throughout the U.S.; and (4) other areas of discussion.

29

THE ECONOMICS OF TECHNOLOGICAL CHANGE AND THE DEMISE OF THE SHARECROPPER
Day, Richard H.
The American Economic Review, 57: 427-449. 1967.

Technological changes in the Mississippi Delta farm economy between 1940
and 1960 resulted in a two-stage push of people off the farm and then out
of the rural area. The first stage pushed the sharecropper off the farm
and into villages and small towns where he lived as a farm wage worker.
The second stage pushed this worker from the rural to the urban sector of
employment.

30

EDUCATION, INNOVATION, SOCIOPOLITICAL CULTURE, AND DEPRESSED RURAL
COMMUNITIES
Boyd, William L. and Glenn L. Immegart
The Journal of Educational Administration, 15(1): 49-66. 1977.

The findings of this study indicate that the assumptions underlying
prevailing strategies for change are often poorly in tune with the
social and political realities of depressed rural communities.

31

ESTIMATING THE RELATIVE RURALITY OF U.S. COUNTIES
Smith, Blair J. and David W. Parvin
Southern Journal of Agricultural Economics, 7(2): 51-60. 1975.

Develops a technique which can more accurately delineate between urban or
rural. Applies this to five representative states and found that this
procedure is the best yet devised for identifying and defining rurality.

32

FACTORS INHIBITING APPALACHIAN REGIONAL DEVELOPMENT
Hale, Carl W.
The American Journal of Economics and Sociology, 30(2): 133-158. 1971.

The author concludes that the major problem in Appalachia regional development is one of attitudes, not resources. These attitudes have prevented
the development of a "growth" psychology in the area.

33
FACTORS RELATED TO EMPLOYMENT OF WIVES IN A RURAL IOWA COUNTY
Burchinal, Lee G.
Ames: Iowa Agricultural Experiment Station Research Bulletin 509.
October 1962.

Sampled 111 farm and 175 nonfarm families in Greene County, Iowa, to
establish factors which influence the employment of wives. Findings
suggest that nonfarm wives have higher employment rates. Employment of
women with high school diplomas was greater than for those with less
education. The employment of wives was related to: (1) greater household tasks performed by husband; (2) greater dominance of wives in family
purchasing decisions; and (3) greater dominance of husbands in family
social activity decisions. Wives working was unrelated to family dis-
cord or emotional characteristics.

34
FAMILY AND COMMUNITY ACTIVITIES OF RURAL NONFARM FAMILIES WITH CHILDREN
Bollman, Stephen R., Virginia M. Moxley and Nancy C. Elliott
Journal of Leisure Research 7(1): 53-62. 1975.

Six factors - resource level, stage of family life cycle, presence of a
preschool child, family size, geographic mobility, and employment
status of the mother - were analyzed in terms of their effect on nonwork
activities of families with children.

35
FARM SIZE, RURAL COMMUNITY INCOME, AND CONSUMER WELFARE
Heady, Earl O.
American Journal of Agricultural Economics 56(3): 534-542. 1974.

This paper analyzes general alternatives in rural community income generation and welfare in relation to farm-size alternatives.

36
GATEKEEPERS: AGENTS IN ACCULTURATION
Kurtz, Norman
Rural Sociology 33(1): 64-70. 1968.

A process of acculturation is described in regard to Spanish-surname
persons who migrated from rural areas to Denver. The urban newcomers
relied on helpers or "gatekeepers" for access to resources needed to
solve problems encountered in the urban setting. The study indicates
that informal channels in the community are used to transfer resources
to people in trouble.

37
A GOOD LIFE FOR MORE PEOPLE
1971 Yearbook of Agriculture
Washington, D.C.: United States Department of Agriculture. 1971.

Examines how American agriculture and the rest of the nation can deal with
a big increase in the U.S. population. Rural areas need more housing,
better community facilities, more industry and jobs, better planning and
training, improved education and vocational training.

38

GROWTH AND CHANGE IN RURAL AMERICA
Fuguitt, Glenn V., Paul R. Voss and J. C. Doherty
Washington, D.C.: The Urban Land Institute, 1979.

This book provides very useful information on recent nonmetropolitan
population trends. Structural factors associated with and migrant
characteristics of these trends are analyzed.

39

IDENTIFYING THE STRUCTURE OF COMMUNITY POWER - SOME SUGGESTIONS FOR
RURAL SOCIAL WORKERS
Colliver, Mac
In Second National Institute on Social Work In Rural Areas Reader. 35-53.
Buxton, Edward B., ed.
Madison: University of Wisconsin--Extension Center for Social Service, 1978.

This paper examines three aspects of community power: 1) the need for
community power structure information on the part of rural social workers
based upon the emerging rural social work literature; 2) the different
forms or structures of community power; and 3) information on the different approaches the rural social worker could use to identify those key
community influentials who could provide vital support in human service
organization and delivery.

40

THE IMPACT OF THE RURAL SOUTHERN CULTURE OF WHITE PARENTS ON THE HEALTH,
EDUCATION, AND WELFARE OF THEIR CHILDREN
Dillman, Caroline M.
ERIC: ED160265.

This article demonstrates that white children of the rural South are
caught between two cultures--the middle class value system taught at
school and the rural lower/working class values held by their parents.
Differences in values and the attitudes of parents present an impediment to the children's education as well as to the successful implementation of health, education, and welfare programs.

41

THE INTEGRATION OF RURAL MIGRANTS IN NEW SETTINGS
Rieger, Jon H. and J. Allan Beegle
Rural Sociology, 39(1): 42-55. 1976. ERIC: EJ104741.

The integration process of rural migrants was plotted over time through a
cross-sectional analysis of 688 residences for a sample from Michigan's
Upper Peninsula.

42

KEEPING UP WITH CHANGE IN RURAL SOCIETY
Neiderfrank, E. J.
Washington, D.C.: United States Department of Agriculture, January 1970.
36 pp. ERIC: ED049426.

This document summarizes the facts and ideas about agriculture and community
life in the U.S. with some implications for the future. It reviews changes

in farm structure as well as changes in rural economics due to the tremendous impact of economic and technological change upon local institutions and community living.

43
LINKAGES OF MEXICO AND THE UNITED STATES
Loomis, Charles, Zona Loomis and Joanne Gullahorn
East Lansing: Michigan State University, 14, Research Bulletin,
Agriculture Experiment Station, 1966, 89 pp.

This bulletin studies cooperation and conflict between Mexico and the U.S. and notes cultural and social differences and similarities, especially as they impinge on social change.

44
LIFE IN RURAL AMERICA
Washington, D.C.: National Geographic Society, 1974.

This book is prepared by the Special Publications Division of the National Geographic Society. It provides a fairly broad picture of life in rural, small-town America.

45
LOCATING THE RURAL COMMUNITY
Sanderson, Dwight
In Perspective on the American Community, Roland L. Warren, ed.
Chicago: Rand McNally and Company, 179-183. 1973.

The author defines the geographical bases of the rural community on the basis of a "community-center" idea.

46
LOCATION PREFERENCES, MIGRATION, AND REGIONAL GROWTH: A STUDY OF THE SOUTH AND SOUTHWEST UNITED STATES
Hansen, Niles M.
New York: Praeger Publishers, 1973.

Growth center and regional policy decisions should give considerable attention to the lagging regions of the U.S. This book examines location preferences, migration patterns, and economic problems in the South and the Southwest. Case studies of Mexican-Americans, Native Americans, and poor whites and blacks are included.

47
LOW INCOMES OF RURAL PEOPLE: THE NATURE AND EXTENT OF THE PROBLEM IN A SOUTH-CENTRAL KENTUCKY AREA
Burkett, W. Keith and James F. Thompson
Lexington: University of Kentucky, Department of Agricultural Economics,
Agricultural Experiment Station, Bulletin 697, April 1965.

The twofold purpose of this five county study in Kentucky was: (1) to indicate the extent and nature of the low-income problem in this and

similar areas and to evaluate possible remedies; and (2) to use this area
as a case study of the relationship of low-income problems to the functioning of the national economy.

48
THE MEANING OF 'RURALITY' IN AMERICAN SOCIETY: SOME IMPLICATIONS OF
ALTERNATIVE DEFINITIONS
Bealer, Robert C., F. C. Willits and W. P. Kuvlesky
Rural Sociology 30(3): 255-266. 1965.

This paper deals "separately with three components of 'rural' and . . .
(examines) some of the logical and practical implications of defining
'rural' only in terms of the ecological, the occupational, or the
sociological facet."

49
MIGRATION: AN OLD SCENE WITH A NEW CAST
Reul, Myrtle R.
East Lansing: Michigan State University, Center for Rural Manpower and
Public Affairs, Special Paper No. 23. September 1974. 63 pp.
ERIC: ED100569.

This monograph discusses migration in a global sense, including both urban
and rural. The monograph's purpose is to: (1) show that when viewed in
its historical perspective, migration has changed only in terms of numbers
and racial, sexual or ethnic composition of the moving groups; and (2)
point out that accurate prediction of social needs can be made years in
advance by examining population trends and the movement of people.

50
MODERN INDIAN PSYCHOLOGY
Bryde, John F.
Vermillion, South Dakota: University of South Dakota, Institute of
Indian Studies. 1971.

Discussed in this book are culture and Indian values, psychology and Indian
psychology, dealing with culture conflict, general Indian history, and
Dakota and Sioux history.

51
MOUNTAIN FAMILIES IN TRANSITION: A CASE STUDY OF APPALACHIAN MIGRATION
Schwarzweller, Harry K., J. S. Brown, and J. J. Mongalam
University Park, Penn.: The Pennsylvania State University Press, 1971.

The authors focus on the migrants and the migration process of Appalachian
people to urban settings. Adjustments in sociocultural systems and the
utilization of mutual-aid networks demonstrate the many factors related
to the successes and failures of these people in the industrial centers
of the Northwest. This book can be applied to most regions of the U.S.
where parallels in the rural-urban migration stream can be easily found.

52
MOVING TO THE COUNTRY: RETURN MIGRATION TO A RURAL AREA
Mapstone, James R.
1975. ERIC: ED138415.

Reports on a study designed to compare in-migrants with non-migrants to
determine the migrants' demographic and socioeconomic contributions to
rural areas. It was determined, by analysis of a survey, that returned
migration constituted the major type of movement; family relations were
paramount; migrants' search for alternative life styles was not supported;
it was determined that a refinement of migration theory to account for
goal-oriented moves and moves resulting from failure to adapt is
necessitated.

53
MY LAND IS DYING
Caudill, Harry M.
New York: E. P. Dutton & Company, Inc., 1971.

In this book Caudill concentrates on the problem of strip mining in
Appalachia. The human misery and political issues presented in the text
are applicable to other parts of the country where resources are being
exploited without regards to people and their natural surroundings.

54
NATIONAL PLAN OF ACTION
National Commission on the Observance of International Women's Year. 1977.

Adopted at National Women's Conference in Houston, Texas, November 18-21,
1977. Section on Rural Women, p. 25. Suggests establishment of federal
rural women and the OMB report beneficiaries according to sex, minority
status and rural urban residence, based on a standard definition.

55
NEGROES IN THE U.S. - SOCIAL, INDUSTRIAL, AND BEHAVIORAL INTERACTION.
VOL. 2 (A BIBLIOGRAPHY WITH ABSTRACTS)
Kenton, Edith
Springfield, Virginia: National Technical Information Service.
1973 - October 1978, 268 pp. NTIS/PS-78/1147/4 ST.

The bibliography includes studies on rural and urban affairs, racial-
labor market conditions, employment and unemployment, family relations,
and the armed services. Discussions are presented on attitudes towards
Blacks, black-white comparisons, regional variations, and cross-cultural
psychology.

56
THE NEW RURAL SOCIETY
Goldmark, Peter C.
Boise, Idaho: Address delivered to the Federation of Rocky Mountain
States, September, 1973. 6 pp. ERIC: ED068215.

The New Rural Society Project concerns itself with the deterioration of
America through urban overcrowding and rural depletion. The paper discusses how communications technology can considerably improve conditions

in employment opportunities; educational services; health care; and social cultural, and recreational pursuits--the major reasons for migration from rural areas.

57
THE NEW RURALISM: THE POST-INDUSTRIAL AGE IS UPON US
Ellis, William N.
The Futurist 10(4): 202-204. 1975.

A new ruralism, which may mark the beginning of a post-industrial age aimed at meeting man's psychic needs rather than his material wants, may require shifts in government and business policies.

58
NIGHT COMES TO THE CUMBERLANDS: A BIOGRAPHY OF A DEPRESSED AREA
Caudill, Harry M.
Boston: Little, Brown and Company, 1962.

This book focuses on the ignorance, demoralization and suffering of the inhabitants of the Cumberland region of eastern Kentucky.

59
OUR CHANGING RURAL SOCIETY
Iowa State University Center for Agricultural and Economic Development.
Ames: Iowa State University, The Iowa State University Press, 1964.

This book discusses changes in populations, power structure, community organization, and social change in rural America. The work is considered "a landmark in rural sociology".

60
OUR LAND TOO
Dunbar, Tony
New York: Pantheon Books, 1971.

This two-part study of poverty consists of conversations with poor black families, tenant farmers in the Mississippi Delta and thoughts on the problems of poor whites in eastern Kentucky.

61
PATTERNS OF LIVING RELATED TO INCOME POVERTY IN DISADVANTAGED FAMILIES
Ames: Iowa State University, Iowa Agricultural and Home Economics
Experiment Station, Special Report 74, August 1974.

Samples from cross sections of rural small places, urban low-income areas, and special populations (black families, rural migrants, and open-country farm and nonfarm families) were taken in this study of low-income families of 13 states. Four general types of family characteristics were examined: demographic attributes, resource factors, social structure and process, and value orientations to education and employment.

62
PATTERNS OF LIVING RELATED TO INCOME POVERTY IN DISADVANTAGED FAMILIES,
A BASEBOOK
Liston, Margaret I., ed.
Washington, D.C. U. S. Department of Agriculture, Cooperative State
Research Service, 1974. ERIC: ED098011.

A basebook which identifies patterns of living among relatively disadvantaged families and determines factors significantly associated with these
patterns of living for purposes of definition and measurement applicable
to descriptive interpretation and intensive analysis related to selective
aspects of family disadvantagement. An overview of findings from 2,650
rural and urban families is presented.

63
PATTERNS OF SOCIAL PARTICIPATION OF RURAL AND URBAN MIGRANTS IN AN URBAN
AREA
Usui, Wayne M., et al.
Sociology and Social Research 61(3): 337-349. 1974. ERIC: EJ159328.

Participation in religious and non-religious voluntary associations and
visitation with relatives, neighbors, and friends were examined.

64
THE PEOPLE OF CUMBERLAND GAP
Felterman, John
National Geographic 140: 591-620. November 1971.

This article examines the independent and self-sufficient living of
mountaineers, the children of the pioneers who came to the Appalachians.

65
PEOPLE, PROFIT, AND THE RISE OF THE SUNBELT CITIES
Perry, David and Alfred Watkins
In The Rise of the Sunbelt Cities.
Beverly Hills: Sage Publications. 1977.

In this paper the divergent conceptions of the fundamental role of the
city in America are discussed. Also discussed are the emergence of the
city as first and foremost a center of profit, the waves of migration to
American cities, and a diversion of the adherence to the dominant role
for the American City.

66
POLITICAL ATTITUDES AND THE LOCAL COMMUNITY
Putnam, Robert D.
American Political Science Review 60(3): 640-654. 1966.

This article examines the influence of the local political environment
on the attitudes and behavior of community members. It is found that
community influence is mediated through primary and secondary influences
in the community. These influences are important to understanding parti-
san politics in the local community.

67

POLITICAL STRUCTURE OF RURAL AMERICA
Knoke, David and Constance Henry
In the Annals of the American Academy of Political and Social Science,
F. Clemente, ed. 251-262. January 1977.

Historical rural American political behavior has revolved around the three
themes of radicalism, conservatism, and apathy. Future trends suggest a
diminishing political difference between rural and urban populations.
Leaving aside the possibility of an unforeseen crisis, rural interests
are unlikely to capture national policy attention.

68

POPULATION REDISTRIBUTION, MIGRATION, AND RESIDENTIAL PREFERENCES
DeJong, Gordon and Ralph Sell
In The American Academy of Political and Social Science 429. F. Clemente, ed.
130-144. January 1977.

In this article, the impact of residential preferences on population
dispersal migration is analyzed by means of data from a longitudinal
study. Recent data from the Census Bureau indicate that the rural to
urban pattern of population change may have halted or even been reversed.

69

POWER CORRUPTS
Segerberg, Osborn, Jr.
Esquire, 138-143. March 1972.

The author discusses the history of the Tennessee Valley Authority power
agency and its effect on the environment and on the people. The strip
mining procedures of T.V.A. are discussed and its power corrupting
consequence.

70

THE QUALITY OF RURAL LIVING. PROCEEDINGS OF A WORKSHOP
Washington, D.C.: National Academy of Sciences--National Research
Council, 1971. 139 pp. ERIC: ED072880.

Formal papers presented during the initial sessions of the workshop
included: "What Constitutes Quality of Living?," "Rural Health in the
United States," "Nutritional Levels in Rural United States: New Approaches
Needed," "Urban-Rural Contrasts in Public Welfare," "Possibilities for
Improving Rural Living: An Economist's View," "Quality of Rural Education
in the U.S.," "Rural Housing in the U.S. . . .", and "Employment and
Income of Rural People."

71

RACIAL INTEGRATION IN A TRANSITION COMMUNITY
Molotch, Harvey
American Sociological Review 34(6): 878-893. 1969.

An attempt is made to record conditions under which various forms of racial
integration occur in a changing community and the relationship between

those conditions and the means by which members of the two races (black and white) attempt to cope with the challenges of sharing biracial social environments. Racial integration is found to be very limited in frequency and intensity.

72

REAL, REGULATED AND RELATIVE POVERTY IN THE U.S.-MEXICO BORDERLANDS
Stoddard, Ellwyn R.
Revised/expanded paper presented at the Annual Meeting of the Rural Sociological Society. San Francisco, California. August, 1975, 42 pp.
ERIC: ED113102.

The essay explores the extent to which poverty exists among the residents of the U.S.-Mexico borderlands. It examines economic criteria, differential rates of poverty existing among the dominant and minority of borderlands population, and non-economic criteria for determining the degree of economic well-being.

73

REFLECTIONS ON FORTY YEARS WITH THE RURAL CHURCH MOVEMENT
Greene, Shirley E.
In Social Work in Rural Areas: Issues and Opportunities. Joseph Davenport, III, Judith A. Davenport and James R. Wiebler, eds. Laramie: The University of Wyoming, Department of Social Work, 173-180, 1980.

The author discusses and explains the Rural Church Movement and her part within it. The Rural Church Movement had two principal foci: 1) the rural church as an institution; and 2) the rural community.

74

RELIGION AND SOCIAL CHANGE IN THE SOUTH
Maddox, George L. and Joseph H. Fichter
Journal of Social Issue, 22(1): 44-59. 1966.

This paper argues that the religious heritage of the Southern region is a factor which provides a likely explanation of why the region has kept its identity as the most conservative section of the U.S. in spite of substantial changes in transportation, urbanization, industrialization, and education.

75

RESIDENTIAL PREFERENCES AND RURAL DEVELOPMENT POLICY
Zuiches, J. J. and E. H. Carpenter
In Rural Development Perspectives.
Washington, D.C.: U.S. Department of Agriculture, Economic Development Division, RDPI, 12-17. November 1978.

Reviews migration trends and discusses social economic, and attitudinal explanations for these trends. Implications for rural policy are also considered.

76

RESIDENTIAL SHIFTS AND ETHNICITY: A STUDY OF ADJUSTMENT OF HOUSEHOLD
HEADS RECENTLY MOVED FROM FARMS TO SMALL TOWNS IN CENTRAL ARIZONA
Leonard, Olene
1975. ERIC: ED111551.

This study surveyed the magnitude of the adjustment process for a sample
of Anglo, Mexican American, Black, and American Indian families that had
shifted their residences from farms to small towns in western (Pinal
County) Arizona.

77

THE REVIVAL OF POPULATION GROWTH IN NONMETROPOLITAN AMERICA
Beale, Calvin
Washington, D.C.: U. S. Department of Agriculture, Economic Research
Service, Rept. ERS-605, June 1975. ERIC: ED108813.

This article deals with the migration of people from cities to rural areas
during the 1970's. Among the reasons cited are: (1) decentralization of
manufacturing and other industry; (2) increased settlement of retired
people; (3) expansion of state colleges; (4) more recreation activity;
and (5) apparent higher birth rate in nonmetro areas.

78

RURAL AMERICA: OUR GROSS NATIONAL PRODUCT
Schultz, LeRoy G.
Iowa Journal of Social Work 3(2): 48-57. 1970.

The author presents data on the decline of rural America, and suggests some
solutions to problems of human suffering.

79

RURAL COMMUNITIES IN ADVANCED INDUSTRIAL SOCIETY AND DEVELOPERS
Bradshaw, T. K. and E. J. Blakely
New York: Praeger Special Studies, 1979.

The authors review the effects of advanced industrial society on the rural
community. They argue that it is no longer adequate for community developers to work just at the level of assisting individuals or establishing
groups to work for needed improvements. What is needed now is a rural
developer who can work in an entire region, coordinating people and
resources and using technological-based assistance.

80

RURAL COMMUNITY CHANGE
Wilkinson, Kenneth P.
In Rural U.S.A.: Persistence and Change. Thomas R. Ford, ed.
Ames: The Iowa State University Press, 115-125. 1978.

The author focuses on changes in rural community interaction and the
future prospects of the rural community in an increasingly urban society.

81
A RURAL COMMUNITY ON THE FRINGE
Schaffer, Albert
Rural Sociology, 23(3): 277-285. 1958.

Examines a rural community which maintained its stability due to prox-
imity to two industrialized centers, where farmers could work and still
maintain farming. Analyzes social structure of the community, boundary
mechanisms, neighborhoods, and school district; discusses changes which
occurred in each.

82
THE RURAL COMPONENT OF AMERICAN SOCIETY
Hassinger, Edward W.
Danville, Ill.: The Interstate Printers and Publishers, Inc., 1978.

This is one of the most current texts on rural sociology today. The
author examines dimensions of rural society, aspects of the rural community, the agricultural industry and establishment, the institutional
organizations of rural society, and rural poverty.

83
A 'RURAL' INDIAN COMMUNITY IN AN URBAN SETTING
Dowling, John H.
Human Organization, 27(3): 236-240. 1968.

The present paper is concerned with the demographic attributes of the
Oneida community and with some of the historical and contemporary forces
which have structured the community demographically in a way which
conforms to the model appropriate for hinterland communities. To
anticipate, the data suggest that in the Oneida community social distance
is the fundamental equivalent of territorial distance in remote
communities.

84
RURAL LIFE: PATTERNS AND PROCESSES
Jones, Gwyn
London: Longman Group Limited, 1973.

While much of this book is focused primarily on patterns and processes
of rural life in Britain, the author provides much information which
can be easily applied to rural American life. Discussions on the
family, the neighborhood, and the rural community are particularly
useful.

85
RURAL POVERTY
Burchinal, Lee G. and Hilda Siff
Journal of Marriage and the Family, 26(4): 339-405. 1964.

Characteristics of rural poverty in the 1960's described in this article
are useful for comparing them with present conditions.

86
RURAL POVERTY AND THE URBAN CRISIS: A STRATEGY FOR REGIONAL DEVELOPMENT
Hansen, Niles M.
Bloomington: Indiana University Press, 1970.

The interrelationships among lagging, intermediate, and congested regions
are examined. Regional planning roles in manpower and human resource
development are considered. Special consideration is given to the
problems and needs of Native Americans and Mexican Americans.

87
RURAL RENAISSANCE IN AMERICA? THE REVIVAL OF POPULATION GROWTH IN
REMOTE AREAS
Morrison, Peter A. and Judith P. Wheeler
1976. ERIC: ED138406.

This bulletin describes the characteristics of the population growth in
rural areas, it considers their possible causes, and suggests some
problems and outlines potential benefits. Tabular data presented included
demographic statistics on population mobility, migration, and interchange
covering the period between 1950-1975.

88
RURAL SOCIAL ORGANIZATION IN A SPANISH-AMERICAN CULTURE AREA
Johansen, Sigurd
Albuquerque: The University of New Mexico Press, 1948.

This study examines the nature of rural social organization in a Spanish-
American area in New Mexico and the role social-cultural processes play
in determining such social organizations.

89
RURAL SOCIAL SYSTEMS
Loomis, Charles P. and J. Allan Beegle
New York: Prentice-Hall, Inc., 1950.

This rural sociology textbook, which is outmoded in several areas, provides
an in-depth analysis of rural social systems, including the family,
informal groups, religious groups, educational groups, political and
occupational groups, and service agencies.

90
RURAL SOCIETY
Sanders, Irwin T.
Englewood Cliffs, N.J.: Prentice Hall, 1977.

This book on rural society is unique in its comparative treatment of rural
life on a world-wide scale. The author examines all major aspects of
rural life in the United States and in most nations of the world.

91
RURAL, SUBURBAN, AND CENTRAL CITY CHILDREN: SEX-TYPE ROLES IN OCCUPATION
Scheresky, Ruth F.
Psychological Reports, 43(2):   407-411.   1978.

Children's views of occupational roles which are traditional sex-typed by
society were explored as differences among the views of children located
in rural, suburban, or central city areas.

92
THE RURAL-URBAN CONTINUUM: REAL BUT RELATIVELY UNIMPORTANT
Dewey, Richard
In Perspectives on the American Community, Roland L. Warren, ed.
Chicago: Rand McNally and Company, 184-192.   1973.

The author argues that, while influences of rural and urban environments
upon social organization and individual behavior are important sociological facts, there is need for the rural-urban continuum to be reduced in
importance.

93
RURAL-URBAN MIGRATION AND POVERTY: A SYNTHESIS OF RESEARCH FINDINGS AND
A LOOK AT THE LITERATURE, FINAL REPORT
Price, Daniel O.
Washington, D.C.:   Office of Economic Opportunity, Tracor Project 073-
014, 1971.   ERIC: ED114236.

This report, which is the result of a literature survey in the general
area of rural-urban migration and poverty, presents both a synthesis of
current research findings and an annotated bibliography.

94
SHILOH: A MOUNTAIN COMMUNITY
Stephenson, John B.
Lexington: University of Kentucky Press, 1968.

This book is a study of family and community life in the Kentucky mountain
town of Shiloh.   The changes and adjustments of this community to
modernization provide the central focus to the study.

95
THE SMALL COMMUNITY
Morgan, Arthur E.
New York: Harper & Brothers, 1942.

This book is a brief survey of small community life--what it is and how
to work within it.

96
SMALL TOWN IN MASS SOCIETY
Vidich, Arthur J. and Joseph Bensmen
Princeton, N.J.:   Princeton University Press, 1968.

This is the revised edition of the classic study of Springdale which "described the penetration of the 'isolated' community by agencies and culture of mass institutions." Issues of class, power, and religion provided focal points for the study.

97
SMALL TOWNS AND SMALL TOWNERS
Swanson, Bert E., R. A. Cohen, and E. P. Swanson
Sage Library of Social Research, Vol. 79.
Beverly Hills: Sage Publications, 1979.

This book explores the physical, economic, governmental, and social conditions of small towns.

98
SOCIAL CHANGE IN RURAL SOCIETIES
Rogers, Everett M. and Rabel J. Burdge
New York: Appleton-Century-Crofts, 1972. 2nd edition.

This book is really an introduction to rural sociology. Particularly useful for the rural social workers are the chapters which describe rural social institutions and the process and consequences of planned change in disadvantaged rural communities.

99
THE SOCIAL ECOLOGY OF A RURAL COMMUNITY
Young, Ruth and Olaf Larson
Rural Sociology, 35: 337-353. 1970.

A village-centered New York rural community provides a natural group to test hypotheses about the interworking of structural and interactional variables in shaping community identification and the participation of male household heads and homemakers. The findings give the social importance of neighborhood-like groups new meaning for efforts to relate rural and urban people to the larger society.

100
SOCIAL IMPLICATIONS OF INCREASING FARM TECHNOLOGY IN RURAL LOUISIANA
Constandse, Adrian K., P. F. Hernandez, and A. L. Bertrand
Baton Rouge: Louisiana State University, Agricultural and Mechanical College, Agricultural Experiment Station, Bulletin 628, August 1968.

This study is one of the few research efforts to examine the impacts of changes in farm technology upon the structure and functioning of rural social organizations such as the family, the church, local government, education, and the economy.

101
SOCIAL POWER IN A RURAL COMMUNITY
Ferrell, Mary Zey, O. C. Ferrill and Quentin Jenkins
Growth and Change, 4(2): 3-6. 1973.

This article explores the nature of social power relationships at the community level, with particular focus upon the distribution of power through the utilization of the monomorphic-polymorphic perspective and upon the kinds of relationships which tend to produce power in a particular community.

102
SOCIAL PROBLEMS IN RURAL AMERICA
Ginsberg, Leon H.
In Social Work Practice.
New York: Columbia University Press, 176-186. 1969.

This article is an overview of the major social problems facing rural America. Most of the discussion is focused on the following areas: housing, crime, and social services.

103
SOCIAL PSYCHOLOGICAL IMPACT OF GEOGRAPHICAL LOCATION AMONG DISADVANTAGED RURAL AND URBAN INTERMEDIATE GRADE CHILDREN
Olsen, Henry D. and Donald E. Carter
Child Study Journal 4(2): 81-91. 1974.

This article reports a study that ascertained differences in perceived self-concept of academic ability due to residential setting (rural vs. urban).

104
THE SOCIAL ROLE OF A COUNTY SHERIFF
Esselstyn, T. C.
Journal of Criminal Law, Criminology and Police Science 44: 177-184. August 1953.

The author maintains that open country crime does not conform to general ideas of crime in urban areas. He also argues that, in part because of these differences, the social role of the county sheriff is different in rural areas.

105
THE SOCIOCULTURAL SETTING OF INDIAN LIFE
McNickle, D'arcy
American Journal of Psychiatry 125(2): 115-132. 1968.

It is commonly assumed that the American Indian is faced with (inevitable) assimilation, either voluntary or involuntary, into the majority culture. As this author points out, however, the Indian has managed to find alternatives in the past when, in his relations with the white man, he has faced seemingly inevitable choices. Illustrations from recent workshops for Indian students are used to demonstrate that, despite many problems, it may be possible for the young Indian to use skills acquired from the majority culture in support of his traditional society.

106
SOCIOLOGICAL DIMENSIONS OF AGRICULTURAL STRUCTURES IN THE UNITED STATES
Heffernan, William D.
Sociologia Ruralis 12: 481-499. 1972. ERIC: ED071794.

The social implications of the changes in agricultural structures in
rural America are examined. The findings indicated that (1) the corporate farmhand workers were less involved in community activities than the
corporate-integratee or the family farm workers; (2) the world perceptions
held by the corporate-farmhand workers were more similar to those held
by alienated workers; and (3) little difference existed between corporate-
integratee and family farm workers with regard to community involvement.

107
THE SOUTH GOES NORTH
Coles, Robert
Children in Crisis, Vol. 3.
Boston: Little, Brown. 1971.

Coles traces the migration of millions of whites and blacks from the rural
south to northern cities. Focus is on the readjustment problems endured
by the entire family.

108
SPANISH-SPEAKING MIGRANTS IN SEATTLE, WASHINGTON
Sepulveda, Sargio and Ralph A. Loomis
Washington, D.C.: U. S. Department of Agriculture, Economic Research
Service, 1973. ERIC: ED089903.

The urban-associated adjustment problems of Spanish-speaking migrants to
Seattle, Washington were examined. An effort was made to ascertain from
the migrant's vantage point the role and effectiveness of public agencies
in facilitating adjustment, policy recommendations for alleviating some
of the individual and societal dysfunctions of transition are outlined.

109
STINKING CREEK
Fetterman, John
New York: F. P. Dutton & Co., 1967.

A report of family life in a mountain hollow of eastern Kentucky.

110
THE SUNNING OF AMERICA: MIGRATION TO THE SUNBELT
Biggar, Jeanne C.
Population Bulletin
Washington, D.C.: Population Reference Bureau, 34(1): 1979.

The author summarizes recent migration trends that have favored the South
and Southwest. Sections of the essay focus on elderly migrations, urban-
to-rural migrations, and migration movements throughout the world.

111

SURVEY OF NAVAJO COMMUNITY STUDIES 1936-1974
Henderson, Eric B. and Jerrold E. Levy
Tucson: University of Arizona. Department of Anthropology, March 1975.
158 pp. NTIS/PB 251 676/1ST.

This bulletin is a survey of most of the extant studies which have been
made of Navajo communities since the 1930's. Data for a selected number
of social, economic, and demographic variables as reported in these
studies are compared.

112

TECHNOLOGY, POWER AND SOCIALIZATION IN APPALACHIA
Aquizap, Roman and Ernest A. Vargas
Social Casework, 51: 131-139. March 1970.

The author argues that to intervene in and change a community, a family,
or an individual effectively requires a keen understanding of how technology, power, and socialization are related. The purposes of the
article are to describe the economic and social class distribution within
a rural non-farm coal-mining community in Appalachia and its underlying
socialization practices, and to show how the subtleties of socialization
within the lower stratum actually complement and perpetuate dependence
on the elite of the upper stratum.

113

TERRITORIAL BOUNDARIES OF RURAL POVERTY: PROFILES OF EXPLOITATION
Reul, Myrtle R.
East Lansing: Michigan State University, Center for Rural Manpower and
Public Affairs and the Cooperative Extension Service, 1974.

This book examines rural poverty in various parts of the country, with
particular emphasis mainly on one segment of the rural poor--namely
migrant farm laborers. A major contribution of the book is the development of a framework for understanding psycho-social-cultural commonalities and differences of the rural poor--whether they be American Indians,
Appalachian and southern whites, southern blacks, or Chicanos.

114

THREE DECADES OF CHANGE IN A STABLE RURAL COMMUNITY
Copp, James H.
University Park, Pa.: The Pennsylvania State University,
Agricultural Experiment Station, Progress Report 261, July 1965.

Remarkable stability was found in a rural community of Pennsylvania when
data gathered in 1937, 1949, and 1960 were compared.

115

THE UNSETTLING OF AMERICA: CULTURES AND AGRICULTURE
Berry, Wendell
San Francisco: Sierra Club Books, 1977.

This book is a moving account of how exploitation of resources in agriculture has destroyed both the land and the different cultures which
have been intimately wedded to it.

116
THE WESTERN ASPECT OF RENEWED NONMETROPOLITAN GROWTH IN THE UNITED STATES
Beale, Calvin L.
Corvallis, Oregon: Western Rural Development Center, December 1975. 6 pp.
ERIC: ED121551.

U.S. Census data (1970-1974) comparing population trends in the West were
analyzed in reference to the recent urban to rural migration patterns
exemplified by a total U.S. metropolitan growth of 3.4% versus a nonmetropolitan growth of 5.6%. The remainder of the article focuses
primarily on rural growth in the West such as the growth of recreational
and retirement communities, the increasing of Native American populations,
etc.

117
WHO'S RUNNING THIS TOWN?
Lowry, Ritchie P.
Trans-action 3(1): 31-36. 1965.

The myths behind small-town conservatism are examined in this article.

118
YESTERDAY'S PEOPLE
Weller, Jack E.
Lexington: The University of Kentucky Press, 1965.

Based on thirteen years experience as a missionary in Southern Appalachia,
the author describes the life of the mountaineer. The book is particularly useful to social workers by aiding them in their understanding of
the mountaineer family and social life.

CHAPTER 2

RURAL SOCIAL RESEARCH

General Topics

Agricultural Research

Community Development

Community Satisfaction

Community Services

Data Sources

Evaluation

Farm Labor

Health

Housing

Income Assistance

Management Information Systems

Manpower Development

Policy Research

Population Distributions

Quality of Living

Rural Development

Rurality

Rural Sociology

Small Towns

1
AN ANNOTATED BIBLIOGRAPHY OF SMALL TOWN RESEARCH
Smith, Suzanne M.
Madison: University of Wisconsin, Department of Sociology, 1970, 142 pp.
ERIC: ED042562.

This annotated bibliography lists books, articles, and bulletins (written from 1900-1968) related to small towns in the U.S.

2
ASSESSMENT OF RURAL HEALTH RESEARCH
Washington, D.C.: U.S. Department of Agriculture, Office of Planning and Evaluation, 1974, Vol. I, 180 pp., Vol. II, Part 2, 352 pp.

Comprehensive inventory of rural health care services research. Problem-oriented research of depth and quality for use in decision making is identified and a selection is evaluated.

3
COMMUNITY DEVELOPMENT MANAGEMENT INFORMATION SYSTEM
Kuennen, Daniel S.
Georgetown, Delaware: University of Delaware, Cooperative Extension Service, March 1979.

Presents a management information system for use in community development programs, although the materials are primarily intended for Community Development Block Grants Programs.

4
COMMUNITY RESEARCH RESULTS FOR POLICY PURPOSES
Moe, Edward O.
In Rural Policy Research Alternatives.
Ames: The Iowa State University Press, 78-91, 1978.

This chapter attempts to explore the problems of communicating research results, analyzes promising links between researchers and users of policy information, and proposes some institutional innovations that will more effectively link the two groups.

5
COMMUNITY SATISFACTION IN A RURAL SETTING: DIMENSIONALITY AND CORRELATES
Rojeck, D. G., F. Clemente and G.F. Summers
Working paper, Center for Applied Sociology.
Madison, Wisconsin: Wisconsin University, April 1974.

In addressing the issue of community satisfaction as a viable extension to the search for social indicators, the following hypotheses were tested:

1) community satisfaction is a multidimensional variable; 2) satisfaction with community services is a municipality-oriented phenomenon that will vary according to size and place of residence; and 3) the assessment of community satisfaction is not dependent on objective economic, demographic, or social status indicators.

6

DATA SOURCES FOR COMMUNITY STUDIES: THE UNITED STATES
Clubb, Jerome M. and Michael W. Traugott
Archival Data Resources for the Study of Nonmetropolitan Areas: The United States. ERIC: ED162777.

Lists a very substantial number of empirical data resources which are available for the study of nonmetropolitan social, political and economic phenomenon.

7

DECISION MAKING AT THE HOUSEHOLD LEVEL
Morse, Richard L. D.
In Rural Development: Research Priorities.
Ames: The Iowa State University Press, 46-55, 1973.

Since family life patterns and the quality of family life are ultimately affected by rural development, any rural development proposal should include an analysis of its probable effects on the family. Areas of research could include family life cycle, time factors, family economy, and family functions.

8

DECISION-MAKING AT THE NATIONAL LEVEL
Paarlberg, Don
In Rural Development: Research Priorities.
Ames: The Iowa State University Press, 20-26, 1973.

Directions for appropriate macro-level research in rural development are presented in this article.

9

DELIVERY OF RURAL COMMUNITY SERVICES: SOME IMPLICATIONS AND PROBLEMS
Carruthers, Garrey, et al.
Las Cruces: New Mexico State University, AES-635, July 1975, 49 pp.
ERIC: ED116860.

Summarizing research conducted under the Western Regional Research Project in the delivery of rural community services, this report presents explications of the following generalizations which have been supported by research: 1) many rural service institutions need reorganization and renewal; 2) regionalization increases organizations' ability to provide some rural community services; 3) rural development depends directly on citizen participation and representation of various population segments; 4) effective leaders view development as a community process, not a personal one; and 5) public leaders seem to be drawn primarily from certain community segments.

10

DEVELOPING A MANAGEMENT INFORMATION SYSTEM IN A RURAL COMMUNITY MENTAL
HEALTH CENTER
Maypole, Donald E.
Administration in Mental Health, 6(1): 69-80, 1978.

This paper describes how one rural community mental health center developed
a management information system and responded to the pressures for accountability from funding bodies and collateral agencies in the community.

11

ECONOMIC RESEARCH PROBLEMS
Maki, Wilber R.
In Rural Development: Research Priorities.
Ames: The Iowa State University Press, 56-65, 1973.

The author discusses the information requirements and knowledge needs with
respect to optimal management scale of service delivery and widespread
citizen participation in social priority settings in rural areas.

12

ESTIMATING THE RELATIVE RURALITY OF U.S. COUNTIES
Smith, Blair J. and David W. Parvin
Southern Journal of Agricultural Economics 7(2): 51-60, 1975.

Develops a technique which can more accurately delineate between urban or
rural. Applies this to five representative states and found that this
procedure is the best yet devised for identifying and defining rurality.

13

AN EVALUATION TO DETERMINE THE EFFECTIVENESS OF COORDINATION, ADMINISTRATION,
AND DELIVERY OF SERVICES BY A MULTI-SERVICE CENTER IN RURAL ARKANSAS
Fayetteville: University of Arkansas, Graduate School of Social Work,
1973, 119 pp. NTIS/PB-240 390/5ST.

The project evaluated the first year attempt at developing a multi-service
center to deliver comprehensive social services in rural Arkansas. Recommendations concerning structure, management, training and information systems
are included. Community image, constituent organizations, and consumer
attitudes are discussed in depth.

14

AN EVALUATION MODEL FOR A MANPOWER DEVELOPMENT PROJECT
Wetherill, G. Richard
Paper presented at the Annual Meeting of the Southern Association
of Agriculture Scientists. New Orleans, Louisiana, 1975.

Author is proposing a model for the evaluation of a manpower development
program for a specific rural area of the state of Texas. The manpower
program is a multi-phased rural development project aimed at eleven High
Plains rural counties in the Texas Panhandle. A bi-dimensional evaluative
design has been formulated in order to accomplish ongoing evaluation.

15
EVALUATION EXTENSION
Byrn, Darcie, et al.
ERIC: ED161885.

This is a manual to aid rural community workers to better understand and
apply the principles and methods of evaluation. Although the manual is
directed toward extension workers, it is very practical and applicable to
social work practitioners in rural community settings.

16
FACTORS RELATED TO COMMUNITY RESIDENTS EVALUATION OF LOCAL SERVICES
Singh, Raghu Maath and Billy Webb
Commerce: East Texas State University, August 22, 1979, 26 pp.

The extent to which citizens are knowledgeable about and satisfied with
major services in their communities is important in effective community
development. Five small rural communities in Hopkins County, Texas, were
selected to investigate the availability of and residents' satisfaction
with institutional services.

17
FALSE ASSUMPTIONS ABOUT THE DETERMINANTS OF MEXICAN-AMERICAN AND NEGRO
ECONOMIC ABSORPTION
Shannon, Lyle W.
Sociological Quarterly, 16(1): 3-15, 1975. ERIC: EJ159731.

Examines longitudinal data on Mexican American and Negroes to determine if
they have become more like their Anglo hosts in terms of occupation, income,
and level of living.

18
FEDERAL RESEARCH AND INFORMATION NEEDS
Daft, Lynn M.
In Rural Policy Research Alternatives.
Ames: The Iowa State University Press, 3-22, 1978.

This chapter explores some dimensions of the rural development issue from
a national policy perspective, examines the policy-making process itself,
and describes some research and information needs.

19
A FIELD-THEORY PERSPECTIVE FOR COMMUNITY DEVELOPMENT RESEARCH
Wilkinson, Kenneth P.
Rural Sociology, 37(1): 43-207, 1972.

This article provides a conceptualization of community development within
the general framework of social field theory and indicates critical areas
of needed research as received from that perspective.

20
A FRAMEWORK FOR RESEARCH. THE EDUCATION OF MIGRANT WORKERS - WHERE DO WE
STAND?
Alphandery, Helene Gratiot
Prospects, 4(3): 364-368, 1974.

Themes for comparative research work and cautionary remarks on the artificial
simplication of research situations are presented in relation to the educational problems of migrant children.

21
GATHERING COMPLETE RESPONSES FROM MEXICAN-AMERICANS BY PERSONAL INTERVIEW
Zusman, Marty E., et al.
Indianapolis: Indiana State Department of Public Instruction, 1975.
ERIC: ED104612.

Responses to personal interviews among Mexican-American migrants were
evaluated to determine whether high quality data can be obtained through
personal interviews within the migrant culture. Analysis was based on
(1) sample mortality; (2) item non-response; and (3) details used to
open-ended items.

22
HOUSING
Southern Rural Development Center
Mississippi State: Southern Rural Development Center, Rural Development
Bibliography Series No. 5, September 1977.

This document reviews recent housing research and provides an annotated
bibliography of housing literature.

23
HUMAN SERVICES IN RURAL AMERICA: AN ASSESSMENT OF PROBLEMS, POLICIES, AND
RESEARCH
Bauheier, Edward C., Janet M. Derr, and Robert W. Gage.
Denver, Colorado: University of Denver, Social Welfare Research Institute,
May 1973, 101 pp.

Findings of an investigation of social and economic problems, social
policy issues, and service delivery systems in sparsely settled rural
areas are presented by the Social Welfare Research Institute of the
University of Denver. The literature review and analyses were conducted
with particular regard for problems of minority and ethnic groups, including
Indians and Mexican-Americans, and migrant and seasonal farmworkers.

24
THE IMPACT OF GOVERNMENT TRANSFER PAYMENTS ON HUMAN RESOURCE DEVELOPMENT
Southern Rural Development Center
Mississippi State: Southern Rural Development Center, Rural Development
Series No. 8, January 1979, 32 pp.

A synthesis of research literature (1969-1977) on the impacts of government
transfer payments.

25
INCOME AND WELFARE OF RURAL PEOPLE - AGRICULTURAL RESEARCH SIGNIFICANT
TO PUBLIC POLICY, PUBLIC WELFARE, AND COMMUNITY IMPROVEMENT
Larson, Olaf F.
Rural Sociology, 30(4): 452-461, 1965.

This paper reviews and illustrates the contributions of agriculturally-
related social science research to the welfare of rural people, with
primary attention given to research which contributes to decision-making
on public problems within public programs.

26
ISSUES ON AGRICULTURAL RESEARCH
Washington, D.C.: Rural America, Inc., 1977. 26 pp. (75¢).

Comments on USDA research and recommends new directions.

27
LESSONS FROM RESEARCHING RURAL NEEDS
Leonardson, Gene and David Nelson
Worklife, 12-15, September, 1977.

In rural areas, only agriculture produces more earnings than government
jobs. Government employment is therefore basic to any attempt to alleviate
rural poverty and promote rural development.

28
LOCAL RESEARCH AND INFORMATION NEEDS
Huie, John M.
In Rural Policy Research Alternatives.
Ames: The Iowa State University Press, 23-31, 1978.

This chapter concentrates on the development of research and information
for local policymakers, and draws some implications for research and the
organization of research efforts.

29
A METHODOLOGICAL REVIEW OF RESEARCH IN RURAL SOCIOLOGY SINCE 1965
Stokes, C. Shannon and Michael K. Miller
Rural Sociology, 40(4): 411-434, 1975.

The methodological adequacy of research in Rural Sociology since 1965 is
examined, and suggestions are made for improving both the quality of
research and the reporting of research findings.

30
NATIONAL CONFERENCE ON NONMETROPOLITAN COMMUNITY SERVICES RESEARCH.
Prepared for the Committee on Agriculture, Nutrition, and Forestry,
United States Senate.
Washington, D.C.: Department of Agriculture, Economic Research Service,
348 pp. NTIS/PB-276 444/7 ST.

The purpose of the conference was to facilitate the improvement of the quality of nonmetropolitan community services research for public decision-making at all levels of government. Three sections constituting the delivery sessions were: needs and use assessment at national and local levels; conceptual bases and measurement of quantity, quality, and consumer satisfaction; and service cost-quality-quantity relationships.

31
AN OVERALL QUALITY OF LIVING INDEX
Cleland, Charles L. and Y. N. Lin
Paper presented at the Meeting of the Rural Sociology Section of the Southern Association of Agricultural Scientists, Houston, Texas, February 6, 1978, 10 pp. ERIC: ED149941.

This study of the quality of life in the rural South developed a weighted index of the overall quality of living based on subjective evaluations by rural residents of such concerns as the local government's quality, politics, political organizations, schools, educational system, churches, civic organizations, recreational facilities, job opportunities, income, and the transportation system.

32
PLIGHT OF UNEMPLOYED SINGLE FARM WORKERS: THE RESPONSE OF THE UNIVERSITY TO A SOCIAL PROBLEM THROUGH IN-CULTURE RESEARCH
St. John, Edward
Research Monograph No. 14, 1974. ERIC: ED093543.

This monograph emphasizes the process in which the single-men projects were developed, briefly describing the projects and discussing research results and implications of the process for future research. Findings indicated that members of the single-male subculture can be organized into self-help groups and that in-culture research approach works.

33
PRACTICE, METHOD AND THEORY IN EVALUATING SOCIAL ACTION PROGRAMS
Rossi, Peter H.
In On Fighting Poverty: Perspectives for Experience. James L. Sundquist, ed. New York: Basic Books, 217-234, 1969.

Concerned with the War on Poverty. It also focuses on the Community Action Program and reactions of individuals in Appalachia and South Carolina to this program, and the development and consequences of government policy in the field. Rossi's chapter focuses on an explanation of why evaluation research has fallen short of its potential and suggests some ways in which these difficulties can be overcome. He suggests that evaluation of social action programs is best conducted by the use of experimental research designs.

34
PRINCIPLES IN DESIGN AND MANAGEMENT OF POLICY RESEARCH
Eberts, Paul R. and Sergio Sismondo
In Rural Policy Research Alternatives.
Ames: The Iowa State University Press, 42-77, 1978.

This chapter examines four central issues in the design and management of
policy research: the distinction between various kinds of policy research
and their respective roles in the decision making process; the distinction
between policy research in the social sciences from other types of social
research; the major dimensions and implications of a proposed scheme for
policy research; and the meaning and usefulness of policy research to
policy-makers to whom it is communicated.

35
PROBLEMS, ISSUES AND PROGRESS OF RURAL DEVELOPMENT RESEARCH
Jehlik, Paul J.
Paper presented at the Annual Meeting of the Rural Sociologic Society,
Baton Rouge, Louisiana, 1972.

An attempt is made to explain the problems and issues of carrying out rural
development research in the context of an institutionalized production-
oriented research system.

36
PROGRAM AND RESEARCH ISSUES IN RURAL DEVELOPMENT
Marshall, Ray
Southern Economic Journal, 41(4): 559-569, 1975.

In reviewing some of the problems of rural areas, the author demonstrates
that, with the exception of agribusiness interests, rural development has
received very limited attention by policymakers and scholars. The article
reviews some research and conceptual issues related to the problem.

37
THE QUALITY OF RURAL LIVING
Proceedings of a Workshop.
Washington, D.C.: National Academicy of Sciences -- National Research
Council, 1971, 139 pp. ERIC: ED072880.

Formal papers presented during the initial sessions of the workshop in-
cluded: "What Constitutes Quality of Living?," "Rural Health in the
United States," "Nutritional Levels in Rural United States: New Approaches
Needed," "Urban Rural Contrasts in Public Welfare," "Possibilities for
Improving Rural Living: An Economist's View," "Quality of Rural Education
in the U.S.," "Rural Housing in the U.S." and "Employment and Income of
Rural People."

38
RESEARCH AND COMMUNITY DEVELOPMENT: A PRACTITIONER'S VIEWPOINT
Yoak, Margaret O'Neill
Journal of the Community Development Society, 10(1): 39-47, 1979.

Practitioners in community development depend on research results as a
theoretical foundation and for support in practice. In order to meet
research needs, there must be a clarification of the concept of research
both by practitioners and social scientists. Broad types of research
include case studies, methodological guides, and theoretically based
research of practical value. Topical areas of research may be classified
as: community structures, dynamics, and reactions; human behavior research;
methodology, process, teaching and training; and evaluation of community
development effectiveness. Obstacles to meeting research needs may be
overcome through increased communication and understanding between researchers and practitioners; clarification and sharing of roles; and through
the creation of new roles to help bridge the gap between research and
practice.

39
RESEARCH AND DEVELOPMENT PROJECTS
Washington, D.C.: U. S. Department of Labor, Employment and Training
Administration, 1978.

This annual edition summarizes the projects funded by the Office of
Research and Development of the Employment and Training Administration
between July 1, 1975 and September 30, 1978.

40
RESEARCH PRIORITIES FOR MICROPOLITAN DEVELOPMENT
Tweeten, Luther
In Rural Development: Research Priorities.
Ames: The Iowa State University Press, 78-94, 1973.

A conceptual normative systems framework for allocating research resources
to promote micropolitan (i.e., nonmetropolitan) development is discussed
in this article.

41
THE RESEARCH REVIEW - 1971
Polenske, Karen
Washington, D.C.: Economic Development Administration, June 1971, 83 pp.
ERIC: ED058410.

This report is published to help inform employees of the Economic Development Administration and Regional Commissions of the nature, results, and
application of regional development research. One article in this issue
discusses implications of rural-urban migration for regional development
and growth center policies.

42
A RESEARCH UTILIZATION PROGRAM TO SERVE REGION VIII
Welch, Henry H.
Denver, Colorado: University of Denver, Center for Social Research and
Development, July 31, 1975, 46 pp. NTIS/PB-254 907/9ST.

This program (RUP) was established in 1972 to address the problems of
research utilization in a rural region characterized by geographic expansion,
dispersed populations and scarce resources. A research utilization specialist (RUS) was hired to (1) serve as a catalyst for application of research,
(2) develop and maintain research related communication with appropriate
agencies and resources, (3) encourage policy planning, and (4) serve as a
resource, consultant and change agent within the region.

43
RESOURCES IN EVALUATION FOR RURAL DEVELOPMENT
Southern Rural Development Center
Mississippi State: Southern Rural Development Center, Series No. 2,
April 1978, 55 pp. ($1.00).

This manuscript responds to the rural development practitioner's need for
knowledge on the subject of evaluation research. There are six articles
focused on rural development which deal with issues such as the process
of evaluation, the concept and philosophy of evaluation, alternative modes
of evaluation, sources of information, and the responsibilities of the
evaluation researcher.

44
RESOURCES IN EVALUATION FOR RURAL DEVELOPMENT
Southern Rural Development Center
Mississippi State: Southern Rural Development Center, Bibliography
Series No. 2, April 1977, 90 pp. ($3.00).

This partially annotated bibliography is an excellent resource guide to
materials on evaluative research and rural development.

45
THE ROLE OF RESEARCH IN COMMUNITY DEVELOPMENT
Hendriks, G.
In Social Welfare Policy, II.
The Hague: Mouton and Company, 1963.

Community development as an instrument of social policy needs the contribution of applied social research. In each stage of the process of
community development there is a need for a specific type of survey; and
good communication and mutual understanding between research workers,
community developers, and policy-makers is necessary.

46
RURAL DEVELOPMENT RESEARCH: CONCEPTUALIZING AND MEASURING KEY CONCEPTS
Jansma, J. Dean and Frank M. Goode
American Journal of Agricultural Economics, 58(5): 922-927, 1976.

The objective of this paper is to present suggestions concerning how one
might improve the operationalization and measurement of rural development
research.

47
RURAL DEVELOPMENT RESEARCH AND EDUCATION
Southern Rural Development Center
Mississippi State: Southern Rural Development Center, undated.

Feature articles in this new journal focus on four major research areas
in rural development: community services and facilities, people building,
economic improvment, and environmental improvement.

48
RURAL DEVELOPMENT RESEARCH AT LAND-GRANT INSTITUTIONS IN THE SOUTH
Southern Rural Development Center
Mississippi State: Southern Rural Development Center, September 1974.

Lists research activities at land-grant institutions undertaken in the
1970's with brief descriptions of each project (some were completed, others were
not). Helpful tool for obtaining unpublished material.

49
RURAL DEVELOPMENT RESEARCH IN THE NORTHEAST FOR THE NEXT FIVE YEARS: A
FRAMEWORK
Task Force Report to the Northeastern Regional Agricultural Research
Planning Committee.
Ithica, New York: Northeast Regional Center for Rural Development, 1973.

Report identifies priority problem areas for research over the next five
years. Priority problems were ranked by the task force, based on significance, researchability, applicability, etc. Gives framework for researching problems. Major problems identified were: (1) land use, (2) community
services, and (3) economic development through creation of more employment
opportunities.

50
RURAL DEVELOPMENT: RESEARCH PRIORITIES
North Central Regional Center for Rural Development.
Ames: The Iowa State University Press, 1973.

This is a collection of papers presented during a symposium in Zion, Illinois.
The papers cover a variety of research priority areas in community development, ranging from sociological to economic considerations. Much of the
focus is on the future research role of land-grant institutions.

51
RURAL DEVELOPMENT RESEARCH IN SOCIOLOGY: WHERE DO WE GO FROM HERE?
Southern Rural Development Center
Mississippi State: Southern Rural Development Center, Series Publication
No. 19, August, 1977.

The articles in this publication deal with three rural research issues:
the lack of correspondence between social research and field situations;
a needed research orientation for rural sociologists in the South; and
the problems of using and applying sociological knowledge in seeking
solutions to major community and societal issues.

52
THE RURAL HEALTH INITIATIVE - PRIMARY CARE RESEARCH AND DEMONSTRATION
Washington, D.C.: U.S. Department of Health, Education and Welfare,
Rural Health Systems, 1979, 30 pp.

This bulletin describes how a variety of local projects are pursuing five
of the principal themes reflected throughout the Rural Health Initiative
effort. These are: (1) coordination of resources; (2) community involvement; (3) comprehensive care; (4) response to need; and (5) quality care.

53
RURAL INCOME MAINTENANCE EXPERIMENT
Setzer, Florence, et al.
Madison: University of Wisconsin. Institute for Research on Poverty.
November 1976, 119 pp. NTIS/SHR-0002383.

This is a summary report of the second of four DHEW experiments to test
the behavioral consequences of a universal income-conditional cash
transfer program. Two locations were selected for the experiment, one
in North Carolina and one in Iowa, to represent areas with differing
proportions of poor persons and to permit the testing of regional and
ethnic differences in work incentive and other behavioral characteristics.

54
RURAL INDUSTRIALIZATION: A MONOGRAPH
Southern Rural Development Center
Mississippi State: Southern Rural Development Center, July 1979, 72 pp.

In this monograph are three rural research articles: "Rural Industrial-
ization Research Needs and Priorities: An Economic Assessment";
"Research Needs and Priorities in Rural Industrialization"; and "What
Research Tells About the Effects Rural Communities Will Face if They
Successfully Industrialize."

55
RURAL ORIENTED RESEARCH AND DEVELOPMENT PROJECTS: A REVIEW AND SYNTHESIS
Washington, D.C.: U.S. Department of Labor, Employment and Training
Administration. Monograph 50, 1977.

This document is intended primarily for use by researchers, planners and
operators of employment and training programs in rural areas. It provides
suggestions and techniques for carrying out planning and program operation
responsibilities; identifies potential research opportunities; and surveys
a number of reports on previous projects.

56
RURAL POLICY RESEARCH ALTERNATIVES
Rogers, David L. and Larry R. Whiting, eds.
Ames: The Iowa State University Press, 1978.

The papers in this volume deal with improving research design and methods
for the study of public policy issues in rural development as well as the
application of different kinds of techniques in policy research.

57
RURAL RESEARCH IN USDA.
Hearings Before the Subcommittee on Agricultural Research and General
Legislation of the Committee on Agriculture, Nutrition, and Forestry.
Washington, D.C.: U.S. Senate, 95th Congress, 2nd Session, May 4 and 5,
1978. ERIC: ED162814.

These hearings centered on the state of rural development research in the
U.S. Department of Agriculture (USDA). Topics were: (1) what is nonfarm,
nonfood and fiber rural development research; (2) analyses of research
priority system for USDA and the land-grant system; and (3) applicability
and availability of research to rural people--issues of access and usefulness. Research areas mentioned include housing, quality of life, transportation, leadership, energy, community development, health, employment,
service delivery, land use, and identification of need through citizen
participation.

58
RURAL SOCIOLOGICAL RESEARCH, 1966-1974: IMPLICATIONS FOR SOCIAL POLICY
Nolan, Michael F. and Robert A. Hagen
Rural Sociology, 40(4): 436-454, 1975.

After reviewing the articles published in Rural Sociology during the period
1966-1974, the authors conclude that rural sociologists have had little
to offer policy makers in the way of recommendations.

59
RURAL SOCIOLOGICAL RESEARCH AND SOCIAL POLICY: HARD DATA, HARD TIMES
Nolan, Michael F. and John F. Galliher
Rural Sociology, 38(4): 491-499, 1973.

In this commentary the authors discuss why research of rural sociologists
has little impact on social policy decisions relevant to present social

problems. Using Hightower's recent book, <u>Hard Tomatoes, Hard Times</u>, as an example, some directions for future research are suggested.

60
RURAL SOCIOLOGY AND RURAL DEVELOPMENT
Copp, James H.
<u>Rural Sociology, 37(4): 515-533, 1972.</u>

Rural sociologists' contributions in rural development have been minor because of deficits in substantive knowledge and system-oriented emphasis on infrastructure and provision of services within recent federal admini- stration. The author examines this condition and suggests other conditions under which rural sociologists could contribute substantially.

61
RURAL-URBAN PROBLEMS IN NORTH CAROLINA, THROUGH OUR EYES
Christenson, J. A.
<u>Five Miscellaneous Extension Publications No. 113,</u>
<u>Raleigh: North Carolina State Agricultural Extension Service, 1974.</u>

Information was gathered on the opinions of North Carolinians' perceptions of problems in their communities. Results showed that North Carolinians see the cost of living, the use of illegal drugs, and the availability of recreational and entertainment facilities, medical facilities, and trans- portation as major problems in their communities.

62
SATISFACTION WITH COMMUNITY SERVICES IN NORTHERN WEST VIRGINIA
Kuehn, John P.
<u>Morgantown: West Virginia University, Agricultural Experiment Station,</u>
<u>Bulletin 649, October 1976. ERIC: ED141062.</u>

Study objectives were to determine the levels of satisfaction with selected community services in an eleven-county area of northern West Virginia and to compare these levels to those of twelve other selected sites in non- metropolitan northeastern United States. Satisfaction items were: local ambulance, housing situation, local road maintenance, medical services, dental services, local schools, neighborhood, local fire department, local police, sports and recreation programs, telephone service, public transportation, and media.

63
SOCIAL CHANGE AND PUBLIC POLICY IN RURAL AMERICA: DATA AND RESEARCH NEEDS
FOR THE 1970'S
Madden, J. Patrick
<u>American Journal of Agricultural Economics, 52(2): 308-313. 1970.</u>

Lists six major trends which are dissolving the cultural dichotomy between rural and urban people. Lists research and data problem areas. Concludes that most failures of social reform programs are the result of poor communi- cation and failure to take into account the culture of the area. Stresses

the importance of an awareness of sociocultural attributes of the area.
Discusses avoidance of "pitfalls" when preparing rural development policies.

64

SOCIAL AND ECONOMIC CHARACTERISTICS OF THE METROPOLITAN AND
NONMETROPOLITAN POPULATION: 1977 AND 1970
Littman, Mark S., et al.
ERIC: ED166110.

This report analyzes data on population groups living in central cities,
suburbs, and nonmetropolitan areas in 1977, and examines changes that have
occurred since 1970. Subjects featured in the report are population, marital status, household relationship, family size, migration, educational
attainment, labor force status, occupation, industry, income and poverty.

65

SOCIAL IMPACTS OF NONMETRO INDUSTRIAL GROWTH: ANNOTATED BIBLIOGRAPHY OF
U.S. CASE STUDIES
Selvik, Arne and Gene F. Summers
Mississippi State: Southern Rural Development Center, Series Publication
No. 18, March 1977, 55 pp.

This bibliography presents annotations of a number of articles dealing with
the social impacts of nonmetropolitan manufacturing. One criterion for
the selection of articles was the reporting of empirical data on some
aspect of community response to the location of a new manufacturing plant.

66

SOCIAL SCIENCE RESEARCH ON RURAL HEALTH CARE DELIVERY: A COMPILATION OF
RECENT AND ONGOING STUDIES
Cordes, Sam M.
University Park: Pennsylvania State University, Agricultural Experiment
Station, Report No. AE&RS 131, August, 1977, 60 pp. ERIC: ED153777.

Summaries of 89 studies on rural health care (underway or recently completed)
in the U.S. as of December 1976 are reported.

67

SOURCES OF INFORMATION FOR EVALUATING RURAL DEVELOPMENT: AN OVERVIEW
Grayburn, Laura, Marilyn Magee and Myrna Hoskins
Paper presented at the Annual Meeting of the Southern Association of
Agricultural Scientists. Mobile, Alabama, 1976.

A handbook of evaluative research on rural development sources of information. It is intended as an evaluator's guide to material which the
authors have found to be helpful for locating evaluative research reports,
articles and reference books. Included in this handbook is a discussion
about computerized information retrieval systems whose subject matter is
relevant to evaluative research and a brief selected bibliography of
references for further information.

68
TECHNOLOGICAL CHANGE AND WOMEN'S ROLE IN AGRIBUSINESS
Hacker, Sally
Human Services in the Rural Environment, 5(5): 6-14, 1980.

The author argues that the role of critical action should be reunited with
research to strengthen the discipline of sociology. Using the role of
women in agribusiness as an example, the author demonstrates the uncon-
ventional methodological approach of the activist/researcher.

69
THROUGH OUR EYES, COMMUNITY PREFERENCES AND POPULATION DISTRIBUTION
Christenson, J.A.
Miscellaneous Extension Publications No. 112, 4
Raleigh: North Carolina State Agricultural Extension Service, 1973.

Information on population distribution in North Carolina and the people's
community preferences with comparison to other areas of the United States
is presented in this report. Population and location did not seem to be
crucial in selecting a community and a good place to raise children;
quality of water, air, schools, health facilities, and job opportunities
were of major importance.

70
TOTAL RESEARCH EFFORT
Emery, Margaret
Morgantown: University of West Virginia, School of Social Work,
June 1972, 34 pp. NTIS/PB-212 991/4.

This research project concentrates primarily on the employment of subprofes-
sionals in human service agencies. The ultimate goal of the effort is to
provide knowledge to help alleviate shortages of adequate jobs and adequate
human services in rural Appalachia.

71
UNEMPLOYMENT ESTIMATION IN RURAL AREAS: A CRITIQUE OF OFFICIAL
PROCEDURES AND A COMPARISON WITH SURVEY DATA
Korshing, Peter F. and Stephen G. Sapp
Rural Sociology, 43(1): 103-112, 1978.

This article examines the validity of procedures used by governmental
agencies for estimating unemployment in rural areas. The results of the
study support the contention that in a rural area the official procedures
lack some degree of validity and may radically underestimate the actual
level of employment.

72
WESTERN REGION AREA DEVELOPMENT RESEARCH CENTER
Padfield, H. I.
Corvalis, Oregon: Oregon State University, Agricultural Experiment Station,
216-15-98. (Research Program).

The program objectives are: (1) to investigate economic, psychological and
cultural processes by which rural areas become marginal from the American
mainstream economy and society; (2) to identify patterns of adaptation to
conditions of marginality and how these patterns vary; (3) to determine the
most effective policies, programs and services for reintegrating marginal-
ized people and areas; and (4) to evaluate existing policies and programs
in terms of contributing to or preventing marginalization.

73
WHERE HAVE ALL THE FARM WORKERS GONE?
Washington, D.C.: Rural America, Inc., September 1977, 81 pp. ($5.00).

The statistical annihilation of migrant and seasonal farm workers by
federal agencies is examined. An analysis of the federal effort to define
and count migrant and seasonal farm workers is provided.

CHAPTER 3

RURAL SOCIAL POLICY

General Topics

Agricultural Policy	Medicaid
Balanced National Growth	Migrant Programs
Farmers Home Administration Loans	Older Americans Act
Farm Labor	Public Assistance
Farm Subsidies	Rural Development Act of 1972
Federal Indian Policies	Rural Justice
Food Stamps	Rural/Urban Fiscal Policy
Health	Title V Rural Development Programs
Housing and Community Development Act	Unemployment Insurance
Land Use	Welfare

1
ACCULTURATING THE INDIAN: FEDERAL POLICIES 1834-1973
Cingolani, William
Social Work, Vol. 18, 24-28, November 1973.

This article discusses the extent to which Indian policies have been
successful in converting the Indian to European culture.

2
AGRICULTURAL SELF-GOVERNMENT
Lowi, Theodore
In Agrarianism in American History. Louis H. Douglas, ed.
Lexington, Kentucky: D. C. Heath and Company, 1969.

This article depicts how decentralization in the name of "grass roots"
democracy and self-government became the political process through which
the status quo of American agriculture came to dominate farm policies and
programs at federal, state, and local levels of government.

3
AN ALTERNATIVE AGRICULTURE POLICY
Washington, D.C.: Rural America, Inc., December 1977 (60¢).

Gives a brief overview of the alternative agriculture movement. Several
policy issues are outlined, and long range political strategies are
discussed.

4
AMERICAN INDIANS AND FEDERAL AID
Sorkin, Alan L.
Washington, D.C.: The Brookings Institution, 1971.

To develop the economic potential of the reservation and to ease the burden
of adjustment for those Indians who want to relocate, the federal government conducts a variety of assistance programs. The purpose of this book
is to describe and evaluate those programs, and to identify their strengths
and weaknesses.

5
AN ANALYSIS OF THE HUD NON-METROPOLITAN COMMUNITY DEVELOPMENT PROGRAM
Ball, Terry E. and Leonard F. Heumann
Journal of the Community Development Society 10(1): 49-65. 1979.

The 1974 Housing and Community Development Act established a new approach
to funding community development programs based on local needs rather
than national directives. The majority of eligible participants covered
by the CD Act compete in the nonmetropolitan discretionary CDBG Program
for funding. This article focuses upon the record of the nonmetropolitan
discretionary CDBG Program with emphasis on Illinois. The analysis un-
covered two major problems in the program. First, the program apparently

discriminates against the smaller communities applying for funds, and second, the program duplicates or exceeds some of the worst features of the old categorical grant system. It requires competitive applications, limits applications to one year grants, and leaves most of the screening formula used to award grants to the discretion of HUD Area Offices.

6
AN ANALYSIS OF LAND USE LEGISLATION IN SELECTED STATES
Mitchell, John B.
Ohio Agricultural Research and Development Center. 1978. 25 pp.

Examines the land use legislation and policies of selected states and the organizational structures evolved to carry out these policies. Intended for decision makers and professionals.

7
ANNUAL REPORT OF THE PRESIDENT TO THE CONGRESS ON GOVERNMENT SERVICES TO RURAL AMERICA
Washington, D.C.: U.S. Department of Agriculture, Rural Development Service, Available for the years 1970-1976.

These annual reports are required under Section 901 (4) of the Agricultural Act of 1970. Each report outlines the distribution of federal outlays to rural and urban areas by program groups. Recent federal incentives and regulations are also reported.

8
APPALACHIA: THE DISMAL LAND
Caudill, Harry M.
Dissent. 715-722. November/December 1967.

The author examines how planned government intervention can have both positive and negative effects on Appalachia.

9
BENEFITS AND BURDENS OF RURAL AMERICA
Ames: Iowa State University Press. 1970.

A collection of essays covering a wide array of problems in rural areas, with suggested government policy actions and local courses of action.

10
CABINET COMMITTEE ON OPPORTUNITIES FOR SPANISH-SPEAKING PEOPLE REVIEW: NATIONAL COORDINATION OF MIGRANT PROGRAMS
1974. ERIC: ED098005.

The thesis of this report is that the coordination of migrant programs requires national responsibility. Numerous studies and selected research proposals of projects are overviewed.

11

CAPACITY BUILDING FOR HOUSING, COMMUNITY DEVELOPMENT ACT IN NONMETROPOLITAN CITIES
Blakely, Edward J. and Martin Zone
Journal of the Community Development Society, 7(1): 116-131. 1976.

Paper analyzes the basic administrative structures of the Community Development Act, the external assistance and fiscal resources as they relate to local problem solving and community development. Concludes that for cities over 5,000 community development programs are possible, but for cities under 5,000 they may need outside expertise to take advantage of the new "creative federalism."

12

CHANGE IN RURAL AMERICA: CAUSES, CONSEQUENCES, AND ALTERNATIVES
Rodefeld, Richard, et al.
St. Louis, Missouri: The C. V. Mosby Co., 1978.

This volume is the most comprehensive collection of articles available on twentieth century changes in the rural sector of the U.S. Changes that occurred in the following six areas are examined: agricultural technology, farm organizational and occupational structure, transportation, community urban population distribution, and rural economic base.

13

CHARACTERISTICS OF FARMERS HOME ADMINISTRATION MORTGAGES AND THEIR EFFECTS ON LOCALITIES
Wiseman, Patricia and James T. Lindley
Paper presented at the Southern Regional Science Association Meetings, Birmingham, Ala., April 14-15, 1977.
Richmond, Va.: Office of Housing, Commonwealth of Virginia, 6 N. Sixth St. Suite 202.

This paper is based on a study of 508 Farmers Home Administration mortgages in a rural Virginia county. The main purpose of the study was to determine the effects of subsidized housing on a local tax base. The results showed that subsidized single-family home mortgagers did pay their fair share for services received and many times resulted in increased tax revenues.

14

COMMUNICATING RESEARCH RESULTS FOR POLICY PURPOSES
Moe, Edward O.
In Rural Policy Research Alternatives.
Ames: The Iowa State University Press, 78-91. 1978.

This chapter attempts to explore the problems of communicating research results, analyzes promising links between researchers and users of policy information, and proposes some institutional innovations that will more effectively link the two groups.

15

COMPREHENSIVE PLANNING ASSISTANCE IN THE SMALL COMMUNITY
Washington, D.C.: U.S. Government Printing Office, United States
Department of Housing and Urban Development, HUD-28-RT, 1969.

This is an evaluation of the federal government's Section 701 Urban
Planning Assistance Program in communities of less than 50,000 in population size. Forty-one communities across the country were studied.
The results as far as citizen participation is concerned were not opti-
mistic. Some of the findings were that citizen involvement in the planning process was most notable by its absence, that consultants were used
extensively to prepare plans and that, under these circumstances, significant citizen involvement seldom occurred. When it did it was directed at
obtaining approval of consultant's recommendations more than at obtaining
citizen views. Another finding was that the citizen views that were
represented in 701 planning were primarily those of local elites. The poor
and minorities were virtually never involved.

16

COURT ADMINISTRATION IN RURAL AREAS
Fetter, Theodore and E. Keith Stott, Jr.
Public Administration Review 40(1): 34-39. 1980.

Differences in rural and urban settings support the conclusion that strategies for providing improved judicial services to rural areas need to be
based on institutional precepts that will help strengthen existing communities and their traditions rather than turn them into dependent components
of larger regions.

17

CURRENT POLITICAL REALITIES OF RURAL AREAS
Tsutros, Frank
In Social Work in Rural Areas: Preparation and Practice. R. K. Green and
S. A. Webster, eds.
Knoxville: The University of Tennessee, School of Social Work, 36-44. 1978.

The author describes the function of the Congressional Rural Caucus and
the current political realities as they relate to rural development.

18

THE DECLINE OF AGRARIAN DEMOCRACY
McConnell, Grant
Berkeley, Calif.: University of California Press, 1953.

The political history of agricultural adjustment legislation and the decentralization of policy-making power is reviewed. The pitfalls of local
control in decision-making are carefully revealed.

19
THE DESTRUCTION OF AMERICAN INDIAN FAMILIES
Unger, Steven, ed.
New York: Association of American Indian Affairs, 1977. 90 pp.

Unwarranted and unjust governmental interference with Indian family life
is perhaps the most flagrant infringement of the right of Indian tribes
to govern themselves. The essays included in this book examine the
Indian child-welfare crisis, document the human cost of the crisis, and
report on innovative programs designed and implemented by the Indian
tribes themselves.

20
DIFFERENTIAL PERCEPTIONS OF IMPACT OF A RURAL ANTI-POVERTY CAMPAIGN
Sutton, Willis A., Jr.
Social Change Quarterly, 50(3): 657-667. 1969.

One of the country's major rural community action programs during OEO days
was located in Knox County, Kentucky. This article describes differential
perceptions--ranging from most to least favorable views--of the impact of
the program on the conditions of the rural poor.

21
A DIRECTORY OF RURAL ORGANIZATIONS
National Rural Center
Washington, D.C. (undated).

This is a directory of major national organizations involved in various
aspects of rural development and policies.

22
DIRECTORY OF STATE TITLE V RURAL DEVELOPMENT PROGRAMS
National Rural Center
Washington, D.C.: National Rural Center (undated).

A 400 page book listing 900 Title V projects in the 50 states and Puerto
Rico.

23
DIRECTORIO DE AGENCIAS FEDERALS Y ESTATALES PARA AMERICANOS DE HABLA
ESPANOLA EN KANSAS
Romero, J. Christian, et al.
Washington, D.C.: Department of Health, Education and Welfare, Office of
Education, Bureau of Post Secondary Education, Oct. 1978. ERIC: ED154964.

This directory, which is written in Spanish, contains information related
to Federal and State agencies which may be considered important to Spanish-
speaking people.

24

DISTRIBUTION AMONG RURAL PEOPLE OF BENEFITS AND COSTS OF SELECTED
GOVERNMENT PROGRAMS
Youmans, R. C.
Corvalis, Oregon: Oregon State University, Department of Agricultural
Economics, July 1975.

The paper reviews how the benefits and costs of selected government
programs are distributed among rural people.

25

THE DISTRIBUTION OF FARM SUBSIDIES: WHO GETS THE BENEFITS?
Schultze, Charles L.
Washington, D.C.: The Brookings Institution, 1971.

An economic analysis of the distribution of price and income supports
demonstrates clearly that subsidies have benefited primarily large
farmers rather than their smaller counterparts.

26

DOLLAR HARVEST: THE STORY OF THE FARM BUREAU
Berger, Samuel L.
Lexington, Kentucky: Heath Lexington Books, 1971.

This book is a revealing account of how the American Farm Bureau
Federation--the most powerful farm organization in the history of
American Agriculture--has shaped farm policies and programs in ways
which benefit the larger, more productive farmers.

27

DYNAMICS IN RURAL POLICY DEVELOPMENT: THE UNIQUENESS OF COUNTY
GOVERNMENT
Giles, William A., Gerald T. Gabris, and Dale A. Krane
Public Administration Review 40(1): 24-34. 1980.

The problems encountered by county officials in the day-to-day operation
of an ever increasing complex government are analyzed. The analysis
touches upon the issues of whether the administrative development is
significantly related to the policy of local government.

28

THE ECONOMIC IMPACT OF A BUSINESS AND INDUSTRIAL GUARANTEED LOAN IN A
RURAL COMMUNITY
Seaton, Kendell L.
Washington, D.C.: American University, Institute for Applied Public
Financial Management. July 1977. 93 pp. NTIS/SHR-0001979.

The Business and Industrial loan guarantee program is a result of the passage and implementation of the Rural Development Act of 1972. Its primary purpose is to revitalize rural areas. This study attempts to improve understanding of how development proceeds in a rural area, emphasizing the economic benefits and the problems encountered with industrialization.

29
ECONOMIC IMPACT OF PUBLIC POLICY AND TECHNOLOGY ON MARGINAL FARMS AND ON THE NON-FARM RURAL POPULATION
Tweeten, Luther and Dean Schreiner
In Benefits and Burdens of Rural Development.
Ames: Iowa State University Press. 1970.

This chapter discusses the impact of technology and public policies on marginal farms, structural transformation of the rural nonfarm sector, and the distribution of federal assistance programs to rural populations.

30
THE ECONOMIC AND SOCIAL CONDITION OF RURAL AMERICA IN THE 1970'S, PART 2: IMPACT OF DEPARTMENT OF HEALTH, EDUCATION, AND WELFARE PROGRAMS ON NON-METROPOLITAN AREAS, FISCAL 1970.
Washington, D.C.: U.S. Government Printing Office, Dept. of Health, Education and Welfare. 101 pp. ERIC: ED056799.

The report was prepared by DHEW for Senate hearings on a bill to Revital-ize Rural and Economically Distressed Areas. The report contains: 1) an analysis of DHEW programs which were included in Title IX of the USDA's rural report to Congress; 2) a summary of criteria used in determining the development location, and construction of DHEW facilities and services; 3) a list of all programs having potential for encouraging distribution of future industrial growth and expansion more evenly throughout the U.S.; and 4) other areas of discussion.

31
THE ECONOMIC AND SOCIAL CONDITION OF RURAL AMERICA IN THE 1970'S, PART 3: THE DISTRIBUTION OF FEDERAL OUTLAYS AMONG U.S. COUNTIES.
Washington, D.C.: U.S. Government Printing Office, Department of Agriculture, Economic Research Service, December 1971. ERIC: ED062055.

The distribution of federal outlays within the U.S. in fiscal year 1970 is summarized in this report. One major conclusion of the report is that non-metropolitan residents do not share proportionately in the distribution of outlays of many federal programs; larger, higher income urban areas are heavily favored.

32
ECONOMIC AND SOCIAL CONSIDERATION IN EXTENDING UNEMPLOYMENT INSURANCE TO
AGRICULTURAL WORKERS
Northeast Agricultural Experiment Stations, Regional Research Project
Committee, NE-58
Washington, D.C.: U.S. Government Printing Office, 1973. 113pp.

The possibility of extending unemployment insurance to farm workers
generates considerable debate among federal policy-makers. The economic
and social issues of that debate are discussed in this report.

33
EFFECTS OF FEDERAL PROGRAMS ON RURAL AMERICA
Hearings - 90th Congress, 1st Session, July 10-12, 1967. U.S. Congress,
House Committee on Agriculture, Subcommittee on Rural Development.
Washington, D.C.: U.S. Government Printing Office. 1967.

Statements and correspondence from over 100 persons are presented pertaining to many general and specific rural problems in light of federal programs
in operation.

34
THE EFFECTS OF MEDICAID ON STATE AND LOCAL GOVERNMENT FINANCES
Gayer, David
National Tax Journal 25(4): 511-519. 1972.

The study discussed the effect Medicaid has had on states with respect to:
1) stimulating state expenditures, 2) equalizing quality of care and 3)
equalizing the burden on states for the program's support. Although expenditures on medical care for low income persons have been stimulated
the remaining objectives have not been achieved.

35
EMERGING ISSUES FOR SPARSELY POPULATED AREAS AND REGIONS UNDER A NATIONAL
GROWTH POLICY
Tweeten, Luther G.
American Journal of Agricultural Economics 55(5): 840-850. 1973.

National growth policy seeks to stabilize and re-distribute population and
income. Therefore, rural areas, spurred by federal assistance, must be
made more attractive to industry. The main emphasis suggested is on
developing better educational systems, and other public services.

36
EMPLOYMENT, INCOME, AND WELFARE IN THE RURAL SOUTH
Rungeling, Brian, et al.
New York: Praeger, 1977.

The purpose of this study was to document by primary data gathering the
structure, operation, and behavior of southern rural labor markets.

Factors which may inhibit the adjustment of the labor market of the rural South--including the welfare system--are analyzed. One section of the book is devoted to Chicanos (migrants and non-migrants) and agricultural workers, another section to welfare reform.

37
EQUAL OPPORTUNITY IN FARM PROGRAMS: AN APPRAISAL OF SERVICES RENDERED BY AGENCIES OF THE UNITED STATES DEPARTMENT OF AGRICULTURE
U.S. Commission on Civil Rights
Washington, D.C.: U.S. Government Printing Office. 1965. ERIC: ED06826.

Focusing on the extent and quality of services rendered to black rural families, the study evaluated the degree of equal opportunity in the Cooperative Extension Service, the Farmers Home Administration, the Soil Conservation Service, and the Agricultural Stabilization and Conservation Service. Findings were that blacks received less service, and were requested to participate on agency committees less than whites.

38
FACTORS INHIBITING APPALACHIAN REGIONAL DEVELOPMENT
Hale, Carl W.
The American Journal of Economics and Sociology 30(2): 133-158. 1971.

The author concludes that the major problem in Appalachia regional development is one of attitudes, not resources. These attitudes have prevented the development of a growth psychology in the area.

39
FAMILIES BEHIND THE AFDC STEREOTYPE
Grendering, Margaret P.
Journal of Extension 14:8-15. January/February 1976.

This article demonstrates that the majority of AFDC recipients in both urban and rural areas do not fit the public's stereotype. Implications and future directions for extension programs are also discussed.

40
THE FAMILY FARM IN CALIFORNIA
Small Farm Viability Project
Sacramento, California: Department of Economic Development. A cooperative effort with the Department of Economic Development, the Governor's Office of Planning and Research, the Department of Food and Agriculture, and the Department of Housing and Community Development. November 1977.

The purpose of this project was to determine what could be done to increase the viability of family farms in California. The report indicates specific policies and actions which would reduce certain obstacles to the viability of small family farms. Several interesting findings are gi regarding the social impacts that could be expected if small farms were encouraged to proliferate.

41
FARM LABOR
Fuller, Varden and Bert Mason
In the Annals of the American Academy of Political and Social Science,
Vol. 429. F. Clemente, ed., 63-80. January 1977.

Estimates of farm occupations for 1974 imply that the nation's agriculture
is dominantly a self-employment industry. Farm labor in the U.S. lacks
market structure and is seldom a chosen lifetime occupation. Recent
developments in federal policies indicate that farm workers are likely to
receive federal protection equal to non-agricultural workers.

42
FARM LABOR HOUSING
Washington, D.C.: Rural America, Inc. ($35.00, for sale only).

This film gives an introduction to the FMHA Farm Labor Housing Program for
groups interested in providing better housing for low-income families.
Major steps in preparing a 515 loan and grant application are reviewed.
Eighty slides plus cassette that has both audible signal and inaudible
pulsed signal are provided.

43
FARM PRESERVATION
Washington, D.C.: Rural America, Inc., 4 pp. (10¢).

This fact sheet illustrates the difficulties of minority farmers in acquir-
ing and retaining farm land. Some recommendations for improving the situation are offered.

44
FARMWORKERS IN RURAL AMERICA, 1971-1972: PARTS 1-5.
Hearings before the Sub-Committee on Migratory Labor of the Committee on
Labor and Public Welfare. U.S. Senate, 92nd Congress, 1st and 2nd Sessions,
Throughout 1971 and 1972.
Washington, D.C.: Congress of the U.S., Senate Committee in Labor and
Public Welfare. ERIC: ED118327.

This series of hearings covered many topics, a few of which were: general
problem areas affecting the rural poor, particularly the migrant laborer
and his family; the policies and effects of federal agencies responsible
for providing rural programs; the syndication of farmlands by conglomerates; and the quality of rural life.

45
FEDERAL ASSISTANCE AND NONDISCRIMINATION: IDENTIFYING ELIGIBLE
PARTICIPANTS IN USDA PROGRAMS
Hammill, Anne and Percey R. Luney
Rural Sociology, 37(1): 98-102. 1972.

All USDA administered farm programs are subject to Title VI of the Civil
Rights Act of 1964. In response to the many problems in identifying

eligible populations, the authors present guidelines for reducing identification problems.

46
FEDERALLY ASSISTED HOUSING PROGRAMS FOR THE ELDERLY IN RURAL AREAS:
PROBLEMS AND PROSPECTS
Washington, D.C.: Housing Assistance Council, Inc. 1978.

Describes, analyzes and makes recommendations on federal housing that
can serve the elderly in rural areas. Includes federal agency and programs
involved.

47
FEDERAL BUDGET AND RURAL AMERICA
Washington: D.C.: Rural America, Inc., April 1975. 13 pp. ($1.00).

Presents data showing that rural areas do not get a fair share of federal
funds especially in the areas of housing, welfare, job training, education,
and assistance for the elderly.

48
FEDERAL HEALTH POLICIES IN RURAL AREAS
Hearings before the Subcommittee on Family Farms and Rural Development of
the Committee on Agriculture.
Washington, D.C.: U.S. Government Printing Office, Part I, 287 pp.,
Part II, 174 pp. 1975.

Comprehensive overview of the state of rural health programs, progress,
and needed action and testimony from experts in related fields are included.

49
FEDERAL INDIAN POLICIES . . . FROM THE COLONIAL PERIOD THROUGH THE EARLY
1970'S
Bureau of Indian Affairs, U.S. Department of the Interior
Washington, D.C.: U.S. Government Printing Office, Superintendent of
Documents. (50¢).

This pamphlet provides a brief history of federal Indian policies. Also
included in the back is a short bibliography of books and studies on Indian
history, problems, and the Indians' relationship to the federal government.

50
FEDERAL RESEARCH AND INFORMATION NEEDS
Daft, Lynn M.
In Rural Policy Reserach Alternatives
Ames: The Iowa State University Press, 3-22. 1978.

This chapter explores some dimensions of the rural development issue from
a national policy perspective, examines the policymaking process itself,
and describes some research and information needs.

51
FEDERAL SPENDING IN RURAL AREAS: A FAIR DEAL?
Reid, J. Norman, et al.
In Rural Development Perspectives. RDPI.
Washington, D.C.: U.S. Department of Agriculture, Economic Development
Division. 27-29. November, 1978.

This article briefly compares the distribution of federal funds to metropolitan and non-metropolitan areas. The author concludes that while some
differences exist, a lack of data makes it impossible to draw accurate conclusions about the equity of distribution.

52
FISCAL IMPACTS OF PUBLIC PROGRAMS ON TWO TYPES OF RURAL RESIDENTS IN
BOUNDARY COUNTY, IDAHO
Stubbs, David E. and Gerald Marousek
Moscow: Idaho Agricultural Experiment Station, Bulletin 573, March 1977.
24 pp. NTIS/PB-281 787/2ST.

The objectives of the research project include the following: 1) to
estimate the proportions of Boundary County's rural population that are
back-to-the-land people and conventional rural people; 2) to identify the
economic variables and collect data that will enable estimation of the
revenue contribution made by the two rural subpopulations toward the support of county services.

53
FOOD STAMPS FOR RURAL AMERICANS
Vrechek, Nancy M. and E. Evan Brown
In Rural Development Research and Education, 1(3): 6-7. 1977.
Mississippi State, Miss.: Southern Rural Development Center.

The article summarizes a study done by the Georgia Title V research staff
on the characteristics of Food Stamp recipients in Ware County, Georgia.
Several important characteristics were revealed. Working poor families
participated at a higher rate than did welfare families. Females dominate
the public assistance roles. A majority of the heads of households were
45 years or older and faced more severe training barriers for more highly
skilled jobs. The size of the Food Stamp bonus did not necessarily
decrease as the family size increased.

54
FORCES INFLUENCING RURAL COMMUNITY GROWTH
Rainey, Kenneth D.
American Journal of Agricultural Economics, 58(5): 959-962. 1976.

This paper examines how demographic changes in rural areas may impact on
public policy and programs.

55
THE FORGOTTEN FARMER: THE STORY OF SHARE CROPPERS IN THE NEW DEAL
Conrad, David E.
Urbana: The University of Illinois Press, 1965.

New Deal policies and attendant programs facilitated the demise of the sharecropper, the migration of his family to the city, and the subsequent hard-
ships that followed.

56
FOURTH ANNUAL REPORT OF THE PRESIDENT TO THE CONGRESS ON GOVERNMENT
SERVICES TO RURAL AMERICA
Washington, D.C.: U.S. Government Printing Office, United States
Department of Agriculture, 1974.

Analysis of 209 federal programs which accounted for 77 percent of funds
allocated to rural areas. Per capita outlays favor fast growing and/or
high-income counties. Apparently, counties which need the money are not
getting enough. Per capita outlays in rural areas were highest respectively,
in agriculture, natural resources, and community development. Rural areas
consistently received less federal outlays per capita than did metro areas
for housing, human resources, and defense and NASA spending.

57
GEOGRAPHY OF SECTION 8
Washington, D.C.: Rural America , Inc., 1978. 40 pp. ($2.00)

Tells how HUD's Section 8 housing assistance program discriminates against
rural areas.

58
GOALS AND VALUES IN AGRICULTURAL POLICY
Iowa State University Center for Agricultural and Economic Adjustment
Ames: Iowa State University Press. 1961.

This book is a collection of papers presented at a conference designed to
bring agricultural economists, political scientists, sociologists and
other social scientists together to examine problems of goals and values.
Papers are concerned with the value/goal system of American society generally as well as for agriculture in particular, and finally goals of farm
people for their own industry.

59
GUIDE TO FEDERAL PROGRAMS FOR RURAL DEVELOPMENT
Baker, John Austin
Washington, D.C.: U.S. Department of Agriculture, Rural Development
Service, Unnumbered, 1971.

A comprehensive list with some description of all federal programs designed
to aid in rural development. Includes programs designed to assist in

business stimulation, job creation, income expansion, facilities and service expansion in rural areas, community operations, and preparation for future development.

60
HARD TOMATOES, HARD TIMES
Hightower, Jim
Cambridge, Mass.: Schenkman Publishing Co., 1978.

This book provides an excellent account of how land grant universities are oriented toward enhancing the capacity of larger farmers, while neglecting and/or diminishing that of smaller farmers and farm workers. Special focus is on the development of the tomato harvester and the subsequent decline in small farms and farm workers in California.

61
HEW PROGRAMS FOR RURAL AMERICA: DEPARTMENT OF HEALTH, EDUCATION, AND WELFARE PROGRAM ASSISTANCE FOR NONMETROPOLITAN AREAS FOR FY 1972.
Washington, D.C.: U.S. Congress, Senate Committee on Agriculture and Forestry, February 6, 1975.

This volume focuses on HEW dollar obligations to nonmetropolitan areas for programs related to: public health services; rural education development; and to aging, child development, and youth programs; social welfare and rehabilitation services; social security administration; and other joint programs funded or managed by HEW.

62
HEALTH SERVICES IN RURAL AMERICA
Matthews, Tresa H.
Washington, D.C.: U.S. Department of Agriculture, Rural Development Service, Economic Research Service, Bulletin No. 362, 1974. 40 pp.

Health care needs and services in rural areas are compared with those in urban areas. Federal health legislation and its effect on rural areas are discussed. Examples of successful public and private experimental health delivery programs are given.

63
HUMAN SERVICES IN RURAL AMERICA: AN ASSESSMENT OF PROBLEMS, POLICIES AND RESEARCH
Bauheier, Edward C., Janel M. Derr, and Robert W. Gage
Denver, Colorado: University of Denver, Social Welfare Research Institute, May 1973. 101 pp. NTIS/SHR-0000209.

Fundings of an investigation of social and economic problems, social policy issues, and service delivery systems in sparsely settled rural areas are presented by the Social Welfare Research Institute of the University of Denver. The literature review and analysis were conducted with particular regard for problems of minority and ethnic groups, including Indians and Mexican Americans, and migrant and seasonal farmworkers.

64
A HISTORY OF INDIAN POLICY
Tyler, S. Lyman
Washington, D.C.: U.S. Government Printing Office, 1973.

A comprehensive history book of federal Indian policy form the colonial
period to the present, with emphasis on the period since 1930, to enable
the reader to see the processes involved in the adoption, administration,
and eventual changes of Indian policy.

65
THE IMPACT OF FEDERAL POLICIES ON RURAL SOCIAL SERVICE PROGRAMS
Honour, Robert
Human Services in the Rural Environment 1(1): 12-19. 1979.

In this article the author examines the nature of the "rural problem," the
unique aspect of social work administration in rural areas, and policy/
planning efforts needed to deliver social services in rural areas with
greater equity.

66
THE IMPACT OF GOVERNMENT TRANSFER PAYMENTS ON HUMAN RESOURCE DEVELOPMENT
Southern Rural Development Center
Mississippi State, Miss.: Southern Rural Development Center, Rural
Development Series, No. 8. January 1979. 32 pp.

A synthesis of research literature (1969-1977) on the impacts of government
transfer payments.

67
THE IMPACTS OF PRICE SUPPORT POLICIES AND PROGRAMS ON FARM SCALE AND THE
NATURE OF FARM FAMILY LIFE
Poole, Dennis L.
Ann Arbor, Mich.: University Microfilms International, A Doctoral
Dissertation. 1979.

The author identifies the chain of causal impacts extending from price support policies and programs to the changing scale of American farms, to the
changing nature of farm family life. The political and economic history of
price supports are examined in terms of the demise of small farms and the
upsurge of large farm operations in the United States. Then changing farm
scale is examined in terms of its possible impact on five dimensions of farm
family life: economic status, role responsibilities, kinship orientation,
social participation and the quality of interpersonal relationships.

68
INCOME AND WELFARE OF RURAL PEOPLE - AGRICULTURAL RESEARCH SIGNIFICANT
TO PUBLIC POLICY, PUBLIC WELFARE, AND COMMUNITY IMPROVEMENT
Larson, Olaf F.
Rural Sociology 30(4): 452-461. 1965.

This paper reviews and illustrates the contributions of agriculturally related social science research to the welfare of rural people, with primary attention given to research which contributes to decision making on public problems within public programs.

69
THE INDIAN: AMERICA'S UNFINISHED BUSINESS, REPORT OF THE COMMISSION ON THE RIGHTS, LIBERTIES, AND RESPONSIBILITIES OF THE AMERICAN INDIAN
Brophy, William A. and Sophie D. Aberle
Norman: University of Oklahoma Press, 1969.

This book brings the dilemma of the modern Indian into sharp focus, and is the first comprehensive investigation of the condition of the American Indian since the publication of the Meriam Survey Report in 1928.

70
INEQUALITY: A PORTRAIT OF RURAL AMERICA
Tamblyn, Lewis R.
Washington, D.C.: Rural Education Association.

This document demonstrates that federal spending on human resources development disproportionately favors metropolitan areas.

71
THE INITIAL EFFECTS OF SOCIAL SECURITY ON MONTANA FARM AND RANCH OPERATORS
A'Delbert, Samson
Bozeman, Montana: Agricultural Experiment Station, Bulletin 558, 1961.

Farmers' and ranchers' attitudes toward retirement reveal points of profitable concentration for those agencies interested in furthering the farmers' security. A look at the extent of ranchers' and farmers' information or misinformation reveals areas needing attention by the Agricultural Experiment Station and other agencies concerned with the enlightenment of farm people. The findings and sources of information on OASI should reveal useful material to extension groups, farm publishers and other agencies engaged in the diffusion of information.

72
IT'S TIME TO RETHINK OUR FARM POLICY
Bergland, Bob
Human Services in the Rural Environment 5(1): 1-5. 1980.

Bergland argues that national public discussion should be directed toward learning how public policy might be changed to reshape farm structure and redirect its course.

73
KEEPING THE MIGRANT STREAM FLOWING
Alegria, Fernando, Jr.
Manpower 6(10): 25-27. 1974.

In a cooperative effort government agencies and worker groups prevented migrant workers from becoming early casualities of the energy crisis through various help programs.

74

LAND POLICY IMPLEMENTATION: DESIGN AND MANAGEMENT OF RURAL ECOSYSTEMS
Alter, T. R.
East Lansing: Michigan State University, July 1976. 143 pp.
NTIS/PB-284 187/2ST.

The study is relevant to policy debates surrounding issues of land use. It focuses on policy implementation in the context of state land policies that influence land use decisions and that are initiated by state or local government units.

75

LIMITED ACCESS: A REPORT OF THE COMMUNITY DEVELOPMENT BLOCK GRANT PROGRAM IN NONMETROPOLITAN AREAS
Washington, D.C.: Rural America, Inc., December 1977. 412 pp.
NTIS/PB-275 817/5ST.

The report presents a summary of a one-year monitoring study of the operation of the community development block grant program in nonmetropolitan areas. The findings show that the smallest and poorest communities have the most trouble in finding out about and applying for funds of this program.

76

LINKAGES OF MEXICO AND THE UNITED STATES: STUDY BASED ON MODIFIED PROBABILITY SAMPLES OF RURAL MICHIGAN, THE U.S. GENERAL PUBLIC, SPANISH-SPEAKING LATINOS OF THE SOUTHWESTERN U.S., URBAN MEXICO, AND RURAL MEXICO
Loomis, Charles, et al.
East Lansing: Michigan State University, Agricultural Experiment Station,
AES-R-BULL-14, 1976. 90 pp. ERIC: ED075124.

This study was based on modified probability samples of rural Michigan, the U.S. general public, Spanish-speaking Latinos of the southwestern U.S., urban Mexico, and rural Mexico. Hypotheses concerning the potential collaboration of citizens of the U.S. and Mexico were tested. The findings are discussed under the following chapter titles: "Factors of Knowledge and Mass Communication," "Actual Behavioral Linkages," "Attitudes Toward the Across the Border Linkages with that Country," "Desire for Linkages and Collaboration," and "The Meaning of the Linkage--Contrasts of Mexico and the United States."

77

LONG-TERM COST IMPLICATIONS OF FARMERS HOME ADMINISTRATION SUBSIDIZED AND GUARANTEED LOAN PROGRAM
Washington, D.C.: General Accounting Office, Program Analysis Division
April 24, 1979. 75 pp. NTIS/PB-295 319/8ST.

The Farmers Home Administration provides loans for rural housing, family, and community and industrial development. The report discusses the nature and operation of each program and develops an approach for estimating its long-term costs.

78
LOW-INCOME HOUSING PROGRAMS FOR RURAL AMERICA
Washington, D.C.: Rural America, Inc., February 1978. 20 pp. ($1.00).

Provides a brief description of subsidized housing programs of FHA and HUD.

79
LOW INCOME PERSPECTIVES ON BALANCED NATIONAL GROWTH AND ECONOMIC DEVELOPMENT
Berkeley, California: National Economic Development Law Project,
January 1978. 56 pp. NTIS/PB-276 293/8ST.

This paper contains a review of present federal commitments to the poor; and analysis of information on where low-income families and individuals are located; a discussion of the special vulnerabilities of low-income rural families; and suggestions for programs and strategies that will retain the best elements of commitment to low-income families within the context of Balanced National Growth and Economic Development.

80
MAKING FEDERALISM WORK
Sundquist, James L. and David W. Davis
Washington, D.C.: Brookings Institution, February 1969. 353 pp.
NTIS/COM-74-11444/8.

The study examines the problems of coordination experienced by regional, state and local agencies in their efforts to cooperate in the implementation of several federal programs legislated during the 1960's for the purpose of assisting community economic planning and development. The review includes an examination of programs in rural areas.

81
MANPOWER POLICIES AND RURAL AMERICA
Marshall, Ray
Manpower 4(4): 14-19. 1972.

This article discusses what occurs when nonfarm industries locate in rural areas. Very often workers are employed from outside the area, having little impact on the unemployed and underemployed. There is support for relocating people to job opportunities rather than free migration. Relocation assistance projects are reviewed.

82

MARGINAL FARMS: A MICRO DEVELOPMENT OPPORTUNITY

Schneeberger, K. D. and J.G. West

Southern Journal of Agricultural Economics 4: 97-100. 1972.

This paper focuses on rural development programs which were designed to help marginal farm operators realize higher net earnings from resources managed through extension-type programs using paraprofessionals.

83

MENTAL HEALTH OF RURAL AMERICA: THE RURAL PROGRAMS OF THE NATIONAL INSTITUTE OF MENTAL HEALTH

Segal, Julius, ed.

Washington, D.C.: U.S. Government Printing Office, August 1973.

The problem of supplying mental health services to rural areas in the U.S. and the involvement of the National Institute of Mental Health (NIMH) in the solution of these problems are reported. The text is composed of studies of rural life and mental health which include demographic and epidemiological studies; approaches to service based on hospital and community resources; a discussion of community mental health centers in rural U.S.; five case histories of rural mental health centers; programs for State hospitals with rural patients; and programs for supplying the manpower to meet rural needs.

84

MIGRANT WORKERS: A BIBLIOGRAPHY WITH ABSTRACTS

Young, Mary E.

Springfield, Virginia: National Technical Information Service, April 1978. 74 pp.

Needs and problems of the migrant worker are reviewed. Aspects include medical and health care, housing, employment, education needs, and the interaction of the migrant and the community. This updated bibliography contains 69 abstracts.

85

MULTI-JURISDICTIONAL AREA DEVELOPMENT: A MODEL AND LEGISLATIVE PROGRAM

Institute for Rural America in Association with Spindletop Research, July 1969. 126 pp.

This book concentrates on the establishment of an improved national delivery system. A national development policy is proposed which consists of two parts. The first involves the need for an improved delivery system. The second part consists of the reformulation of the various programs (education, health, welfare, etc.) which are to be conveyed through an improved delivery system.

86
NEW DEAL POLICY AND SOUTHERN RURAL POVERTY
Mertz, Paul E.
Baton Rouge: Louisiana State University Press, 1978.

The inability of the Roosevelt administration to alleviate the plight of
some of the United States most destitute citizens--sharecroppers and tenant
farmers--is carefully described and analyzed in this study. Some of the
more liberal social welfare reform programs designed to help this segment
of the population are examined, and the reasons for failure considered.

87
NEW DIRECTIONS IN EXTENSION
Summers, James C.
Conference Papers Series 4.
Morgantown, W. Va.: West Virginia University, Office of Research and
Development, Appalachian Center, September 1973.

A pilot program at West Virginia University Extension was initiated for the
purpose of developing new and modified university extension educational
programs that would contribute to an improved quality of living among the
rural poor. This volume, which consists of conference papers and remarks,
examines outcomes of the program and explores the changing social, economic,
and community-based roles of Extension.

88
THE NEW RURALISM: THE POST INDUSTRIAL AGE IS UPON US
Ellis, William N.
The Futurist 10(4): 202-204. 1975.

A new ruralism, which may mark the beginning of a post-industrial age aimed
at meeting man's psychic needs rather than his material wants, may require
shifts in government and business policies.

89
NONMETROPOLITAN SOCIAL PLANNING
Wylie, Mary L.
In Social Work in Rural Communities, Leon H. Ginsberg, ed.
New York: Council on Social Work Education, 48-61. 1976.

Most social planning is urban-oriented. The author of this article
discusses some of the problems of rural social planning and describes how
social planning technology can be applied to nonmetropolitan communities.

90
THE OLDER AMERICANS ACT AND THE RURAL ELDERLY
Hearings before the Special Committee on Aging, U.S. Senate, 94th Congress,
First Session.
Washington, D.C.: Congress of the United States, Special Committee on
Aging. ERIC: ED116839.

The older Americans Act of 1965 has not met the needs of the rural elderly and was consequently the subject of these hearings which considered proposed legislation under Title III of the Act which gave support for demonstration programs to assist older rural people and to improve the delivery system of rural America.

91
THE PEOPLE LEFT BEHIND
Washington, D.C.: President's National Advisory Commission on
Rural Poverty, 1967.

Matters pertinent to the participation of Mexican-Americans in the political life of California are discussed. These matters include the issue of reapportionment and its effect on the Mexican-American community; water rights; influence in major political parties; political use of police and the courts; and Mexican-American political problems in both rural and urban areas.

92
OF THE PEOPLE, BY THE PEOPLE, FOR THE PEOPLE: COOPERATIVE HOUSING FOR RURAL AMERICA
Washington, D.C.: Rural America, Inc., April 1979.

Provides a comprehensive study of cooperative housing for rural America.

93
PEOPLE, PROFIT AND THE RISE OF THE SUNBELT CITIES
Perry, David and Alfred Watkins
In the Rise of the Sunbelt Cities.
Beverly Hills: Beverly Hills Sage Publication, 1977.

In this paper the divergent conceptions of the fundamental role of the city in America are examined.   Discussed are the emergence of the city, as first and foremost a center of profit, the waves of migration to American cities, and a diversion of the adherence to the dominant role for the American city.

94
A PERSPECTIVE IN TITLE V RURAL DEVELOPMENT PROGRAMS IN THE WESTERN STATES
Sorensen, Donald M.
Corvallis, Oregon: Western Rural Development Center, Special Report No. 2.
December 1975.   17 pp. ERIC: ED116840.

Based on the available documentation of Title V (Rural Development Act of 1972) rural development programs currently underway in the western region, this report summarizes project endeavors to: 1) improve income and employment; 2) enrich environmental quality; 3) enhance social and health amenities; and 4) improve the quality of government processes and services.

95
PLATFORM FOR RURAL AMERICA
Washington, D.C.: Rural America, Inc., Revised at the Third National
Conference), December 1977.

This revised edition of the original platform for Rural America reflects
the findings and recommendations which emerge from the second and third
national conferences on Rural America. This document outlines a proposal
of action for concerned citizens.

96
POLICY IMPLICATIONS OF THE MOVEMENT OF BLACKS OUT OF THE RURAL SOUTH
Lee, Anne S. and Gladys K. Bowles
Washington, D.C.: U.S. Department of Agriculture, Economic Research
Service, 1974. ERIC: ED096023.

In recent decades, the heavy movement of blacks out of the rural south has
produced shifts in service needs. This out-migration effected compositional
changes in both rural and urban populations, affecting the urban south, the
urban non-south, and the rural south. The paper also examines some policy
implications related to service needs caused by this movement.

97
THE POLICY PROCESS IN AMERICAN AGRICULTURE
Talbot, Ross E. and Don F. Hadwiger
San Francisco: Chandler Publishing Co., 1968.

A political science perspective is given in this analysis of the policy-
making process in American agriculture. The book is an excellent text for
understanding the interplay of ideology, political actors, and legislative
processes.

98
POLITICAL ECONOMICS OF RURAL POVERTY IN THE SOUTH
Ford, Arthur M.
Cambridge, Mass.: Ballinger, 1973.

Integrating economics, political theory and sociology the author traces the
major characteristics of the agrarian revolution experienced by the Core
South and Appalachia since the mid-thirties. The political power of the
upper income farmer is carefully contrasted with the relative powerlessness of low-income farmers and unskilled farm laborers in the South.

99
POLITICAL PARTICIPATION OF MEXICAN AMERICANS IN CALIFORNIA
A Report of the California State Advisory Committee to the U.S. Commission
on Civil Rights
Washington, D.C.: Commission on Civil Rights, August 1971. ERIC: ED062061.

Matters pertinent to the participation of Mexican Americans in the political
life of California are discussed. These matters include the issue of reapportionment and its effect on the Mexican American Community; voter rights;
influence in major political parties; political use of police and the courts;
and Mexican American political problems in both rural and urban areas.

100
POLITICAL STRUCTURE OF RURAL AMERICA
Knoke, David and Constance Henry
In The Annals of the American Academy of Political and Social Science,
51-62. January 1977. F. Clemente, ed.

Historical rural American political behavior has revolved around the themes
of radicalism, conservatism, and apathy. Future trends suggest a diminishing political difference between rural and urban populations. Leaving
aside the possibility of an unforeseen crisis, rural interests are unlikely
to capture national policy attention.

101
POVERTY AND POLITICS: THE RISE AND DECLINE OF THE FARM SECURITY
ADMINISTRATION
Baldwin, Stanley
Chapel Hill: The University of North Carolina Press, 1968.

The Farm Security Administration supported some of the most innovative and
liberal New Deal programs to combat poverty of rural people, particularly
small farm owners, tenants, and farmworkers. This book reviews these
programs and gives a revealing account of how conservative forces purged
these programs and the administrative bureaucracy which sponsored them.

102
POWER CORRUPTS
Segerberg, Osborn, Jr.
Esquire, 138-143, March 1972.

The author discusses the history of the Tennessee Valley Authority Power
Agency and its effect on the environment and on the people. The strip
mining procedure of TVA is discussed and its power corruption consequences.

103
PRINCIPLES IN DESIGN AND MANGEMENT OF POLICY RESEARCH
Eberts, Paul R. and Sergio Sismondo
In Rural Policy Research Alternatives.
Ames: The Iowa State University Press, 42-77, 1978.

This chapter examines four central issues in the design and management of
policy research: the distinction between various kinds of policy research
and their respective roles in the decision making process; the distinction
between policy research in the social sciences from other types of social
research; the major dimensions and implications of a proposed scheme for
policy research; and the meaning and usefulness of policy research to
policymakers to whom it is communicated.

104
PROCEEDINGS OF A NATIONAL CONFERENCE ON RURAL DEVELOPMENT
United States Senate
Washington, D.C.: U.S. Government Printing Office, 1974.

Conference dealt with congressional views on rural development, past
responses of the land grant system to rural development needs, case
studies of some successful efforts, and policies which may lead to
conflict.

105
PROGRESS AND PLANS FOR IMPLEMENTATION OF RURAL DEVELOPMENT ACT OF 1972
Subcommittee on Rural Development
Washington, D.C.: U.S. Government Printing Office, Committee on
Agriculture and Forestry, 1973.

A report on the functions the Rural Development Act will perform, and when
and how these functions will be implemented. The Rural Development Act is
analyzed and explained so that local rural officials and leaders can understand and use provisions to aid their people and communities.

106
PUBLIC POLICY OF RURAL HEALTH
Swanson, Bert E. and Edith Swanson
In Rural Health Services: Organization, Delivery, and Use.
Ames: The Iowa State University Press, 137-163. 1976.

Contemporary health policy issues as they relate to rural America are
discussed in this article.

107
PUBLIC POLICY AND RURAL SOCIAL CHANGE
Schaller, W. Neill
In Rural U.S.A.: Persistence and Change, Thomas R. Ford, ed.
Ames: The Iowa State University Press, 199-210. 1978.

How public policies have influenced change in rural America and how overall change has shaped public policy are examined.

108
THE QUEST FOR RURAL EQUITY
Margolis, Richard
Human Services in the Rural Environment 1(2): 1979.

The author discusses the discrimination that many Americans are facing
because of the fact that they live in a rural setting. The author
emphasizes organizing rural America to give political, economic, and
social equity to those who reside in rural settings.

109
RAISING RESPONSIBLE HELL
Vincent, Gary
Successful Farming, 76: 24-25. November 1976.

Article on farm women's increased involvement in politics. Describes
three organizations: Women Involved in Farm Economics, American Agri-
Women and Concerned Farm Wives of Kansas.

110
A RECRITIQUE AND ANALYSIS OF THE RURAL DEVELOPMENT ACT OF 1972
Stanfield, G. G.
Rural Sociology 40(1): 75-79. 1975.

Sees the Rural Development Act of 1972 as being an appeasement. Cites
the fact that federal government has not made a more vigorous financial
commitment to rural industrial expansion as one reason. Says that
national legislators do not see rural industrial plant location as a
relatively high priority and are disinclined to expand budgets for low
priority programs.

111
REDMAN'S LAND/WHITE MAN'S LAW: A STUDY OF THE PAST AND PRESENT STATUS
OF THE AMERICAN INDIAN
Washburn, Wilcomb E.
New York: Charles Scribners' Sons, 1971.

This book is the study of the process by which the Indian moved from
sovereign, to ward, to citizen. The author describes and analyzes the
steps in the relationship that developed between whites and Indians and
shows the historical evolutions of the assumptions underlying the
Indian's present status.

112
RENEWED GROWTH IN RURAL COMMUNITIES
Beale, Calvin L.
The Futurist, 196-202. August 1975.

Factors contributing to the migration of people from urban to rural areas
are examined.

113
REPORT ON URBAN AND RURAL NON-RESERVATION INDIANS (TASK FORCE EIGHT:
URBAN AND RURAL NONRESERVATION INDIANS. FINAL REPORT TO THE AMERICAN
INDIAN POLICY REVIEW COMMISSION)
Washington, D.C.: U.S. Government Printing Office, Congress of the
United States. ERIC: ED141011.

This report presents the results of a 12 month investigation of rural and
urban nonreservation American Indian needs, including legal services
social services, housing, health, elderly care, alcoholism counseling,
and transportation.

114
RESIDENTIAL AND REGIONAL DISTRIBUTION OF BENEFITS UNDER THE ALLOWANCE FOR
BASIC LIVING EXPENSES: ABLE WELFARE REFORM PROPOSAL
Carlin, Thomas A., Gary Hendricks and Faye F. Christian
Washington, D.C.:   U.S. Department of Agriculture, Agricultural
Economic Report No. 374.

A broad-based welfare reform program, proposed in 1974 by the Joint Economic Committee of the U.S. Congress, is compared to the current Aid to
Families with Dependent Children (AFDC) and Food Stamp programs. The
proposal is termed ABLE (Allowance for Basic Living Expenses). The study
finds that the primary impact of ABLE would be to increase substantially
the number of welfare-eligible families without changing the distribution
of eligible families among regions or urban and rural areas. However,
there would be a substantial reduction in benefits to eligible families
in the Northeast and to a lesser extent in the North Central region and
the West. Eligible Southern families would gain substantially. Metropolitan areas would lose benefits under ABLE, but rural areas, except
in the Northeast, would gain.

115
RESIDENTIAL PREFERENCES AND RURAL DEVELOPMENT POLICY
Zuiches, J. J. and E. H. Carpenter
Washington, D.C.:   U.S. Department of Agriculture, Rural Development
Perspectives, RDPI, 12-17. November 1978.

Reviews migration trends and discusses social, economic, and attitudinal
explanations for these trends. Implications for rural policy are also
considered.

116
RESOURCE GUIDE FOR RURAL DEVELOPMENT
Washington, D.C.:   National Rural Center.

The guide provides information about public and private funding source
for rural development.

117
THE REVERSAL IN MIGRATION PATTERNS - SOME RURAL DEVELOPMENT CONSEQUENCES
Ploch, Louisia A.
1977. ERIC: ED144743.

The focus of this publication is on the consequences of reverse migration on
rural areas of Maine. Maine's rural in-migrants are having impact on both
the economy and local services. This impact is mainly on the demand for
better education, better libraries, etc. The consequences of these
demands cannot be ignored by rural policymakers.

118
REVISED GUIDE TO THE RURAL DEVELOPMENT ACT OF 1972
Committee on Agriculture and Forestry
Washington, D.C.: U.S. Government Printing Office, United States Senate,
1975.

Report discusses additions to the Rural Development Act of 1972 up to 1975.
Also, it lists and describes the financial and technical assistance available to local officials in their efforts to develop rural areas.

119
REVITALIZATION OF RURAL AND OTHER ECONOMICALLY DISTRESSED AREAS, PART I.
Hearings before the Committee on Government Operations, 92nd Congress,
1st Session on S.10, a Bill to Establish a National Policy Relative to
the Revitalization of Rural and Other Economically . . .
Washington, D.C.: U.S. Senate, 200 pp. ERIC: ED056800.

Bill S.10 testimony was to revitalize rural and other economically distressed areas by 1) establishing incentives for a more even and practical
distribution of industrial growth and activity, and 2) developing manpower
training to meet the needs of industry.

120
THE ROLE OF COMMUNICATION AND ATTITUDES IN SMALL FARM PROGRAMS
Southern Rural Development Center
Mississippi State, Miss.: Rural Development Series No. 4, SRDC ($1.00).

The author discusses how lack of access to resources, limited access to
information, and farmer values and attitudes affect small farmers
and the adoption of new farm practices.

121
RURAL AMERICA: OUR GROSS NATIONAL PRODUCT
Schultz, LeRoy G.
Iowa Journal of Social Work 3(2): 48-57. 1970.

The author presents data on the decline of rural America, and suggests
some solutions to problems of human suffering.

122
RURAL DEVELOPMENT ACT, 1972
Collinsville: Southwestern Illinois Metropolitan Area Planning Commission,
November 1972. 6 pp. NTIS/PB-214 817/9.

A brief summary is made of the major elements of the Rural Development Act
of 1972 as they relate to local officials.

123
RURAL DEVELOPMENT ACT OF 1972: STAFF EXPLANATION OF H.R.12931
Washington, D.C.: U.S. Senate, The Rural Development Act of 1972,
passed by the Senate April 20, 1972, Committee Print, 92nd Congress,
2nd Session, April 21, 1972. 9 pp. ERIC: ED118285.

Designed to assist in the development of rural areas in the U.S., the
Rural Development Act of 1972 is divided into seven titles which are
named and explicated in this staff explanation.

124
RURAL DEVELOPMENT: FIRST ANNUAL REPORT TO THE CONGRESS ON THE AVAILABILITY
OF GOVERNMENT SERVICES TO RURAL AREAS
Washington, D.C.: U.S. Department of Agriculture, February 1971.   34 pp.
ERIC: ED124344.

Information derived from the Federal Information Exchange System on
federal outlays in rural America provides the basis for this initial annual
report. The narrative discussions in the report cover socioeconomic trends
and program availability. The latter discussion includes reference to the
following services: telephone, electricity, water, sewer, medical,
educational, manpower, housing, small business, law enforcement, food
assistance, and income maintenance.

125
RURAL DEVELOPMENT: PART 5
Hearings before the Subcommittee on Rural Development of the Committee
on Agriculture and Forestry.
Washington, D.C.: United States Senate, September 9, 1971.   409 pp.
ERIC: ED118280.

Transcripts of the 1971 Senate hearings on rural development held in
Stillwater, Oklahoma and Lincoln, Nebraska are presented in this docu-
ment: 1) Balanced National Growth Policy; 2) National Rural Development
Program; 3) 5.1612, The Rural Community Development Revenue Sharing Act
of 1971; 4) Reorganization of U.S. Department of Agriculture and Related
Agencies.

126
RURAL DEVELOPMENT: PART 6
Hearing before the Subcommittee on Rural Development of the Committee on
Agriculture and Forestry.
Washington, D.C.: United States Senate, 92nd Congress, 1st Session,
September 20, 1971. 1612-A Bill to Establish a Revenue Sharing Program
for Rural Development. 126 pp. ERIC: ED118281.

Transcripts of the 1971 Senate hearings on 5.1612, a bill to establish a
revenue sharing program for rural development, are presented in this
document.

127
RURAL DEVELOPMENT AND POLICY COORDINATION ACT OF 1979
Washington, D.C.: U.S. Senate, Committee on Agriculture, Forestry and
Nutrition. May 16, 1979.

Recommends passage, with an amendment of the Rural Development Act of
1972. It would require USDA to establish a rural development policy

management process in concert with state and local government, other federal
agencies, and the private sector as well as the submission of a comprehensive
five-year assessment of rural conditions and interim biennial progress reports.

128
RURAL ELECTRIC COOPERATIVES: THE CHANGING POLITICS OF ENERGY IN RURAL AMERICA
Doyle, Jack and Vic Reinemer, eds.
Washington, D.C.: Environmental Policy Institute, 317 Pennsylvania Ave.,
S.E. 20003. ($12.50, plus $1.50 handling)

A collection of case studies of rural electric co-ops in 14 states written by
local citizens and co-op members.

129
RURAL GOVERNMENT AND LOCAL PUBLIC SERVICES
Rainey, Kenneth D. and Karen D. Rainey
In Rural U.S.A.: Persistence and Change, Thomas R. Ford, ed.
Ames: The Iowa State University Press, 126-144. 1978.

The author reviews current problems of local governments and concludes that
the major policy issues for rural communities are land use controls, public
service districts and planning districts, local finances, education, health
care, and transportation.

130
THE RURAL HOUSING AND COMMUNITY DEVELOPMENT DELIVERY SYSTEM
Washington, D.C.: Rural America, Inc., December 1977. 11 pp. (55¢).

Reviews the present rural housing delivery systems, recent efforts to improve systems in cooperation with state governments, and suggests future
improvements.

131
RURAL INDUSTRIALIZATION: PROBLEMS AND POTENTIAL
North Central Regional Center for Rural Development
Ames: The Iowa State University Press, 1976.

This book reviews and explores the need for and methods of attracting
industry to rural areas as well as the social and economic benefits and
liabilities that exist after industrialization occurs.

132
RURAL JUSTICE AND LEGAL ASSISTANCE
Paper presented at the National Conference on Rural America, Washington, D.C.
Washington, D.C.: Rural America, Inc., April 1975. 11 pp. ERIC: ED104583.

Poor rural residents are often denied equal protection, due process, and
other constitutional rights given to every American. This demonstrates
that the application of justice in rural America is lacking in 1) law
enforcement quality, 2) judicial process functions, and 3) participation
by the poor and ethnic minorities residing within its jurisdiction. Part
of the problem stems from an unequal distribution of program funds between
rural and urban areas.

133
RURAL POLICY RESEARCH ALTERNATIVES
Rogers, David L. and Larry R. Whiting, eds .
Ames: The Iowa State University Press, 1978.

The papers in this volume deal with improving research design and methods
for the study of public policy issues in rural development as well as the
application of different kinds of techniques in policy research.

134
THE RURAL POOR UNSEEN BY POLICYMAKERS
Goodstein, Jeanette, ed.
Tempe: Arizona State University, Center for Public Affairs, 1977.

Consists of papers and discussions from a conference held in Phoenix. The
content is focused on issues which dominate rural poverty in the Southwest, including migrants, delivering human services, employment and undocu-
mented workers.

135
RURAL POVERTY AND THE POLICY CRISIS
Coppedge, Robert O. and Carlton G. Davis, eds.
Ames: The Iowa State University Press, 1977.

This text focuses on conceptual dimensions of poverty issues and problems,
the cost of rural poverty in America, alternative frameworks for viewing
poverty and income distribution, and institutional policies. Ideas that
will be influencing policy decisions and the survival of rural life for
decades to come are also considered.

136
RURAL POVERTY IN THE UNITED STATES: A REPORT BY THE PRESIDENT'S NATIONAL
ADVISORY COMMISSION ON RURAL POVERTY
Wilber, George L. and C. E. Bishop, eds.
Washington, D.C.: U.S. Government Printing Office, May 1968. 606 pp.
ERIC: ED078985.

Major topics covered in this report include: the structural changes taking
place in rural areas and the inter-relationship between rural and urban
America; occupational mobility and migration; health care and family
planning; the developmental nature of agriculture and other natural resources; the economics of poverty; and policies and programs to alter income
distribution.

137
RURAL SOCIOLOGICAL RESEARCH AND SOCIAL POLICY: HARD DATA, HARD TIMES
Nolan, Michael F. and John F. Galliher
Rural Sociology, 38(4): 491-499, 1973.

In this commentary the authors discuss why research of rural sociologists
has little impact on social policy decisions relevant to present social
problems. Using Hightower's recent book, Hard Tomatoes, Hard Times, as
an example, some directions for future research are suggested.

138
THE RURAL STAKE IN PUBLIC ASSISTANCE
Washington, D.C.: National Rural Center.

This policy analysis report provides a statistical profile of the nation's
rural poor and compares benefits and participation between rural and urban
states.

139
RURAL WOMEN FIGHT FOR RIGHTS: NEW GROUP ACTION OVERCOMES ISOLATION AND
NEGLECT
Ott, Carol
Working Women, 3: 17-64, June 1978.

Farm, migrant and Appalachian women's advocacy coalition formed, Rural
American Women, Inc. Organization's priorities are: enabling rural women
to benefit from national women's movement achievements and to strike down
discriminatory tax laws, especially detrimental to farm women.

140
RURAL WOMEN--IGNORED BUT NO LONGER SILENT
Threatt, Jane
Christian Science Monitor, 9: 26, February 1979.

Cites interesting statistics on rural women. Problems faced by rural
women are: financial inequality, lack of educational benefits and feelings of isolation. Lack of resources in rural areas further intensifies
these problems. Cites coalition, Rural American Women, Inc., whose
purpose is to help give rural women a voice in expressing and articulating
their needs.

141
SCOPE AND NATIONAL CONCERNS
Waters, Jerry B.
In Rural Development: Research Priorities.
Ames: Iowa State University Press, 9-19. 1973.

The author outlines some of the more recent shifts in national policies
and legislative concerns which have implications for rural development
priorities.

142
A SHORT HISTORY OF AGRICULTURAL ADJUSTMENT, 1933-1975
Rasmussen, Wayne D., G. L. Baker, and J. S. Ward
Washington, D.C.: U.S. Department of Agriculture, Economic Research
Center, Agricultural Information Bulletin 391. March 1976.

This bulletin is a brief account of all agricultural policies and programs
implemented between 1933 and 1975.

143

SMALL FARM FAMILY NEWSLETTER
Copies available from Ovid Bay, Science and Education Administration
Washington, D.C.:   U.S. Department of Agriculture.

The purpose of this new USDA newsletter is to provide timely and new
information of interest to small and part-time farmers and their families.
The first issue contains a variety of information including a report on
low interest loans for limited resource farmers, several brief articles
on various state and federal small farm programs, a report on the ACSW
small farm demonstration projects, and other general information of interest to small farmers.

144

SOCIAL CHANGE AND PUBLIC POLICY IN RURAL AMERICA: DATA AND RESEARCH
NEEDS FOR THE 1970'S.
Madden, J. Patrick
American Journal of Agricultural Economics 52(2): 308-313. 1970.

Lists six major trends which are dissolving the cultural dichotomy between
rural and urban peoples. Lists research and data problem areas. Concludes
that most failures of social reform programs are the result of poor communication and failure to take into account the culture of the area.
Stresses the importance of an awareness of sociocultural attributes of
the area. Discusses avoidance of "pitfalls" when preparing rural development policies.

145

SOCIAL IMPLICATIONS OF ACTION PROGRAMS: SOCIOLOGICAL ASPECTS AND
IMPLICATIONS OF U.S. FARM POLICIES
Heady, Earl O.
Sociologia Ruralis, Vol. 8, 362-382. 1968.

The author argues that U.S. farm policies have been subjected to a large
amount of economic investigation and too little sociological analysis.
Then he proceeds to examine some of the important sociological aspects
related to farm policies which are promising avenues for future research.

146

SOME EFFECTS OF PRICE AND INCOME SUPPORT PROGRAMS ON MARGINAL FARMS
Evans, Homer, W. W. Armentrout and R. I. Jack
Morgantown: West Virginia University, Agricultural Experiment Station,
Bulletin 451, February 1961.

Price and income support benefits were distributed to the larger,
wealthier farm states rather than marginal, low-income farm states, such as
West Virginia.

147
SOME EVIDENCE IN SUPPORT OF STATE INDUSTRIAL FINANCING PROGRAMS: THE
SOUTHWESTERN CASE
Williamson, R. B.
Land Economics 44(3):   388-393.   1968.

Case study of state-sponsored industrial financing programs. Examines
southwestern U.S. Growth in new industries is strongest where state
financing is abundant. State-sponsored funding is very effective in
drawing industry to one of three or four possible locations.

148
THE SOUTHWESTERN INDIAN REPORT
Commission on Civil Rights
Washington, D.C.:   U.S. Government Printing Office. May 1973.

This report is an attempt to describe the present day condition of American
Indians. Five problem areas are discussed: employment, education, health
services, the administration of justice, and water rights.

149
TOWARD ECONOMIC DEVELOPMENT FOR NATIVE AMERICAN COMMUNITIES
A Compendium of Papers Submitted to the Subcommittee on Economy in
Government of the Joint Economic Committee, Congress of the U.S.   (91st,
1st Session). Vol. 2, Part II; Development Programs and Plans, Part III:
The Resource Base, Vol. I, Development Prospects and Problems.
Washington, D.C.:   U.S. Government Printing Office, Joint Economic Committee.
ERIC: ED055685.

The study addresses itself to the serious problems of poverty and economic
insecurity found in Native American communities and to the apparent inability of the federal government to provide effective assistance in
improving the economic situations of American Indian and Alaskan Native
groups. The two volume compendium contains papers by invited individual
experts, statements of federal agencies, and statements of native
organization.

150
TOWARD A FEDERAL SMALL FARMS POLICY, PHASE I.
Washington, D.C.:   National Rural Center.

This is a report on Phase I of the Small Farms Policy Project Workshop,
held in Arkansas, October 16-18, 1977.

151
TRICKLE-DOWN AND LEAKAGE IN THE WAR ON POVERTY
Bender, L. D., B. L. Green and R. R. Campbell
Growth and Change 2(4): 34-41. 1971.

A case study of the Ozark region to see what effect in-migration associated
with industrialization has on the rural poor. Concludes that in-migrants
had easier access to the expanding employment market than the rural poor.

152
TVA AND THE GRASS ROOTS
Selznick, Philip
New York: Harper, 1966.

The author analyzes the formal organizational aspects of TVA. The book is
an excellent study of certain pitfalls of decentralized, grass-roots
doctrine for democratic planning.

153
UNEMPLOYMENT ESTIMATION IN RURAL AREAS: A CRITIQUE OF OFFICIAL PROCEDURES
AND A COMPARISON WITH SURVEY DATA
Korsching, Peter F. and Stephen G. Sapp
Rural Sociology 43(1): 103-112. 1978.

This article examines the validity of procedures used by governmental
agencies for estimating unemployment in rural areas. The results of the
study support the contention that in a rural area the official procedures
lack some degree of validity and may radically underestimate the actual
employment.

154
UNITED STATES DEPARTMENT OF HEALTH, EDUCATION, AND WELFARE PROGRAMS FOR
RURAL AMERICA: WELFARE PROGRAM ASSISTANCE FOF NON-METROPOLIGAN AREAS,
FISCAL YEAR 1972.
94th Congress, 1st Session, February 6, 1975.
Washington, D.C.: U.S. Government Printing Office.

This report analyzes HEW's resource distribution in terms of rural
development activities via a program by program examination of the
distribution of funds for fiscal year 1972.

155
URBAN AND RURAL AMERICA: POLICIES FOR FUTURE GROWTH
Advisory Commission on Intergovernmental Relations
Washington, D.C.: U.S. Government Printing Office, Report A-32, 1968.

This report closely examines many dimensions of the continuing process of
urbanization; highlights the intergovernmental policy implications in
its findings; and advances recommendation that the future of American
federalism is inextricably linked with that of urbanization.

156
WAR ON THE POOR: OEO GRANT FOR THE CALIFORNIA RURAL LEGAL ASSISTANCE
PROGRAM VETOED BY STATE
Newsweek, Vol. 77: 18-19, January 1971.

This article focuses on the California Rural Legal Assistance Program.
The program offers legal services for more than 550,000 poor farm workers.
In its four year existence, the agency has won 80 percent of its cases;
however, powerful political forces are threatening the survival of the
program.

157
WATER POLITICS AND PUBLIC INVOLVEMENT
Pierce, John D. and Harvey R. Doerksen, eds.
Ann Arbor, Michigan: Ann Arbor Science Publishers, 1976.

This book presents a series of current articles and research reports
concerning public involvement in water politics. The book has two sections, one dealing with analytical frameworks and one dealing with
participation patterns and evaluation. Finally, there is a long
annotated bibliography which includes many of the more important
materials on public involvement in water politics.

158
WELFARE REFORM: BENEFITS AND INCENTIVES IN RURAL AREAS
Hines, Fred and Max Jordan
Washington, D.C.: U. S. Department of Agriculture, Economic Research
Service, ERS-No. 370. June 1971. 20 pp.

The paper presents an overview of public assistance in the U.S. Secondly,
it looks at the effects the Family Assistance Plan would potentially
have on different regions and places of residence. Twice as many persons
would receive assistance as those now receiving AFDC. State differences
would be decreased. The work incentives of the poor would probably have
effect in the southern region, where benefits would increase substantially.

159
WELFARE REFORM AND RURAL PEOPLE
Washington, D.C.: Rural America, Inc. December 1977. 14 pp. (70¢).

Urban-rural differences in welfare spending and problems with rural
welfare service delivery are outlined in this paper. The Carter
Administration's welfare reform proposal is analyzed, and changes are
recommended in the proposed legislation to serve rural needs equitably.

160
WHO IS A MIGRANT FARM WORKER? QUIENES UN TRABAJADOR AGRICOLA MIGRANTE?
Escamilla, Manuel
Washington, D.C.: Office of Economic Opportunity, 1973. ERIC: ED081530.

This study was concerned with varying definitions of migrants given by
federal agencies helping them. The objectives were to present migrant
definitions utilized by these agencies and to initiate discussion on one
standard definition of a migrant worker.

161
WOMEN IN AGRICULTURE FIGHT FOR THEIR FAMILIES AND THEIR FARMS
Robbins, Wm.
The New York Times, 14: 44. November 1977.

Reports on two newly formed agricultural women's organizations, American Agri-Women and Women Involved in Farm Economics. Organizations hope to dispel myths concerning farm men and women and become recognized and elected in predominantly male oriented farm organizations.

162
WORKING PAPERS FROM THE FIRST NATIONAL CONFERENCE ON RURAL AMERICA
Washington, D.C.: Rural America, Inc., April 1975. 271 pp. ($10.00).

Several subjects were covered in these papers, including rural housing problems, rural health, food policy, agricultural production, and agribusiness research.

163
WORKSHOP ON EVALUATING STATE TITLE V PILOT PROGRAMS IN THE NORTHEAST
Northeast Regional Center for Rural Development
Ithaca, New York: Cornell University, 1974.

The aims of the workshop were clarification of purposes behind evaluation, development of conceptual framework, sharing of evaluation plans among states, exploration of alternative strategies, and identification of follow up activities. Mainly consists of four papers presented at the workshop.

CHAPTER 4

RURAL HUMAN SERVICES

General Topics

Alcoholism

Boom Towns

Community Mental Health

Cross-Cultural Issues

De-Institutionalization

Family Services

Food Stamps

Foster Care

Health Care

Housing

Income Maintenance

Legal Services

Manpower Services

Migrant Family Programs

Natural Helping

Protective Services

Rural Church

Service Delivery Problems

Services Integration

Title XX

Unemployment Compensation

1

ALCOHOLISM SERVICES IN RURAL AREAS: IMPLICATIONS FOR SOCIAL WORK EDUCATION
Dinitto, Diana and Santos H. Hernandez
In Social Work in Rural Areas: Issues and Opportunities. Joseph Davenport,
III, Judith A. Davenport and James R. Wiebler, eds.
Laramie: The University of Wyoming, Department of Social Work, 1980.

This paper surveys the characteristics of rural communities and how these
impact the delivery of alcoholism services. Since a major factor affecting the delivery of services has been the lack of professionally trained
personnel, particular emphasis is placed upon implications for social
work education.

2

AMERICAN INDIAN FAMILIES: PERSPECTIVES ON THE HELPING PROCESS
Red Horse, John
In We Can Help.
Evanston, Illinois: American Academy of Pediatrics, 1979.

This paper presents selected case vignettes derived from child abuse and
neglect proceedings involving American Indian Families. The criterion
guiding case selection was value conflict between human service professionals and Indian family lifestyles. The objective was to capture contrasting "cultural sets."

3

AMERICAN INDIAN MYTHS
Locklear, Herbert H.
Social Work, 17(3): 72-80. 1972.

Mistaken beliefs about American Indians have been thriving for years and
are still being perpetuated. The author presents evidence refuting these
myths, explains major problems of the Indian people in adjusting to urban
life, and tells how American Indian Centers are helping them.

4

ARIZONA JOB COLLEGE: DEFEATING THE DEPENDENCY SYNDROME
Murphy, Betty
Opportunity, 2(5): 4-11. 1972. ERIC: EJ060938.

Describes a comprehensive project aimed at providing multi-services
directed at total family rehabilitation.

5

ARIZONA STATE ECONOMIC OPPORTUNITY OFFICE: ANNUAL REPORT, CALENDAR YEAR
ENDING DECEMBER 31, 1972.
Washington, D.C.: Office of Economic Opportunity, 1973. ERIC: ED082899.

The annual report of the Arizona State Economic Opportunity Office for
1972 is presented. Statistical data related to the state's American
Indian are also presented.

6

ASSESSING THE COSTS OF FOSTER FAMILY CARE IN RURAL AREAS: MYTHS AND
REALITIES
Settles, Barbara H., et al.
Revision of paper presented at the Annual Meeting of the Rural
Sociological Society, New York, N.Y., August 1976. 30 pp. ERIC: ED154968.

This study examined the history and connection of foster care to rural
areas in the U.S., the current situation for foster care in rural America,
and the adaptations necessary to use current data in estimating the costs
of foster care in rural areas.

7

AN ASSESSMENT OF THE EXPERIMENTAL AND DEMONSTRATION INTERSTATE PROGRAM
FOR SOUTH TEXAS MIGRANT WORKERS - THE TEXAS ASSESSMENT
Cambridge, Mass.: Abt Associates, Inc., September 1971. 100 pp.
NTIS/PB-211 190.

The overall purpose of the project was identified as determining the
feasibility and value of an interstate, multi-agency program focusing on
the problems of Mexican-American migrants.

8

A BEGINNING TASK BANK FOR RURAL COMPREHENSIVE HUMAN SERVICES DELIVERY
SYSTEM
Lewis, Robert, Richard Brady and Wayne Pearson
Prepared for Services Integration Project, Office of Planning and
Research, Department of Social Services, Salt Lake City, Utah.
January 1974. 204 pp.

This paper contains a description of the process and preliminary results
of a task analysis of the work of service agencies relating to the Five-
County Integrated Health and Social Services Delivery System, centered in
Cedar City, Utah.

9

BLACKS IN RURAL AREAS: CONSIDERATION FOR SERVICE EFFECTIVENESS
Icard, Larry
In 2nd National Institute on Social Work in Rural Areas Reader.
Edward B. Buxton, ed.
Madison: University of Wisconsin--Extension Center for Social Service,
68-75. 1978.

In this paper the author makes the argument that since a significant number
of blacks reside in rural areas and since disparities exist between blacks
in rural and urban centers, there is a need for professional social work
to identify and address skill and knowledge bases that take into account
the idiosyncracies of these people. Problems, needs, and cultural aspects
of rural blacks are examined in the paper.

10
BOOM TOWNS AND HUMAN SERVICES
Davenport, Judith A. and Joseph Davenport, eds.
Laramie: University of Wyoming, Department of Social Work, 1979.

This volume is a useful resource for familiarizing people with the general
problem areas experienced by many boom towns, particularly in the West.
Problems and issues covered in the text are education, housing, mental
health, community planning, human service politics, grassroots organizing, team approaches, and role of the church.

11
THE BSW DELIVERS SERVICE TO SMALL TOWN AMERICA
Johnson, Louise C.
In Human Services In the Rural Environment Reader. David Bast, ed.
Madison: University of Wisconsin, Center for Social Service.
June 1976-May 1977.

The BSW is the primary social worker in small town rural America. With
this premise, the author discusses roles that a BSW may be expected to
fill and tasks related to those roles.

12
CHILD PROTECTION IN A RURAL SETTING
Shepard, Georgianna
In 2nd Annual Northern Wisconsin Symposium on Human Services in the
Rural Environment Reader. David Bast and Julie Schmidt, eds.
Madison: University of Wisconsin--Extension, Center for Social Science,
21-26, 1977.

This paper deals with the protection of children, with emphasis upon how
the rural context affects the development of a delivery system.

13
COMMUNITY HEALTH CENTER PROGRAM
Washington, D.C.: Rural America, Inc. December 1978. 8 pp. (50¢).

Brief description of HEW's community health center program.

14
COMMUNITY MENTAL HEALTH CENTER ACCESSIBILITY: A SURVEY OF THE RURAL POOR
Lee, Soong H., Daniel T. Gianturco and Carl Eisdorfer
Archives of General Psychiatry 31(3): 335-339. 1974. NTIS/HRP-0011183/1ST

The results of a survey undertaken to evaluate the accessibility of a
community mental health center in a rural poverty area and to identify
barriers to increasing the center's accessibility to the people it
serves are reported. Findings suggest that long-term community education, indigenous workers and backup services to local physicians would
facilitate mental health service.

15

COMMUNITY MENTAL HEALTH IDEOLOGY--A PROBLEMATIC MODEL FOR RURAL AREAS
Berry, Bonnie and Ann E. Davis
American Journal of Orthopsychiatry 48(4): 673-679. 1978.

An examination of the realities of rural community mental health services
is provided. It is pointed out that clinics located in rural areas have
problems that are different from those of urban clinics. Problems related to education and urban-born and trained mental health problems are
cited. The desirability of using indigenous workers is emphasized.

16

COMMUNITY MENTAL HEALTH SERVICES IN RURAL AREAS--SOME PRACTICAL ISSUES
Jeffrey, Michael J. and Ronald E. Reeve
Community Mental Health Journal 14(1): 54-62. 1978.

This study analyzes the special problems, from a systems point of view,
faced by new mental health centers in the social and professional structure
of rural communities.

17

COMMUNITY SATISFACTION: A STUDY OF CONTENTMENT WITH LOCAL SERVICES
Rojeck, D. G., F. Clemente and G. F. Summers
Rural Sociology, 40(2): 177-192. 1975.

The extent of community satisfaction with local services is investigated.
A factor analysis of a 15 item scale relating to satisfaction resulted
in four separate dimensions--satisfaction with medical services, public
services, commercial services and educational services.

18

COMMUNITY SERVICES FOR CHILDREN OF MIGRANT FARM WORKERS: A STATUS REPORT
Stockburger, Cassandra
New York, N.Y.: Ford Foundation, September 1978. ERIC: ED153750.

This report indicates that although community services for migrant children
have increased over the past 15 years, the status of these services is
questionable. For instance, services are restricted to special federal
or state legislation; they are fragmented, no real delivery system exists,
and eligibility and definitions of clients create confusion and duplication of services. The report concludes that in order to effectively
intervene in the needs of migrant children, basic issues relating to
development and delivery of community services must be addressed.

19

COMPREHENSIVE FAMILY-CENTERED TRAINING PROGRAMS: FIVE COMPARATIVE
CASE STUDIES
Bale, Richard L. and C. Fremont Sprague
Cambridge, Mass.: Abt Associates, May 1977. 358 pp. ERIC: ED139593.

The Mountain-Plains Education and Economic Development Program, which exemplifies the comprehensive, residential family-centered approach to serving the economically disadvantaged, was compared to similar programs in the U.S.: Arizona Job Colleges of Arizona; Modern Employment Training Center in California; Manpower, Employment and Training in Texas; and Migrant and Seasonal Farmworkers Association in North Carolina. It was found that the programs followed fundamentally different approaches to rehabilitating the poor. The most comprehensive approach balanced job skill training with a broad array of supportive services and training for all family members.

20
CONSIDERATIONS IN THE CROSS-CULTURAL DELIVERY OF SOCIAL SERVICES TO NATIVE AMERICANS
Duncombe, Patricia
In Social Work in Rural Areas: Issues and Opportunities.
Joseph Davenport, Judith A. Davenport and James R. Wiebler, eds.
Laramie: The University of Wyoming, Department of Social Work, 137-151. 1980.

The author, who has had extensive experience in working with Indian people of the West and Southwest, discusses cultural factors that need to be understood and taken into account if service delivery is to be effective with Native Americans.

21
CROSS-CULTURAL REHABILITATION
Hammond, D. Corydon
Journal of Rehabilitation, 34-44, Sept./Oct. 1971.

This article examines problems which have contributed to the lack of needed rehabilitation services provided by agencies working with Native Americans.

22
DE-INSTITUTIONALIZATION IN RURAL AREAS
Nooe, Roger
Human Services in the Rural Environment, 5(1): 16-20. 1980.

The author argues that in order to maximize success in rural de-institutionalization, greater community involvement compared to the highly formalized service structures of urban areas may be necessary. Maximizing the use of available resources and utilizing natural support systems could enhance de-institutionalization and social justice in rural areas.

23
THE DELIVERY OF MANPOWER AND SUPPORTIVE SERVICES TO RURAL AREAS
Fletcher, Frank M., et al.
Journal of Employment Counseling, 11(4): 167-174. 1974.

This study identified problems by state employment service agencies and other organizations in the delivery of equitable manpower and supportive services to rural and migrant workers, and recommends solutions to these problems.

24
DELIVERING SOCIAL SERVICES IN RURAL AREAS
Buxton, Edward B.
In Social Work in Rural Communities, Leon H. Ginsberg, ed.
New York: Council on Social Work Education, 29-44. 1976.

The author outlines the limitations which apply to the development of social service programs in rural areas, and offers suggestions for effective handling of community social problems.

25
THE DELIVERY OF SERVICES TO MENTALLY RETARDED PERSONS LIVING IN RURAL AREAS: CONTENT, PROBLEMS AND ISSUES
Horejsi, Charles
Paper presented at the Workshop on Service Delivery Models for Rural and Isolated Regions. Sponsored by the National Institute on Mental Retardation and the Saskatchewan Association for the Mentally Retarded. Sasketoon, Saskatchewan, November 27-29, 1978.

This paper focuses on several factors that must be considered in the development of a comprehensive service system for the mentally retarded and elaborates on some of the problems and issues of program development and service delivery in rural areas.

26
DELIVERY OF SOCIAL SERVICES IN HEALTH CARE: A RURAL PERSPECTIVE
Johnson, Louise C.
In Social Work in Rural Areas: Issues and Opportunities. Joseph Davenport, Judith A. Davenport and James R. Wiebler, eds.
Laramie: The University of Wyoming, Department of Social Work, 48-57. 1980.

In this paper the author examines the patterns of medical social service delivery in South Dakota. Attention is also given to developing job descriptions and training programs for BSW's in rural medical settings.

27
DEVILS LAKE COMPREHENSIVE HUMAN SERVICE CENTER
Denver, Colorado: Denver University, Center for Social Research and Development, March 15, 1975. 101pp. NTIS/SHR-0000336/ES.

A comprehensive human services project was sponsored by the Social Service Board of North Dakota to demonstrate that a concerted approach to service delivery can be effectively implemented in rural settings through an integrated, multi-purpose delivery system with satellite centers. The

Devils Lake Comprehensive Human Service Center project in North Dakota
served a large and sparsely populated six-county rural area which
included two Indian reservations.

28
THE DEVILS LAKE HUMAN SERVICES CENTER: FINAL REPORT
Jensen, Thomas A., Duainne S. Bourcy, and Harvey Vreugdenhill
Bismarck: Devils Lake Human Services Integration Project, North Dakota
Social Service Board, June 30, 1975. NTIS/SHR-0000126.

The project provided human service delivery to a six-county rural area
through an integrated multipurpose system, utilizing a core center and a
network of satellite offices. This final report describes all aspects
of the project.

29
DIRECTORY OF SERVICES FOR MIGRANT FAMILIES
Illinois: ESEA Title I, Migrant, 1975. ERIC: ED116834.

This directory presents brief descriptions of services provided to
Illinois migratory agricultural workers and their families. The directory
is written in both English and Spanish.

30
ECONOMIC IMPACT OF THE FOOD STAMP PROGRAM ON MIGRANT FARM LABORERS
Hansen, D.E.
Davis: University of California, Research Project, May 1972.

Measures level of benefits received by migrant farm laborer participants
in the Food Stamp program; determines extent to which migrant laborers
are ineligible for program benefits due to current income and resource
eligibility criteria and other legal provisions; identifies reasons for
failure to participate despite program eligibility; evaluates effect of
program alterations on participation of migrant laborers.

31
EDITED TRANSCRIPTS OF A SERIES OF FOUR UNIVERSITY-COMMUNITY SEMINARS ON
THE RURAL EXPERIENCE: IMPLICATIONS FOR BUILDING EFFECTIVE YOUTH CARE
SERVICES IN RURAL AREAS.
Urzi, Mary
St. Paul: University of Minnesota, Center for Youth Development and
Research, August 1976. 95pp. NTIS/SHR-0002829.

The seminars were part of a short term training and curriculum development
project conducted under the auspice of the center for Youth Development
and Research at the University of Minnesota. Seminar topics were rural
youth and rural adults, rural communities and rural youth, special considerations relative to the rural poor and minority groups, assessing and
delivering services to rural youth, and education and training for rural
service providers.

32

THE EFFECT OF UNEMPLOYMENT COMPENSATION ON A SEASONAL INDUSTRY: AGRICULTURE
Chiswick, B. R.
Journal of Political Economy, 84(3): 591-602, 1976.

It is thought that compensation during off season would be high enough to
inhibit labor force participation during the off season. The Special
Unemployment Assistance program in 1974 was the first to pay benefits
to some agricultural workers. The author feels that the disincentives
to work would be great and that compensation has a greater impact on low
wage earners than on high wage earners. Comparisons were made of the
unemployment rates and the predicted level of employment that would have
existed without SUA in January, 1975. The unemployment rate for off-
season increased 20 percent, employment decreased 5.5 percent.

33

EFFECTIVE MODELS FOR THE DELIVERY OF SERVICES IN RURAL AREAS: IMPLICATIONS
FOR PRACTICE AND SOCIAL WORK EDUCATION
Locke, Barry and Roger A. Lohmann
Proceedings from the Third Annual National Institute on Social Work
in Rural Areas.
Morgantown: West Virginia University, School of Social Work,
August, 1978.

This excellent collection of papers is divided into the following service
categories: aging, communities, corrections, families, health, mental
health and education.

34

ESTABLISHING A SOCIAL SERVICE DEPARTMENT IN A RURAL HOSPITAL
Schlosser, Fred J., Jr.
Hospital Progress, 51(1): 44-45, 1970.

Steps taken and problems encountered in establishing a social service
department in a rural Illinois hospital are described briefly in this
article.

35

AN EVALUATION TO DETERMINE THE EFFECTIVENESS OF COORDINATION, ADMINISTRATION
AND DELIVERY OF SERVICES BY A MULTI-SERVICE CENTER IN RURAL ARKANSAS
Fayetteville: University of Arkansas, Graduate School of Social Work,
1973, 119 pp. NTIS/PB-240 390/5ST.

The project evaluated the first year attempt at developing a multi-service
center to deliver comprehensive social services in rural Arkansas.
Recommendations concerning structure, management, training and information
systems are included. Community image, constituent organizations and
consumer attitudes are discussed in depth.

36
EVALUATION OF DISTRICT V HEALTH AND SOCIAL SERVICES INTEGRATION PROJECT,
THROUGH JUNE 1974.
Cedar City, Utah: Five County Association of Governments.
September 1974, 167 pp. NTIS/SHR-0000033.

The project, undertaken to demonstrate innovative approaches to services
integration in an area which incorporates isolated, rural communities,
uses the Five-County Association as the general purpose government
integrator and management authority. An evaluation of the project is
presented in this report.

37
EXPERIMENTS IN SOCIAL WELFARE: AN EMPIRICAL EVALUATION OF THE MISSISSIPPI
PROJECT
Wilkinson, Kenneth P. and Peggy J. Ross
Mississippi State, Mississippi: Social Science Research Center,
December 1970, 77 pp. NTIS/PB-210 474.

The report describes a project designed to ascertain the differential
effect that higher levels of income, vocational training and/or services
over a period of one year would have on the lifestyles and potential
mobility of selected families receiving AFDC payments in a two-county
rural area of central Mississippi.

38
EXTENSION OF SOCIAL AND HEALTH CARE SERVICES FROM A CENTRALLY LOCATED VA
HOSPITAL TO RURAL AREAS OF ARKANSAS
Sullivan, James E.
In Effective Models for the Delivery of Services in Rural Areas:
Implications for Practice and Social Work Education. Barry L. Locke
and Roger A. Lohmann, eds.
Morgantown: West Virginia University, August 7-10, 1978.

The author discusses the use of community based social workers for
extension of social and health care services from a centrally located
VA hospital complex covering the entire state of Arkansas and serving a
predominantly rural population.

39
FACTORS RELATED TO PARTICIPATION IN THE FOOD STAMP PROGRAM
Hines, Fred
Washington, D.C.: U.S. Department of Agriculture, Economic Research
Service, Agricultural Economic Report No. 298, July 1975.   26 pp.

Correlations between Food Stamp participation rates and higher unemployment, welfare program participation, greater number of low-income households, higher proportion of population under 17 and longer participation
of the county in the Food Stamp program were found to be positive. Negative correlations between participation and greater labor force participation and a higher percentage of population over 65 were found. Rural
counties and counties with higher minority ratios were not as high as
those counties with smaller percentages of minorities or in more urban
counties.

40

FACTORS RELATING TO FOOD STAMP PARTICIPATION OF HIRED FARMWORKER FAMILIES
Smith, Leslie Whitener
Paper presented at the Annual Meeting of Rural Sociological Society,
Madison, Wisconsin, September 1977.
Washington, D.C.: U.S. Department of Agriculture, Economic Research
Service.

Paper presents a socioeconomic profile of farmworker families participating
in the program in 1975 and identifies factors related to program
participation.

41

FAMILIES BEHIND THE AFDC STEREOTYPE
Grendering, Margaret P.
Journal of Extension, Vol. 14: 8-15, January/February 1976.

This article demonstrates that the majority of AFDC recipients in both
urban and rural areas does not fit the public's stereotype. Implications
and future directions for extension programs are also discussed.

42

FAMILY STRUCTURE AND THE USE OF AGENCY SERVICES: AN EXAMINATION OF PATTERNS
AMONG ELDERLY NATIVE AMERICANS
Murdock, Steve H. and Donald F. Schwartz
The Gerontologist, 18(5): 475-481, 1978.

This paper provides information on the levels of perceived service needs,
perceived service availability, and on the use of services in elderly
Native American populations and focuses particularly on the relationships
between family structure and these factors.

43

FAMILY STRUCTURE, VALUE ORIENTATION, AND PURPOSEFUL BEHAVIOR AMONG
AMERICAN INDIANS: A LIFE SPAN FRAMEWORK
Red Horse, John G.
Submitted to Social Casework
Tempe: Arizona State University, School of Social Work.

This article discusses family issues critical to proactive human services
planning and delivery for American Indian communities. A life span conceptual framework serves as a model from which to track value orientations and behaviors as self-revitalizing forces.

44

FEASIBILITY OF SERVICES INTEGRATION, MAY 1975
Henton, Douglas
Submitted in partial fulfillment for the degree of Master of Public Policy.
Berkeley: University of California, Graduate School of Public Policy,
May 1975, 60 pp. NTIS/SHR-0000475.

Human service integration in 33 demonstration projects sponsored by DHEW
was evaluated, and the relationship of specific sets of environmental

and project factors to linkage adoption in six case studies was examined.
One finding was that linkages were more readily adopted in small rural
environments than the large urban areas.

45
FOOD STAMP PARTICIPATION OF HIRED FARMWORKER FAMILIES
Smith, Leslie Whitener and Gene Rowe
Washington, D.C.: U.S. Department of Agriculture, Economics, Statistics,
and Cooperative Services, Agriculture Economics Report No. 403,
April 1977, 77 pp. NTIS/PB-281 610/6ST.

This report presents a socioeconomic profile of approximately 207,000
hired farmworker families (including 9,000 migrant families) participating
in the Food Stamp Program in November 1975 and identifies various factors
related to program participation.

46
FOOD STAMPS FOR RURAL AMERICANS
Vrechek, Nancy M. and E. Evan Brown
Mississippi State, Mississippi: Rural Development Center, Rural Development
Research and Education, 1(3): 6-7, 1977.

The article summarizes a study done by the Georgia Title V research staff
on the characteristics of Food Stamp recipients in Ware County, Georgia.
Several important characteristics were revealed. Working poor families
participated at a higher rate than did welfare families. Females dominate the public assistance roles. A majority of the heads of households
were 45 years or older and faced more severe training barriers for more
highly skilled jobs. The size of the Food Stamp bonus did not necessarily
decrease as the family size decreased.

47
FOURTH ANNUAL REPORT OF THE PRESIDENT TO THE CONGRESS ON GOVERNMENT
SERVICES TO RURAL AMERICA
Washington, D.C.: U.S. Government Printing Office, 1974.

Analysis of 209 federal programs which accounted for 77 percent of funds
allocated to rural areas. Per capita outlays favor fastgrowing and/or
high-income counties. Apparently, counties which need the money are not
getting enough. Per capita outlays in rural areas were highest respectively, in agriculture, natural resources, and community development.
Rural areas consistently recieved less federal outlays per capita than
did metro areas for housing, human resources, and defense and NASA
spending.

48

THE GATEKEEPER CONCEPT: A NEW USE OF AN OLD CONCEPT FOR THE DELIVERY OF
HUMAN SERVICES IN RURAL AREAS
Valenzuela, Wilma Greenfield and Alma G. Hallamore
In Effective Models for the Delivery of Services in Rural Areas:
Implications for Practice and Social Work Education. Barry L. Locke
and Roger A. Lohmann, eds.
Morgantown: West Virginia University, 156-159, 1978.

The gatekeeper concept is an especially useful and flexible concept which
can and hopefully will address the "Balanced Services System" model of
service delivery adopted in New Hampshire.

49

GETTING HUMAN SERVICES TO RURAL PEOPLE
Washington, D.C.: Office of Human Development, June 1976, 147 pp.
NTIS/SHR-001658.

The results of field evaluation of 11 rural human service projects are
reported, barriers to the delivery and receipt of services in rural
areas are identified and implications by DHEW are discussed. Barriers to
effective delivery of DHEW services in rural areas include transportation
problems, lack of information about rural projects, limited flexible
funding and staff capacity at the local area and attitudinal problems.

50

THE GREAT INFORMER: APPALACHIAN NEW YORK'S PEOPLE MOBILE PROJECT
Appalachia, 8(3): 18-27, December 1974 - January 1975. ERIC: EJ116454.

The people mobile is a specifically outfitted 24 foot motor home equipped
with a meeting room, a telephone and a wealth of useful information.
This machine and its staff travel the back roads of Chenango County,
New York supplying rural residents with various social services.

51

HEALTH CARE DELIVERY IN RURAL AREAS
Chicago, Ill.: American Medical Association, Rept. No.-AMA-MP-700,
1972, 41 pp. ERIC: ED076287.

A review of the problems of rural health delivery is presented in this
booklet with selected plans and models of delivery of services in certain
rural areas of the nation.

52

HOMEMAKER SERVICES IN A RURAL SOCIAL SERVICES DEPARTMENT: ONE NOTCH
ABOVE THE NATURAL HELPING RELATIONSHIP
Schultz, Carol
In 2nd National Institute on Social Work in Rural Areas Reader. Edward
B. Buxton, ed.
Madison: University of Wisconsin--Extension Center for Social Service, 10-17
1978

In this paper the author discusses the ways in which the communication patterns established by the Homemaker Services offered in a rural department of social services (in Colorado) related to the communication patterns that occur in the natural helping relationship. The author also discusses the need to keep this helping network as close to the natural helping network as possible and some of the implications for trained social workers who work with these kinds of helpers.

53
HUMAN SERVICES FOR MEXICAN-AMERICAN CHILDREN
Tijerina, Andres A.
Austin: Texas State Department of Human Resources, 1978. ERIC: ED171480.

A compilation of five readings uses the Chicano perspective to analyze the interaction between Mexican American families, their children, and the institutions charged with the child welfare concerns of the society. A variety of strategies for policy makers and practitioners charged with serving the needs of Mexican American families and children are suggested.

54
HUMAN SERVICES IN RURAL ALASKA: HIGHLIGHTS FROM THE EVALUATION OF THE RURAL AREAS SOCIAL SERVICES PROJECT
Feldman, Frances Lomas
Juneau, Alaska: State Department of Health and Welfare, 1971, 224 pp.
ERIC: ED092287.

The purpose of the Rural Social Service Project is to bring public welfare services to Alaska's rural areas. One component of the Project trained and employed qualified native village people as paraprofessionals who could provide the social services needed while living right in the village. This report presents highlights of the evaluation results.

55
HUMAN SERVICES IN RURAL AMERICA: AN ASSESSMENT OF PROBLEMS, POLICIES AND RESEARCH
Bauheier, Edward C., Janet M. Derr and Robert W. Gage
Denver, Colorado: University of Denver, Social Welfare Research Institute, May 1973, 101 pp.

Findings of an investigation of social and economic problems, social policy issues, and service delivery systems in sparsely settled rural areas are presented by the Social Welfare Research Institute of the University of Denver. The literature review and analyses were conducted with particular regard for problems of minority and ethnic groups, including Indians and Mexican-Americans, and migrant and seasonal farmworkers.

56
HUMAN SERVICES IN THE RURAL ENVIRONMENT
Buxton, Edward
Madison: University of Wisconsin Extension Newsletter, 2(2): 1977.

This article is a discussion of a project for limited-resource farmers. The project is a farm management program for 70 limited-resource farmers in central Wisconsin. The goal of the project is upgrading the management skills of these farmers.

57

IDENTIFYING TRAINING NEEDS AND DEVELOPING A TRAINING RESPONSE TO RURAL
SOCIAL WORKERS IN TITLE XX PROVIDER AGENCIES
Edwards, Richard L., Gail Kurtz and Nancy S. Dickenson
In Social Work in Rural Areas: Issues and Opportunities. Joseph
Davenport, Judith A. Davenport and James R. Wiebler, eds.
Laramie: The University of Wyoming Department of Social Work, 1980.

Describes a systematic assessment of training needs of Title XX provider
agency personnel and the concomitant development of a comprehensive
training program aimed at improving service delivery. The training
project was carried on by the Office of Continuing Social Work Education
at the University of Tennessee School of Social Work.

58

THE IMPACT OF FEDERAL POLICIES ON RURAL SOCIAL SERVICE PROGRAMS
Honour, Robert
Human Services in the Rural Environment, 1(1): 12-19, 1979.

In this article the author examines the nature of the "rural problem,"
the unique aspect of social work administration in rural areas, and
policy/planning efforts needed to deliver social services in rural areas
with greater equity.

59

INCOME MAINTENANCE AND THE RURAL POOR: AN EXPERIMENTAL APPROACH
Bawden, D. Lee
American Journal of Agricultural Economics, 52(3): 438-441, 1970.

At the time of the writing of this article, income maintenance experiments
had been conducted in urban areas of New Jersey and Pennsylvania. As
one-third of the poor live in rural areas, the author notes that income
maintenance in rural areas might have different impacts due to the employment opportunities and the proportion of self-employed persons in rural
areas. For a cost determination of any program to be made, the rural
sector must not be overlooked. A rural-OEO funded experiment is
described and expected results are discussed. (Note: See "Rural Income
Maintenance Experiment" in this section.)

60

THE INITIAL EFFECTS OF SOCIAL SECURITY ON MONTANA FARM AND RANCH
OPERATORS
Samson, A'Delbert
Bozeman, Montana: Agricultural Experiment Station Bulletin 558. 1961.

Farmer and rancher attitudes toward retirement reveal points of profitable concentration for those agencies interested in furthering the
farmer's security. A look at the extent of ranchers' and farmers'

information or misinformation reveals areas needing attention by the
Agricultural Experiment Station and other agencies concerned with
the welfare of farm people. The findings and sources of information on
OASI should reveal useful material to extension groups, farm publishers
and other agencies engaged in the diffusion of information.

61
INITIATING COMMUNITY CONSULTATION IN RURAL AREAS
Halpern, Howard and Ronald Love
Hospital and Community Psychiatry, pp. 30-33, September 1971.

In taking services directly to rural areas, the Southeast Nebraska
Psychiatric Clinic developed a program of community based consultation.
The program was designed to bring about a balance between community
demands and changes in disturbed people. The most useful function was
considered to be consultation with the community as a whole rather than to
individuals or individual groups.

62
INNOVATIONS IN RURAL SERVICE DELIVERY
Magel, Don and Cheryl Price
Human Services in the Rural Environment, 1(1): 20-28, 1979.

The authors demonstrate how the Teaching Learning Center model can be an
effective academic/professional training mechanism for innovative social
service delivery in rural areas. Field situations in rural communities
of Arizona are cited as examples.

63
INSTITUTIONAL STRUCTURES FOR IMPROVING RURAL COMMUNITY SERVICES
Mackey, R. G.
Reno, Nevada: University of Nevada, Agricultural and Resource Economics.
(Research Program), undated.

The program objectives include: 1) identifying configuration of institutional structures including elements of the economic, demographic, and
social organization which affect the provision and delivery of community
services; 2) defining objective measures of adequacy of community services;
3) determining the existence and adequacy of community services provided
in selected rural areas of Nevada; 4) determining the relationship between
institutional structures and the existence and inadequacy of community
services; and 5) identifying the policies, alternative patterns of organization and the conditions which are requisite to effective planning and
coordination for the delivery of community services.

64
INTEGRATING THE RURAL WELFARE DEPARTMENT INTO THE COMMUNITY
Falck, Hans S.
In Can Public Welfare Keep Pace? Melvin Morton, ed.
New York: Columbia University Press, pp. 134-150, 1969.

This article applies what is known about group and organizational behavior
to the use of rural community groups in the administration of public welfare.

65
INTERVENTION IN DISINTEGRATING FAMILIES
Wooten, Ray W.
Boise, Idaho: Idaho State Department of Health, 1968, 45 pp. ERIC: ED041433.

A special demonstration project attempted to find means of assisting hard-
core multi-problem families in a predominantly rural Idaho County Agency.
A single agency was formed to coordinate community activities and provide
a variety of services for the needs of the total family. A description
of the project and its results are presented in this report.

66
JOB COLLEGES, INC.: FIRST YEAR EVALUATION, VOL. I AND II.
Glasso, Myfanway I.
La Jolla, California: Systems, Science and Software, Final Report,
September, 1971, 231 pp. NTIS/PB-211 985.

This two-volume report presents a model program to provide families living
in rural areas with basic education, health care, vocational training and
employment opportunities.

67
MAKING WAVES IN A SEA OF PEANUT BUTTER: IMPLICATIONS FOR SOCIAL WORK
PRACTICE IN SPARSELY POPULATED, CONSERVATIVE AREAS
In Social Work in Rural Areas: Issues and Opportunities, Joseph Davenport,
III, Judith A. Davenport and James R. Wiebler, eds.
Laramie: University of Wyoming, Department of Social Work, 1980.

Discusses change related issues that were encountered by a coalition of
Wyoming citizens who attempted to bring the Special Supplemental Food
Program for Women, Infants and Children to their state.

68
MIGRANT ACTION PROGRAM: ANNUAL REPORT, 1972
ERIC: ED072903.

The philosophy behind and the operations of the Iowa Migrant Action Program
(MAP) are discussed in this 1972 Annual Report. Description of various
MAP programs is provided. In addition complete funding data are included.

69
THE MIGRANT: A HUMAN PERSPECTIVE
Rochester, N.Y.: Genesee/Finger Lakes Regional Planning Board,
December 1972, 200 pp. ERIC: ED086412.

Inventorying and analyzing the housing needs of the region's migrant population, the report is presented in two sections. Part I introduces the
migrant, staygrant, and rural agricultural worker. Part II addresses the
particular needs of the agricultural worker, including the rural poor.
Attention is given to education, training, social services, and recreation.
Also discussed is the role the regional planning board must develop to
coordinate agencies which offer services to and conduct studies on migrants
and rural agricultural workers.

70
MIGRANT PROGRAMS IN CALIFORNIA
Washington, D.C.: Office of Economic Opportunity, 1973. ERIC: ED081519.

Services available to migrants in California are listed in this directory.
Information on migrant populations in California are also included.

71
MIGRANT PROGRAMS IN FLORIDA
Washington, D.C.: Office of Economic Opportunity, 1973. ERIC: ED081520.

Services available to migrants in Florida are listed in this directory.

72
MIGRANT PROGRAMS IN TEXAS
Carrasco, Frank, ed.
Washington, D.C.: Office of Economic Opportunity, 1973. ERIC: ED0796295.

Services available to migrants in Texas are listed in this handbook. A
profile for each county is also presented.

73
MODEL FOR THE OPERATION OF INTEGRATED SERVICES IN THE RURAL SETTING
Ottumwa: Southern Iowa Economic Development Association, 1973, 28 pp.
NTIS/SHR-0000543

A model of interagency cooperation to provide integrated human services
in a rural area of Iowa is described.

74
A MODERN RURAL HUMAN SERVICE DELIVERY SYSTEM: AN IOWA EXPERIMENT
Dunn, Lynn
In 2nd Annual Northern Wisconsin Symposium on Human Services in the
Rural Environment Reader, David Bast and Julie Schmidt, eds.
Madison: University of Wisconsin - Extension, Center for Social Science,
pp. 128-133, 1977.

This paper deals with how a public welfare agency in Iowa is attempting
to reorganize to provide more effective services to its rural clientele.
A social service needs survey is included.

75
MONTANA WELFARE LEGAL SERVICES PROGRAM: FINAL REPORT
Helena: Montana Department of Public Welfare, Division of Statistics
and Research, December 1971, 42 pp. NTIS/PB-214 342/8.

The project provided statewide legal service in the predominantly rural
state of Montana and included welfare legal services to Indian reservations
and to the larger urban areas.

76
MONTANA'S RURAL SOCIAL SERVICE DELIVERY SYSTEM
Surdock, Pete W., et al.
Helena, Montana: Montana Department of Social and Rehabilitation Service,
June 1974, 282 pp. NTIS/SHR 0000483/ES.

A project was carried out to design and test methods for coordinating social
service delivery to five sparsely populated Montana counties, including an
Indian reservation. Techniques, functions, procedures, and services are
identified and described.

77
MORE MIGRANTS MAKE IT TO COLLEGE
Murphy, Betty
Opportunity, 7(6): 24-29, 1972. ERIC: EJ060150.

Describes a tuition assistance program offered by the manpower opportunity
program which provides financial assistance and supportive services for
migrant workers, seasonal farm workers, and their children to obtain a
higher education.

78
NATIONAL CONFERENCE ON NONMETROPOLITAN COMMUNITY SERVICES RESEARCH HELD
AT OHIO STATE UNIVERSITY ON JANUARY 11-13, 1977.
Economics, Statistics, and Cooperative Service
Washington, D.C.: Economic Development Division (Sponsored in part by
Committee on Agriculture, Nutrition, and Forestry, U.S. Senate), July
1977, 348 pp. NTIS/PB-276 444/7ST.

The recent turnabout in rural urban migration flows apparently makes
obsolete much of the thought and knowledge about the flow of people from
rural areas to the large urban centers. The conference discusses areas
of needed research.

79
NATURAL HELPING NETWORKS: A STRATEGY FOR PREVENTION
Collins, A. H. and D. L. Pancoast
Washington, D.C.: National Association of Social Workers, 1976.

The authors argue for the efficacy of "natural" or informal helping
systems that operate within communities as opposed to professional and
bureaucratized systems that often seem imposed on communities.

80
NEW APPROACHES TO PLANNING, MANAGING, AND EVALUATING THE IMPACT OF HUMAN
SERVICE DELIVERY SYSTEMS
Proceedings of a Seminar on Human Services Integration.
Denver: University of Denver, Social Welfare Institute, April 1973, 108 pp.

These proceedings are from a three-day seminar which examined indepth the
problems of administering scarce resources for helping dependent and disadvantaged residents of rural areas to develop the capacity for self-
support or self-sufficiency.

81
NON-UTILIZATION OF FAMILY AND RELATED SOCIAL SERVICES
Baker, David and David Colby
Oneonta, New York: Hartwick College, Department of Political Science,
April 1977. 25 pp. NTIS/SHR-0002368.

This study evaluated the utilization of family and related social services
in a predominantly rural area of New York state.

82
NYSSA SERVICE CENTER
Walston, Mary
Salem, Oregon: Department of Human Resources, Quarterly Report,
April 1973, 52 pp. NTIS/PB-254 681/OST

This is the sixth quarterly report of the Nyssa, Oregon, Human Resource
Center Project, which set out to be the first completely integrated
social service facility for migrants in the nation. Most of the population
served is of Mexican-American descent.

83
OUTPOSTING IN THE PUBLIC WELFARE SERVICES
Hoshing, George and Shirley Weber
Public Welfare, pp. 8-14, Winter, 1973.

This article describes the development of the "outposting" approach by the
Social Services Department of the Atlantic County, New Jersey, Welfare
Board and the experience to date with this form of service delivery;
discusses the rationale for outposting; and attempts to set forth the
concepts and principles that underlie it. Among the agencies used as
"outposts" is a migrant farm program which serves a predominantly Puerto
Rican population.

84
PATHWAYS OF RURAL PEOPLE TO HEALTH SERVICES
Hassinger, Edward W.
In Rural Health Services: Organization, Delivery, and Use.
Ames: The Iowa State University Press, pp. 164-187, 1976.

In order to shed light on understanding rural health consumer behavior,
the author examines the characteristics of rural society, the health
care system and the patterned behavior of people in seeking health care.

85
PIONEER EFFORTS IN RURAL SOCIAL WELFARE: FIRSTHAND VIEWS SINCE 1908
Martinez-Brawley, Emilia E., ed.
University Park, Pa.: Pennsylvania State University Press, 1979.

This excellent collection of readings reveals the nature of rural social
work in years past. Its rich history is a tribute to the early pioneers
of social welfare in rural communities, and a valuable resource for the
training and practice of the contemporary rural practitioner.

86
PLANNING COMMUNITY SERVICES FOR THE RURAL ELDERLY: IMPLICATIONS FROM
RESEARCH
Coward, Raymond T.
The Gerontologist, 19(3): 275-282, 1979.

From a review of available research on the elderly, the author discusses
the major implications for the practitioner responsible for planning
community services for the rural elderly.

87
PLANNING AND DELIVERY OF SERVICES IN RURAL AREAS
Ginsberg, Leon
In A Symposium: Planning and Delivery of Social Services in Rural America,
William H. Koch, ed.
Madison: University of Wisconsin, Center for Continuing Education and
Community Action for Social Service, 1973.

This paper discusses some of the characteristics of rural communities as
guides for the effective planning and delivery of services to them.

88
PROVIDING PUBLIC SOCIAL SERVICES IN NONMETROPOLITAN AREAS: EVALUATION OF A
NONTRADITIONAL MODEL
Daley, John Michael, Dennis L. Poole, and Riley Price.
Paper Presented at the Fifth National Institute on Social Work in Rural
Areas. Burlington, Vermont, July 27-30, 1980.

This paper provides the first systematic evaluation of a three year,
federally funded demonstration project in southeastern Arizona, known as
the Satellite Diagnostic Social Service Centers Project. The evaluation
team is testing the concept of SDSSC as a mechansim to serve at a
reasonable cost previously underserved or unserved rural communities.

89
PSYCHIATRIC RESIDENTS PROVIDE EXTRA MANPOWER FOR RURAL COMMUNITY AGENCIES
Withersty, David J.
Hospital and Community Psychiatry, 27(6): 270-271, 1975.

The author describes his experience as a psychiatric resident at the
West Virginia University Medical Center in providing manpower for rural
community agencies. Activities such as psychiatric evaluation, medica-
tion checks, psychotherapy cases, teaching, and consultation were
performed.

90
PUBLIC PERCEPTION OF RURAL COUNTY SOCIAL SERVICE AGENCIES
Bensen, Robert and Robert W. Bilby
In Social Work in Rural Areas: Preparation and Practice, Ronald K. Green
and Stephen A. Webster, eds.
Knoxville: The University of Tennessee, School of Social Work,
243-265, 1978.

Rural county social service agencies are frequently frowned upon by local citizens whose values and perceptions often conflict with social welfare ideology.

91
A PUBLIC WELFARE PLAN TO DEVELOP A PROGRAM IN COMMUNITY PLANNING
Santa Fe: New Mexico Health and Social Service Department, January 1972.
108 pp. NTIS/PB-214 344/4.

A report is made on community social workers working relatively auton-omously in five New Mexico counties in a demonstration project which developed a wide variety of programs in areas such as welfare rights, food demonstration, drug addiction treatment, and child care in coopera-tion with the local communities. The sites included both metropolitan and rural locations and the population included Indian and Spanish-American communities.

92
RELFECTIONS ON FORTY YEARS WITH THE RURAL CHURCH MOVEMENT
Greene, Shirley.
In Social Work in Rural Areas: Issues and Opportunities, Joseph Davenport, III, Judith A. Davenport and James R. Wiebler, eds.
Laramie: The University of Wyoming, Department of Social Work, 173-180, 1980.

Presents some personal reflections on the history of the Rural Church Movement, its problems and successes.

93
REGIONAL AND STATE INSTITUTES: RX FOR HUMAN SERVICES IN BOOM TOWNS
Davenport, Judith Ann and Joseph Davenport, III.
In Boom Towns and Human Services, Davenport and Davenport, eds.
Laramie: University of Wyoming, Department of Social Work, 1979.

This paper briefly examines the social consequences of rapid growth associ-ated with energy development. It describes the purpose and operation of the Wyoming Human Services Project, and proposes the creation and develop-ment of regional and state institutes on energy and human services.

94
REPORT DOCUMENTING THE DESIGN AND DEVELOPMENT OF A FISCAL MANAGEMENT SYSTEM FOR AN INTEGRATED HUMAN SERVICE SYSTEM FOR THE FIVE COUNTY AREAS OF DISTRICT V OF THE STATE OF UTAH
Salt Lake City, Utah: Department of Social Services, 1974, 31 pp.
NTIS/SHR-0001007.

A fiscal management system to support the human services delivery system in a five-county area of Utah is described. The system is designed to centralize functions; to eliminate multi-fiscal agents; to develop a budget and planning methodology; to establish an accounting procedure to allow co-mingling of local, state and federal requirements; and to establish a centralized automated payments system.

95
REPORT ON THE NATIONAL ASSOCIATION OF COUNTIES RESEARCH FOUNDATION
DeJong, Ralph and Mindy L. Good
Human Services Integration Symposium, April 6-8, 1975.
Washington, D.C.: National Association of Counties, 1975.

Representatives of federal, state and county agencies from throughout the
U.S. gathered to discuss program effectiveness. Several issues were
voiced: 1) federal government's regulations inhibit integrated services
at the local level; 2) state commitment enhances accountability and coordination; and 3) county consolidation of programs will not alone achieve
integrated services. Simulations of planning for integrated services were
tested.

96
RIO GRANDE YOUTH CARE CENTER: FINAL REPORT
Los Lunas, New Mexico: Valencia County Commission, 1974, 14 pp.
NTIS/PB-254 8881ST.

A counseling and referral center for youths was established in 1972 to
alleviate delinquency problems in the community, with special reference
to Chicanos.

97
THE ROLE OF MENTAL HEALTH PROGRAMS IN RURAL AREAS
Fink, Richard L.
In Social Work in Rural Areas: Preapration and Practice. R. G. Green
and S. A. Webster, eds.
Knoxville: The University of Tennessee, School of Social Work, 328-340,
1978.

The author appraises the community mental health movement, critiques that
part of the movement in rural areas, and provides some guidelines for a
model redefining and relating rural mental health needs to design and
implementation of programs.

98
RURAL AREAS POSE SPECIAL PROBLEMS FOR PROVIDING SOCIAL SERVICES
Garrett, Mary Louise, David L. Miles and A. G. Lebason
Social Services, Vol. 50, 77-79, November 16, 1976.

A comprehensive health care program implemented in an isolated, medically
underserved, economically depressed, rural Appalachian community had a
major social service component. This article describes the problems
experienced in delivering social services and mental health services,
and demonstrates that delivery must accommodate constraints imposed by
the structure of the community.

99
RURAL GOVERNMENT AND LOCAL PUBLIC SERVICES
Rainey, Kenneth D. and Karen D. Rainey
In Rural U.S.A.: Persistence and Change, Thomas R. Ford, ed.
Ames: The Iowa State University Press, 126-144, 1978.

The author reviews current problems of local governments and concludes
that the major policy issues for rural communities are land use controls,
public service districts and planning districts, local finance, education,
health care, and transportation.

100
RURAL HUMAN RESOURCES PROJECT
Washington, D.C.: National Association of Counties Research Foundation,
1974, 70 pp. NTIS/SHR-0000101/ES.

This quarterly progress report provides descriptions of current activities
of the Rural Human Resources Project, designed to help rural counties
respond to the human service needs of their citizens. These reports
describe the conditions under which human services are delivered in each
state, the principal objectives of each state's project, and current
progress.

101
RURAL HUMAN SERVICES: A PERSPECTIVE ON NEW ENGLAND
Ortiz, James O.
Boston, Mass.: Dept. of Health, Education, and Welfare, Region I,
August 1977, 33 pp. NTIS/SHR-0002084.

The growth of rural communities is discussed in relation to social service
needs and the formulation of social service policies. While social
problems in rural areas of New England are emphasized, difficulties
associated with the provision of human services to resolve these problems
are applicable to almost any rural area of the U.S. Alternative approaches
to the provision of human services in rural areas are described. They
pertain to the development of national and state policies, the role of
local government, and the functioning of human service agencies.

102
RURAL HUMAN RESOURCES PROJECT
National Association of Counties
Washington, D.C.: Office of Economic Opportunity, 1974, 70 pp.

A quarterly progress report from NARC on the Human Resources project.
Several topics including state and county cooperation for integrated
services. Human resource coordinators for the project are listed by
name and address.

103
RURAL INCOME MAINTENANCE EXPERIMENT
Washington, D.C.: U.S. Department of Health, Education and Welfare,
Office of Economic Opportunity, Summary Report, No. SR10, November 1976,
97 pp.

This report is a summary of the rural income maintenance experiments.
Because of the unique characteristics of rural areas with respect to
employment opportunities and the large segment of the poor population in
rural areas, this experiment was conducted to analyze the "rural" reaction
to such programs and administrative requirements that would be necessary.
(Note: This report may be obtained from the Institute for Research on
Poverty at the University of Wisconsin- Madison campus.)

104
RURAL MODELS
Hussey, Hans R.
In Progress in Community Mental Health. Harvey H. Barten and Leopold
Bellak, eds.
New York: Greene and Stratton, 1972.

This article examines rural mental health services models of mental health
care and innovative rural service delivery systems.

105
RURAL PLANNING SPECIALIST: A UNIQUE APPROACH TO THE PROBLEMS OF POVERTY
IN RURAL AMERICA
Harrisburg: Pennsylvania Department of Consumer Affairs, 1973, 127 pp.
NTIS/SHR-0001182.

Guidelines are presented for the implementation of rural planning specialist
(RPS) projects to assist rural communities in developing their human and
organizational resources. Six generalized steps in the RPS process--
introduction and inventory, initial project, working with the community,
defining a problem situation, working toward change, and leaving the
community--are defined, based on the experiences and comments of
Pennsylvania RPS.

106
A RURAL PRACTICE MODEL: EVALUATION
Daley, John Michael, Cheryl Price and Riley Price
In Social Work in Rural Areas: Issues and Opportunities. Joseph Davenport,
III, Judith A. Davenport and James R. Wiebler, eds.
Laramie: The University of Wyoming, Department of Social Work, 1980.

This paper describes a social service model designed to deliver professional social services to previously unserved or underserved rural communities. The process of refinement is traced and changes in the
objectives and evaluation design are discussed.

107

THE RURAL PROTECTIVE SERVICES WORKER AS A COORDINATOR

Buckbee, Russell A.

In Effective Models for the Delivery of Services in Rural Areas:
Implications for Practice and Social Work Education. Barry L. Locke and
Roger A. Lohmann, eds.
Morgantown: West Virginia University, August 1978.

In this paper, the author views and discusses the problems a rural protective service worker faces in order to present a new model for protective services work. The strategy of community organizing in a rural setting is considered and evaluated for the protective services worker.

108

THE RURAL RAPE CRISIS CENTER: A MODEL

Davenport, Judith and Joseph Davenport, III.
Human Services in the Rural Environment, 1(1): 29-39, 1979.

In addition to describing the problems and needs of sexual assault victims
in rural areas, the authors outline a successful crisis intervention
strategy and suggest ways to promote greater rural justice.

109

RURAL SERVICES

Miller, Jon, et al.
Chapel Hill: University of North Carolina, July 1977, 130 pp.
NTIS/SHR-0002313/ES.

A workshop was convened to facilitate the sharing of information among
developmental disabilities councils and identify common problems and issues
that confront developmentally disabled citizens in rural areas; to examine
models of comprehensive service systems in rural areas; and to evaluate
selected rural programs concerning health care.

110

RURAL SOCIAL PROBLEMS, HUMAN SERVICES, AND SOCIAL POLICIES

Derr, Janet Morton
Working Paper 2, Social and Rehabilitation Service, Denver University,
Colorado Center for Social Research and Development.
Washington, D.C.: U.S. Government Printing Office, September 1973, 29 pp.

Discussion of nutrition problems in rural areas. Of five identified high-
risk population subgroups with regard to malnutrition, four are rural.
Evidence indicates that food programs serve rural residents less uniformly
and less adequately than urban residents.

111

RURAL SOCIAL PROBLEMS, HUMAN SERVICES, AND SOCIAL POLICIES

Derr, Janet Morton
Working Paper 3, Poverty and Income Maintenance, Denver University,
Colorado Center for Social Research and Development.
Washington, D.C.: U.S. Government Printing Office, September 1973.

Poverty is more prevalent and more severe in rural than in urban areas, and incomes are generally lower in rural than in urban areas. Although there are a large number of income maintenance and income supplementation programs in rural areas, the programs tend to be less well organized and less extensive than those in urban areas.

112
RURAL SOCIAL PROBLEMS, HUMAN SERVICES, AND SOCIAL POLICIES
Derr, Janet Morton
Working Paper 4, Employment and Manpower, Denver University, Colorado Center for Social Research and Development.
Washington, D.C.: U.S. Government Printing Office, September 1973.

Data indicate that rates of unemployment and underemployment are consistently higher in rural than in urban areas. A variety of manpower and employment services are available to rural areas, but these programs have tended to be poorly organized, to lack realistic assessments of opportunity structures in rural areas, and to be financed at too low a level.

113
RURAL SOCIAL PROBLEMS, HUMAN SERVICES, AND SOCIAL POLICIES
Derr, Janet Morton
Working Paper 6, Education, Denver University, Colorado Center for Social Research and Development.
Washington, D.C.: U.S. Government Printing Office, September 1973.

The educational system, because of its relative "universality" in this country, is in an advantaged position to serve as a change agent in rural areas by providing crucial resources to aid rural residents in their efforts to constructively respond to and guide the change processes which have an impact on them and on their rural environment.

114
RURAL SOCIAL PROBLEMS, HUMAN SERVICES, AND SOCIAL POLICIES
Derr, Janet Morton
Working Paper 7, Housing, Denver University, Colorado Center for Social Research and Development.
Washington, D.C.: U.S. Government Printing Office, September 1973.

The housing problems of the rural poor are great, both in terms of the numbers of rural individuals and families affected and in the severity of the conditions which they experience.

115
RURAL SOCIAL PROBLEMS, HUMAN SERVICES, AND SOCIAL POLICIES
Derr, Janet Morton
Working Paper 8, Health, Denver University, Colorado Center for Social Research and Development.
Washington, D.C.: U.S. Government Printing Office, September 1973.

Comparison of a broad range of rural and urban health care statistics indicates the inadequacy of rural health care systems, particularly with

respect to the rural poor. Included in this report are discussions of
health status, medical manpower and facilities, health services utilization and delivery models and auspices and financing of rural health services.

116
RURAL SOCIAL PROBLEMS, HUMAN SERVICES, AND SOCIAL POLICIES
Derr, Janet Morton
Working Paper 9, Family Planning, Denver University, Colorado Center
for Social Research and Development.
Washington, D.C.: U.S. Government Printing Office, September 1973.

Information on family planning needs and programs in rural areas of underdeveloped nations is available, but information on the United States, both
urban and rural, is less comprehensive. However, more extensive data are
now being collected and there have been a small number of demonstration
rural family projects.

117
RURAL SOCIAL PROBLEMS, HUMAN SERVICES, AND SOCIAL POLICIES
Derr, Janet Morton
Working Paper 13, Social Services, Denver University, Colorado Center
for Social Research and Development.
Washington, D.C.: U.S. Government Printing Office, September 1973.

This paper reports on available literature pertaining to social services
obstacles that hinder the efficient and effective delivery of social
services in rural areas that included a small and widely dispersed
population in combination with adverse economic conditions and an
inadequate service-related resource base.

118
RURAL AND URBAN ATTITUDES TOWARD WELFARE
Osgood, Mary H.
Social Work 22(1): 41-47, 1977.

Suggests that more negative attitudes toward welfare found among rural
populations may account for rural/urban differences in the number of persons
receiving welfare benefits.

119
RURAL-URBAN DIFFERENCES IN THE STRUCTURE OF SERVICES FOR THE ELDERLY IN
UPSTATE NEW YORK COUNTIES
Taietz, Philip and Sande Milton
Journal of Gerontology, 34(3): 429-437, 1979.

This research examines the impact of federal intervention and local community
effort on the development of programs for the elderly.

120
RURAL WIN-INGS
Loomis, Rosemary and Richard Starry
Journal of Employment Counseling, 2(4): 183-186, 1974.

This article explores the experience of two Work Incentive Program (WIN)
staff members in delivering employment related services in a rural WIN
program. It deals with three prevalent rural obstacles to employment:
transportation, flexibility with individual cases, and sex barriers.

121
SATISFACTION WITH COMMUNITY SERVICES IN NORTHERN WEST VIRGINIA
Kuehn, John P.
Morgantown: West Virginia University, Agricultural Experiment Station,
Bulletin 649, October 1976, 41 pp. ERIC: ED141062.

Study objectives were to determine the levels of satisfaction with selected
community services in an 11-county area of northern West Virginia and to
compare these levels to those of 12 other selected sites in non-metropolitan northeastern U.S. Satisfaction items were: local ambulance, housing
situation, local road maintenance, medical services, dental services, local
schools, neighborhood, local fire department, local police, sports and
recreation programs, telephone service, public transportation, and media.

122
SERVICES INTEGRATION ELEMENTS IN THE GLASGLOW, MONTANA SOCIAL SERVICE
AGENCY
DeWitt, John, Janet Derr and Arnold Solomon
Denver University, Colorado Center for Social Research and Development,
Helena, Montana: Montana Department of Social Rehabilitation Services,
September 1974, 91 pp.

This is a report on the services integration project from October 1971 to
July 1974. In an effort to increase participants in social service programs,
such as public assistance, special efforts have been made to bring services
to rural residents through transportation and an increased number of
paraprofessionals.

123
SERVICES INTEGRATION: PART III, AN OVERVIEW
Sampson, Barbara C.
Cambridge, Massachusetts: Abt Associates, Inc., December 1971, 42 pp.
NTIS/SHR-0000160.

Three of twelve services integration projects funded by DHEW in 1971 were
directed specifically toward rural service delivery concerns. In Part III
an overview is presented of project characteristics, strengths, and
weaknesses.

124

SOCIAL SERVICE ACCESSIBILITY: IS LOCATION RELEVANT?

Herrick, John M.

In Social Work in Rural Areas: Issues and Opportunities. Joseph
Davenport, III, Judith A. Davenport, and James R. Wiebler, eds.
Laramie: The University of Wyoming, Department of Social Work, 186-193.
1980.

Service effectiveness is often impaired when the planning of the location
of social service delivery sites are not carefully considered. The
author offers several cost-effective methods for assessing the costs of
both the accessibility and unaccessibility to selected rural social
services.

125

SOCIAL SERVICES TO THE INDIAN UNMARRIED MOTHER

Hostbjor, Stella

Child Welfare, 7-9, 1961.

Discusses Indian attitudes toward illegitimacy and adoption, and the
effect of these attitudes on the delivery of social services to unmarried
mothers.

126

SOCIAL STRATIFICATION AND RURAL ECONOMIC DEVELOPMENT: LESSONS FROM THE
ANTI-POVERTY PROGRAMS IN THE U.S.

Bould-Vantil, Sally

Paper presented at the World Congress of Rural Sociology, (4th),
Torun, Poland: August 1976, 25 pp.   ERIC: ED131972.

Four kinds of U.S. anti-poverty programs were analyzed in terms of their
impact upon the rural poor. Examination of 13 rural community development corporations in terms of prior and present poverty of non-manager
employees indicated the effect of these programs was one of merely
changing the source of income rather than the stratification system,
since the unemployed simply became employed in low skill, low wage jobs.

127

SOCIAL WORK IN RURAL AREAS: ISSUE AND OPPORTUNITIES

Davenport, Joseph, III, Judith Davenport and James Wiebler, eds.

A selection of papers presented at the Fourth National Institute of Social
Work in Rural Areas, July 29-August 1, 1979, Laramie, Wyoming.
Laramie: University of Wyoming, 1979.

This book contains 22 selected papers presented at the conference on social
work in rural areas. Topics include: rural culture, boom towns, health,
aging, mental health, and education and training.

128
SOCIOCULTURAL FACTORS AFFECTING FAMILY PLANNING SERVICES BY NAVAJO WOMEN
Slemenda, Charles W.
Human Organization, 37(2): 190-194, 1978.

This report offers some insights into decision making among Native
Americans, utilizing an ethnological approach to explain contraceptive
behavior among Navajo women in the Fort Defiance area of northeastern
Arizona.

129
A STRATEGY FOR IMPLEMENTING FAMILY PLANNING SERVICES IN THE UNITED STATES
Jaffe, Frederick
American Journal of Public Health, 58(4): 713-725, 1968.

A strategy to make family planning services available to communities in the
U.S. is proposed based upon experience and observations in the U.S., and
upon organizing principles from programs in the developing countries applicable to our situation. Responses of low-income people to family planning
program is of central importance to strategy formulation.

130
STUDY OF ECONOMIC DEVELOPMENT ACTIVITIES IN RURAL COMMUNITY ACTION AGENCIES
Yankelovich, Daniel
New York: Yankelovich, Inc., August 1969, 108 pp. NTIS/PB-185 957.

The report describes the roles played by ten rural community action agencies,
(CAA's) and considers how participation of the poor is affected by the
participation of the CAA in economic development activities and how relationships between OEO and CAA affected the agencies' participation in such
activities.

131
A STUDY OF THE EFFECTS ON THE FAMILY DUE TO EMPLOYMENT OF THE WELFARE
MOTHER: VOLUME I, FINDINGS AND IMPLICATIONS
Feldman, Harold and Margaret Feldman
Ithaca: Cornell University, College of Human Ecology, Report No. DLMA1-
51-34-69-07-1, January 1972, 331 pp.

The study focuses on how employment influences the home and personal life
of the mother. Findings of a comparison of 1,325 women are reported on
problems and concerns about care of the home and relationships with
children. Forty-two recommendations are made, including a training
program to increase women's skill in caring for the home and managing
problems created by their working.

132
A STUDY OF THE EFFECTS ON THE FAMILY DUE TO EMPLOYMENT OF THE WELFARE
MOTHER: VOLUME III.
Feldman, Harold and Margaret Feldman
Ithaca: Cornell University, College of Human Ecology, Report No. DLMA1-
51-34-64-07-03. January 1972, 626 pp.

This report is concerned with multigenerational rural poverty that is seemingly unbreakable. Data were obtained from several years of close observation of 30 families in a small rural community in northern Appalachia. Particular problems faced by low income women relative to their working include child care, transportation, family and home responsibilities, health, interpersonal relations, family life styles, self-image.

133
SUSANVILLE: A COMMUNITY HELPS ITSELF IN MOBILIZATION OF COMMUNITY RESOURCES FOR SELF-HELP IN MENTAL HEALTH
Beier, Ernst, Peter Robinson, and Gino Micheletti
Journal of Consulting and Clinical Psychology, 36(1): 142-150, 1971.

Adult lay members and high school students were trained to work with families selected for having problem children in schools or being under stress. Evaluation of project and community-wide measures applicable for future efforts are discussed.

134
USE OF HEALTH SERVICES IN A RURAL COMMUNITY: MULTIVARIATE PERSPECTIVES
Franta, C. E., et al.
Society for Epidemiologic Research: Abstracts (undated).

This is an abstract of a study of patterns of health service utilization in a rural county of California.

135
VERMONT RURAL AND FARM FAMILY REHABILITATION PROJECT, A BENCHMARK REPORT
Tompkins, E. H., et al.
Burlington: Vermont University, Agricultural Experiment Station, Research Report MP73, May 1973, 48 pp. ERIC: ED086433.

This report presents information about client families and their farms during their contact with the Vermont Rural and Farm Family Rehabilitation (RFFR) Project, which provided rehabilitation and employment services. Interestingly, the contact agency mentioned most frequently by client families prior to involvement with the RFFR Project was the Agricultural Stabilization and Conservation Service of USDA. Later, after association with the Project, the Agricultural County Extension agent had the greatest number of contacts on referral by program aides.

136
THE WYOMING HUMAN SERVICES PROJECT: A MODEL FOR OVERCOMING THE HUGGER MUGGER OF BOOMTOWN
Davenport, Judith Ann and Joseph Davenport, III.
Presented to the Advisory Committees, U.S. Commission on Civil Rights, Denver, Colorado, November 2-3, 1978.

This article examines the social consequences and problems of energy development in small western communities. It describes the history, operation, and results of a model program designed to mitigate the deleterious effect of impact, and pays special attention to the problems of women and minorities in impact areas and also offers implications and recommendations for the future delivery of human services in such communities.

CHAPTER 5

PLANNING, ADMINISTRATION AND COMMUNITY DEVELOPMENT
IN RURAL AREAS

General Topics

Boom Towns

Citizen Participation

Community Action

Community Development Block Grants

Community Development Corporations

Community Organization

Community Power

Community Services

Cooperatives

Energy Development

Extension Service

Federalism

Industrialization

Management Information System

Micropolitan Development

Regional Development

Resource Development

Rural Community Development

Small Town Planning

1

ACTION HANDBOOK: MANAGING GROWTH IN A SMALL COMMUNITY
Murray, James A. and William Lamont, Jr.
Boulder, Colorado: Briscoe, Murray and Lamont, Inc., July 1978, 317 pp.
NTIS/PB-286 911 3/ST.

The Action Handbook is designed to be a detailed how to manage manual for
small communities undergoing or facing the prospect of accelerated growth.

2

AN ACTION SCHEME FOR RURAL COMMUNITY DEVELOPMENT PRACTITIONERS
Jacob, Nelson, Stephen Lilley and Eddie Wynn
In 2nd National Institute on Social Work In Rural Areas Reader. Edward B.
Buxton, ed.
Madison: University of Wisconsin--Extension Center for Social Service,
18-33, 1978.

Drawing on ideas developed by Rothman and on experiences in a target county
of the Title V Project in South Carolina, the authors demonstrate the
utility of a classification scheme for community development in a rural
area. The scheme has several implications for training in rural social work
practice.

3

ADIOS TO MIGRANCY
Carkin, Timothy
Manpower, 6(8): 14-22, 1974. ERIC: EJ102169.

Coca Cola's agricultural labor project was designed to change the migrant's
way of life from unstable to stable by making migrant housing more habit-
able, creating permanent jobs, and providing numerous fringe benefits.

4

THE AMERICAN COMMUNITY: A MULTIDISCIPLINARY BIBLIOGRAPHY
Kinton, Jack F.
Montecello, Illinois: Council of Planning Librarians, September 1970, 56 pp.
ERIC: ED101428.

This is an extensive bibliography of publications dealing with the quest
for community in the United States.

5

AMERICAN INDIANS INDUSTRIALIZE TO COMBAT POVERTY
Sorkin, Alan L.
Monthly Labor Review 92(3): 19-25, 1969.

There are certain barriers which retard industrialization on Indian reservations particularly inadequate transportation. Nonetheless, industrial
development on reservations is seen as probably the most favorable long-run

solution to the economic problems of the American Indians. This article
reviews the factors retarding reservation development and the advantages
of a reservation location. Labor costs, fringe benefits and unionization
are considered.

6

ANALYZING IMPACTS OF COMMUNITY DEVELOPMENT
Bennett, Claude F. and Donald L. Nelson
Mississippi State: Southern Rural Development Center, 1975.

A seven-level chain of events in community development is analyzed in three
phases--planning, specification, and implementation. Determining phase
and level at which evaluation should take place is discussed. These
seven levels are: (1) inputs, (2) activities, (3) people involvement,
(4) reactions, (5) knowledge, attitudes, skill and aspiration change,
(6) practice change, and (7) end results.

7

THE APPALACHIAN COMMUNITY IMPACT PROJECT
Duff, Mike
Lexington: University of Kentucky, Cooperative Extension Service, 1968,
14 pp.

Includes objectives, methodology and evaluation of a project designed to
bridge gaps between the needs of selected Appalachian communities and
available resources to test a new Extension approach to breaking the cycle
of poverty.

8

THE APPALACHIAN COMMUNITY IMPACT PROJECT: A DESCRIPTION OF AN INTEGRATED
APPROACH IN RURAL DEVELOPMENT WITH A DISCUSSION OF INTEGRATED EFFORTS AND
PRINCIPLES VITAL TO COMMUNICATION AND EDUCATION
Duff, Mike
Lexington: University of Kentucky, 1974, 24 pp.

Reports on the project's use of indigenous paraprofessionals to work at
the community level. Includes an evaluation statement on integrative
efforts and a discussion of relevant principles vital to communication and
education.

9

AN APPROACH TO THE UNDERSTANDING OF RURAL COMMUNITY DEVELOPMENT
Mayo, Selz C.
Social Forces, 37(2): 95-101, 1958.

It is the author's contention that community development is a social movement. Using four concepts--change, organization, geographical scope, and
persistence in time--the author demonstrates that community development
is a world-wide movement.

10

APPROACHES TO UNIVERSITY EXTENSION WORK WITH THE RURAL DISADVANTAGED:
DESCRIPTION AND ANALYSIS OF A PILOT EFFORT
Miller, Robert, et al.
Morgantown: West Viriginia University, Office of Research and Development,
Division of Social and Economic Development, September 1972, 205 pp.

This book describes the West Virginia University's Center for Appalachian
Studies and Development pilot project to explore techniques for working
with disadvantaged families in rural areas. The principal goal of the
project was the development of a new and modified university extension
program aimed at providing educational experiences for rural, low income,
non-farm families.

11

AN APPROPRIATE ROLE FOR SOCIAL WORK: SMALL BUSINESS DEVELOPMENT IN THE
RURAL COMMUNITY
Deaton, Robert and Allan Bjergo
In 2nd National Institute on Social Work in Rural Areas Reader. Edward B.
Buxton, ed.
Madison: University of Wisconsin--Extension Center for Social Service,
61-67, 1978.

The author discusses the involvement of social workers in small business
development, an area not traditionally included in social work practice.
Drawing upon experiences in Montana, they demonstrate how rural social
workers can apply their skills in business development, and suggest several
general steps to be considered before establishing an enterprise.

12

ARIZONA BUSINESS DEVELOPMENT PROGRAM
Slinkard, Robert J.
Indian Development District of Arizona, Inc. Final Report, 1971, 67 pp.
NTIS/COM-71-00717.

The report reviews 133 projects processed in efforts to further the growth
of business in Indian reservations by Indian entrepreneurs. An improvised
training manual to suit such areas is reproduced in the report.

13

A BIBLIOGRAPHY OF INDUSTRIALIZATION OF RURAL AREAS
Mississippi State: Southern Rural Development Center, Rural Development
Bibliography Series, No. 1, 1976, ($5.00).

A comprehensive annotated bibliography useful to both practitioners and
scholars with interests in industrialization of rural areas.

14

A BIBLIOGRAPHY OF RURAL DEVELOPMENT: LISTINGS BY TOPIC
Parker, Carrie G., Howard Ladewig, and Edward L. McLean
Clemson, South Carolina: Clemson University. Department of
Agricultural Economics and Rural Sociology, June 1976.

The bibliographic entries are separated into the following categories:
Agriculture, Area Development, Community Economic Development, Environmental Improvement, Facilities and Services, and Human Resource Development.

15

THE BUREAUCRAT AND THE INDIAN: A CASE STUDY IN ORGANIZATIONAL DEVELOPMENT
Gummer, Burton and Paul Driben
Social Work, 1(3): 293-299, 1977.

This paper examines the problems encountered when a nonbureaucratically
structured Indian organization (client-advocacy type) establishes a
relationship with a traditional bureaucracy.

16

CAPACITY BUILDING NEEDS OF RURAL AREAS IN VIRGINIA, EXECUTIVE SUMMARY AND
RECOMMENDATIONS
Farmer, Beckwood, et al.
Richmond, Va.: Virginia Department of Agriculture and Consumer Services.
September 1978, 20 pp. NTIS/PB-289 838/5ST.

The study clearly demonstrates that rural communities must be willing to
sacrifice a certain amount of autonomy for gains in viability. Recommendations are concerned more with approaches that rural local governments,
state governments, and the federal government can take to strengthen the
institutional and resource capability network than with specific actions
to be taken in individual program areas.

17

CDC'S: A DEVELOPMENT ALTERNATIVE FOR RURAL AMERICA
Deaton, Brady J.
Growth and Change, 6(1): 31-37, 1975.

Defines the role, operations, and financing of CDCs (Community Development
Corporations) as well as the basic concepts behind them. Believes the CDC,
through its components of democratic involvement and community participation
in business ownership, could play a vital role in stimulating the depressed
areas in rural America.

18

CENTRAL COAST COUNTIES OF SANTA CRUZ, MONTEREY AND SAN BENITO, CALIFORNIA
Aptos, California: Central Coast Counties Development Corporation.
June 30, 1975, 62 pp. NTIS/PB-262 972/3ST.

This report is based on a variety of programs and resources that have been
combined and coordinated so that a farmworker cooperative might become not

simply a business but a transitional vehicle, a means of assisting members of the farmworker population to gain some influence over the economic and social factors that affect their living conditions.

19
THE CHALLENGES OF A COMMUNITY DEVELOPMENT ROLE FOR THE PUBLIC UNIVERSITY
Marshall, H. Peter and Robert W. Miller
Morgantown: West Virginia University, Center for Extension and
Continuing Education, Bulletin No. 1-2, Series 77, July 1976.

This monograph is a description and evaluation of West Virginia University's attempt to deal creatively with the needs and problems of rural communities through community development efforts.

20
CHANGE IN RURAL APPALACHIA: IMPLICATIONS FOR ACTION PROGRAMS
Photiadis, John D. and Harry K. Schwarzweller, eds.
Philadelphia: University of Pennsylvania Press, 1970.

This book of readings is composed of four parts: the relationships between rural Appalachia and the larger society, some of the major institutions in the region, the role of action programs in the context of change, and the future role of the Extension Service as an instrument for effecting the social reconstruction of Appalachian society.

21
CITIZEN INVOLVEMENT IN LAND USE GOVERNANCE: ISSUES AND METHODS
Rosenbaum, Nelson
Washington, D.C.: The Urban Institute, 1976.

The origins and objectives of citizen involvement in public decision-making are examined in this book. This includes a brief historical overview of citizen participation in the American polity. Then the structure of citizen involvement programs and some basic policy and strategy questions are discussed. Finally, the author discusses the actual implementation of citizen involvement programs in the area of land use and land use decision-making. Rosenbaum proposed citizen involvement with three components; and he discusses these components in some detail. One of the advantages of this presentation is that it is concerned simultaneously with basic policy questions and with practical techniques. There is a selected bibliography.

22
CITIZEN PARTICIPATION CERTIFICATION FOR COMMUNITY DEVELOPMENT: A READER
ON THE CITIZEN PARTICIPATION PROCESS
Marshall, Patricia, ed.
Washington, D.C.: The National Association of Housing and Redevelopment
Officials, February, 1977.

This volume discusses citizen participation in the context of the Community Development Block Grant program. It includes a series of brief statements or essays on citizen participation by some of the more well-known scholars and practitioners concerned with citizen participation, it presents the citizen participation requirements of the Housing and Community Development Act of 1974, and it describes a series of the more popular techniques of citizen participation. The latter part is very similar to the more complete presentation in U.S. Department of Tranportation (page 19). There is also an extensive list of organizations concerned with citizen participation issues.

23
CITIZEN PARTICIPATION IN COMMUNITY DEVELOPMENT: WHY SOME CHANGES ARE NEEDED
Downs, Anthony
National Civic Review, 64(5): 228-248, 1975.

Since passage of the Housing and Community Development Act of 1974 every community seeking related funds has had to make "citizen participation" arrangements. In this article the author reviews some of the problems with these arrangements and offers some suggestions for future citizen participation arrangements.

24
CITIZEN PARTICIPATION IN RURAL DEVELOPMENT CONCEPTS, PRINCIPLES, AND RESOURCE MATERIALS
Mississippi State: Southern Rural Development Center, Rural Development Series, No. 6, November 1978, 39 pp. ($1.00).

Describes the potential as well as the limitations of citizen participation in decision-making processes. The booklet also presents guidelines and strategies for effective citizen participation.

25
CITIZEN PARTICIPATION IN RURAL DEVELOPMENT: A SELECTED BIBLIOGRAPHY
Mississippi State: Southern Rural Development Center. Supplement 1 to SRDC Bibliography Series, No. 6, April 1978, 30 pp. $2.00).

An informative, annotated bibliography on rural citizen participation.

26
A CITIZEN VIEW OF PRIORITY NEEDS IN GRAFTON, WEST VIRGINIA
Ferrise, Anthony and Delmar Yoder
Morgantown: West Virginia University, Cooperative Extension Service, 1977, 15 pp.

Reports the responses of a randomly selected group of citizens in a small town on their view of the problems and priorities as a guide to community leaders and officials.

27
CITIZENS AND NATURAL RESOURCES: A PERSPECTIVE ON PUBLIC INVOLVEMENT
Davis, Lawrence S., et al.
Logan, Utah: Utah State University, Department of Forestry and Outdoor Recreation, 1975.

This is a popular booklet written for the concerned or involved citizen, designed to improve his or her effectiveness in public involvement activities. It is, in effect, an application of the findings brought together by Polchow, et al. and Royer, et al. for use by the citizen.

28
CLINTON COUNTY COORDINATES CRD
White, Donald J.
Extension Review, 4-11, March-April, 1978.

This article explains how Clinton County, New York used rural development Title V funds to deal with problems of inadequate housing, high unemployment and underemployment, and poor-to-nonexistent service delivery systems.

29
COLLOQUY ON CDCs (COMMUNITY DEVELOPMENT CORPORATIONS): A DEVELOPMENT ALTERNATIVE FOR RURAL AMERICA
Growth and Change 7(1): 48-50, 1976.

This article is a debate between D. Jeanne Patterson and Brady J. Deaton on the use of CDCs in the rural community development efforts.

30
COMMUNITIES LEFT BEHIND: ALTERNATIVES FOR DEVELOPMENT
Whiting, Larry R., ed.
Ames: Iowa State University Press. 1974.

A collection of essays and studies on communities, with emphasis on rural communities. Essays deal with the effects of depopulation of rural communities on economic development and social structure. Excellent "manual" on rural community problems. Chapter topics include: consequences of decline and economic adjustment, consequences for leadership and participation, and enhancing economic opportunity.

31
COMMUNITY DEVELOPMENT: A DIRECTORY OF ACADEMIC CURRICULUMS THROUGHOUT THE WORLD
Benson, A. E. and Lee J. Cary
ERIC: ED034134.

Descriptions of academic curriculums and courses for thirty graduate and undergraduate programs in community development are included in this directory.

32
COMMUNITY DEVELOPMENT: HOW TO DO IT
Duff, Mike
Lexington: University of Kentucky Press, Cooperative Extension Service, 1973.

Book provides a self-educational device for leaders in community development. Presents itemized checklists and proposals for community organization and planning as a tool for influencing the development of rural areas. Helps to identify community problems and aids in organizing educational programs to meet the problems.

33
COMMUNITY DEVELOPMENT MANAGEMENT INFORMATION SYSTEM
Kuennen, Daniel S.
Georgetown, Delaware: University of Delaware, Cooperative Extension Service, March 1979.

Presents a management information system for use in community development programs, although the materials are primarily intended for Community Development Block Grants Programs.

34
COMMUNITY DEVELOPMENT IN THE 1970'S
Hildreth, R. J. and W. Neill Schaller
American Journal of Agricultural Economics, 54(5): 764-772, 1972.

A discussion of approaches to improving human well-being through community development. Major emphasis is placed on goal-setting, understanding community institutions, and identifying areas of research. One major area discussed is the paucity of relevant economic theory relating to community and regional economies. A small segment deals with increasing economic activity in the community as a means of increasing well-being.

35
COMMUNITY DEVELOPMENT AS A PROCESS
Cary, Lee J., ed.
Columbia, Missouri: University of Missouri Press, 1970.

This collection of articles is an excellent textbook on community development process and activities.

36
THE COMMUNITY DEVELOPMENT PROCESS, THE REDISCOVERY OF LOCAL INITIATIVE
Biddle, William W. and Loureide J. Biddle
New York: Holt, Rinehart and Winston, 1970.

The development process in two communities, a mining county in rural Appalachia and a deteriorating neighborhood in a northern industrial city, is presented in case-study form. The role of social work in community development is demonstrated.

37
COMMUNITY DEVELOPMENT SERIES
Economic Research Division
Columbus: State of Ohio, Development Department, 1968.

An eight-part series dealing with the development process. Titles are: (1) Getting Started; (2) How to Prepare a Community Survey; (3) How to

Prepare a Site Survey; (4) Industrial Parks; (5) Community Promotion; (6) How to Find and Work with Prospects; (7) Planning; and (8) Zoning.

38
COMMUNITY DEVELOPMENT AND SOCIAL WORK PRACTICE
Warren, Roland L.
New York: National Association of Social Workers, 1962.

These proceedings are from a workshop held in 1962 at the Florence Heller Graduate School for Advanced Studies in Social Welfare, Brandeis University.

39
COMMUNITY DEVELOPMENT: SOME COMMON GROUND, PERFORMANCE CRITERIA, AND EVALUATION
Western Regional CRD Committee
Journal of the Community Development Society, 3(1): 81-86, 1972.

Lists the common ground nature of the conditions surrounding community development efforts. Five categories of common ground: (1) growth and activities of decision-making groups; (2) need for educational inputs; (3) group membership; (4) effective project initiation; and (5) consequences of community development effort. From this the authors developed and explained six major action criteria categories: (1) clientele awareness; (2) use and attraction of needed resources; (3) effective organizational skills; (4) process-content balance; (5) individual skill attainment; and (6) individual study achievements.

40
COMMUNITY DEVELOPMENT SOURCE BOOKS
Lexington: University of Kentucky, Department of Agricultural Economics, 1(3): 1975 and 2(1), 1976.

Designed to provide access to development related information from a variety of sources. Intended for use primarily by community development specialists in CES, their clients and other community agencies. Contains articles on community facilities, economic development, environmental improvement and human development.

41
COMMUNITY DEVELOPMENT . . . SOUTHERN STYLE
Mississippi State: Southern Rural Development Center, Series Publication No. 29 (undated.)

Descriptions of several community development projects in the South, including health care, tourism, recreation, industrialization, land use, youth, government and several other projects.

42
COMMUNITY DEVELOPMENT TRAINING PROGRAMS, PART I
Industrial Development Division
Atlanta: Georgia Institute of Technology, 1969.

This is Part I of a four-part training program in total community development. This training guide describes economic growth potential analysis.
Some "lessons" discussed are: (1) regional economic development; (2)
human resources in regional development; (3) manpower resources analysis;
(4) analysis of natural resources; and (5) analysis of general economy.
The lessons in this publication are designed to instruct laymen in the
area of economic growth analysis.

43
COMMUNITY ORGANIZATION AND THE OPPRESSED
Shaffer, Anatole
Journal of Education for Social Work, 8(3): 65-75, 1972.

A new approach to teaching community organization methods is developed.
The primary element is the consciousness of the workers and oppressed
sharing the goal of ending oppression.

44
COMMUNITY ORGANIZATION IN RURAL AREAS
Morrison, Jim
In Social Work in Rural Communities, Leon H. Ginsberg, ed.
New York: Council on Social Work Education, 57-67, 1978.

The author suggests particular skills necessary for effective community
organizing in rural areas. He offers some criticisms of radical and confrontation approaches stemming from Alinsky-type models of practice.

45
COMMUNITY PLANNING FOR THE SMALL TOWN: A BRIEF GUIDELINE OF KEY
CONSIDERATIONS AND STEPS OF IMPLEMENTATION
Durham: University of New Hampshire, Cooperative Extension Service,
March 1976.

This is a practical "do it yourself" booklet for small town community
planning. It is directed toward busy officials with limited time and
energy for planning. The materials suggest how citizen study committees
can be used to both improve the planning process and assist the Planning
Board.

46
COMMUNITY POWER STRUCTURES AND METHODS ARTIFACTS: A REINTERPRETATION
Seiler, Lauren H.
The Sociological Quarterly, 16(1): 272-276, 1975.

Concludes that from his analysis he cannot determine whether any specific
method for determining power structures is better than another.

47

COMMUNITY PREPARATION FOR ECONOMIC DEVELOPMENT IN ARIZONA--POWER STRUCTURE
ANALYSIS
Mangin, Frank
Norman: University of Oklahoma, Industrial Development Institute.
Thesis Manuscript, 1973.

Author states that effective development hinges on local power structure as
well as on economic factors. Thesis is that not all communities desire
or are capable of growth. Supports this with observed attitudinal patterns
in 29 Arizona communities.

48

THE COMMUNITY PROBLEM SOLVER
Bobowski, Rita Cipalla
American Education, Vol. 13, 16-19, 1977.

The Center for Community Organization and Area Development probed residents
of a tri-state area to understand their problems and then stimulated them to
come up with solutions.

49

COMMUNITY PROBLEMS IN RURAL-URBAN FRINGE AREAS: IMPLICATIONS FOR ACTION
PROGRAMS
Heasley, Daryl K., D. H. Tuttle, and R. C. Bealer
University Park, Pa.: The Pennsylvania State University, Agricultural
and Home Economics Extension Service, Leaflet 270, undated.

A survey of a rural-urban fringe community north of Pittsburgh reveals some
of the "growing pains" of the area. Problems for action programs are
briefly discussed, and guidelines for adjustment are presented.

50

COMMUNITY AND RESOURCE DEVELOPMENT THROUGH GROUP PROCESS
Kuennen, Daniel S.
Newark: University of Delaware, Cooperative Extension Service,
Circular 133, 1973.

Publication deals with more effective community development and rural
development through better use of the group process. Develops a "group
guide outline" to identify functions and techniques of a group in solving
a problem. Sets up a ten-point program to help groups through the basic
requirements of problem-solving.

51

COMMUNITY SERVICE SATISFACTION AND STAGES OF COMMUNITY DEVELOPMENT: AN
EXAMINATION OF EVIDENCE FROM IMPACTED COMMUNITIES
Murdock, S. H. and E. C. Shriner
Journal of the Community Development Society 10(1): 109-124, 1979.

The study attempts to establish how the levels and dimensions of community
service satisfaction differ with stages of economic development and
community population characteristics. This study examines levels of

service satisfaction for 1,400 respondents in nine western communities, by developmental types through descriptive analysis, analysis of variance, and factor analytic techniques. The analysis indicates that both new and longtime residents in currently developing communities are more dissatisfied with community services than residents in either pre- or post-development communities, that differences in levels of satisfaction are not the result of differences in the characteristics of residents, but are significantly related to the stage of community development, and that the dimensions of service satisfaction also vary with the stage of development. Further analysis of the effects of stages of development on service satisfaction are suggested.

52
A COMPARATIVE STUDY OF THE ROLE OF VALUES IN SOCIAL ACTION IN TWO SOUTHWESTERN COMMUNITIES
Vogt, Evon and Thomas O'Dea
American Sociological Review, Vol. 18, 645-654, 1953.

It is the central hypothesis of the values study project that value orientations play an important part in the shaping of social institutions and in influencing the forms of observed social action. Upon a comparison of the Mormon community of Rimrock with the Texas community of Homestead, it is felt that differences in response to situations are related to the differences between the value-orientations central to these communities.

53
COMPREHENSIVE COMMUNITY PLANNING
Carroll, William M., P. Norton, and R. G. Wingard
University Park, Pa.: Pennsylvania State University, College of Agriculture, Cooperation Extension Service, 9 pp. (undated).

Components of the process for developing a comprehenisve community plan are briefly discussed in this booklet.

54
CONSULTING IN RURAL COMMUNITY ORGANIZATION PROCEEDINGS OF THE ANNUAL CONVENTION OF THE AMERICAN PSYCHOLOGICAL ASSOCIATION
Hartung, J. G., et al.
American Psychological Association, 7(2): 803-804, 1972.

The authors discuss five principles of consulting derived from their experience as consultants to a rural health planning organization. A community project is described to illustrate how the authors have used their principles in practice.

55

COOPERATION IN CHANGE: AN ANTHROPOLOGICAL APPROACH TO COMMUNITY DEVELOPMENT
Goodenough, Ward H.
New York: Russell Sage Foundation, 1963.

Social workers are frequently involved in community development projects
which require an understanding of and sensitivity to cultural aspects.
This book provides several case studies on the treatment of cultural
aspects during the initiation of community development projects.

56

COOPERATIVE ARRANGEMENTS WITH RESOURCE CONSERVATION AND DEVELOPMENT
PROJECTS (RC&D) OF THE USDA
Bjergo, Allen and Robert L. Deaton
In Social Work in Rural Areas: Preparation and Practice. R. K. Green
and S. A. Webster, eds.
Knoxville: The University of Tennessee, School of Social Work,
233-242, 1978.

This paper argues that rural community development is an especially effective means for social workers to work with local people and local professionals from the Cooperative Extension Service.

57

COOPERATIVE DEVELOPMENT IN RURAL AREAS
Farmer Cooperatives in the United States
Washington, D.C.: U.S. Department of Agriculture, 1978, 34 pp.

Includes cooperatives organized in the past four decades, new cooperatives
formed by commercial farmers, steps and assistance in organizing a new
cooperative, raising member capital and assistance in financing a new
cooperative.

58

THE COOPERATIVE EXTENSION SERVICE: A NATIONWIDE KNOWLEDGE SYSTEM FOR
TODAY'S PROBLEMS
ERIC: ED099568.

Provides an overview of the Cooperative Extension Service, which has
roughly 3,000 local offices with staff backed up by the land-grant university based specialists. C.E.S. programs emphasize improving the productiv-
ity and the quality of life in rural areas.

59

COOPERATIVES AT THE CROSSROADS: THE POTENTIAL FOR A MAJOR NEW ECONOMIC
AND SOCIAL ROLE
Schaaf, Michael
Exploratory Project for Economic Alternatives, 2000 P St. N.W.,
Washington, D.C., 20036, 1977.

This report offers the reader a view of co-ops' unique role in economic
history and in today's world. It discusses the value that co-ops offer

their participants, and the pitfalls--both internal and external--that co-ops face in the course of their development. The report surveys the variety of co-ops in existence in the United States today, as well as the much stronger, more influential movement that already exists in Sweden; and it concludes with proposals for strengthening cooperatives' role in our economy.

60
COOPERATIVES AND RURAL POVERTY IN THE SOUTH
Marshall, Ray
Baltimore: The Johns Hopkins Press, 1971.

The main economic organizations representing poor people in the South are cooperatives. This book describes the role of cooperatives in rural development, the Poor People's Cooperative Movement, and new cooperatives in the South.

61
AT THE CROSSROADS: AN INQUIRY INTO RURAL POST OFFICES AND THE
COMMUNITIES THEY SERVE
Margolis, Richard J.
Washington, D.C.: U.S. Government Printing Office, Winter, 1980.

The Postal Rate Commission has initiated a series of research papers designed to bring to public attention issues which affect the Postal Service and the Postal community. At the Crossroads, by Richard Margolis, is the first publication of the series. Mr. Margolis reviews the history and development of postal delivery and the postal service, including an historic review of pertinent congressional legislation, as it affects rural areas. An exploratory investigation of sample rural communities is undertaken for the purpose of developing a profile on community life.

62
CURRENT RESEARCH AND PERIODICALS ON RURAL DEVELOPMENT, 1968-1971
Kuennen, Daniel S.
Georgetown: University of Delaware Substation, Cooperative Extension
Service, 1973.

Reviews literature on rural development between 1968 and 1971.

63
DELIVERY OF RURAL COMMUNITY SERVICES: SOME IMPLICATIONS AND PROBLEMS
Carruthers, G. E., E. C.Erickson, and K. M. Renner
Las Cruces: New Mexico State University, Agricultural Experiment
Station, 1975, 49 pp.

This report summarizes research conducted under the western regional research project on the delivery of rural community services. Generalizations which have been supported by research include: 1) many rural service institutions need reorganization and renewal; 2) rural development depends directly on citizen participation and representation of various population segments; and 3) rural people want innovative health care practices.

64
DIFFERENTIAL PERCEPTIONS OF IMPACT OF A RURAL ANTI-POVERTY CAMPAIGN
Sutton, Willis A., Jr.
Social Change Quarterly, 50(3): 657-667, 1969.

One of the country's major rural community action programs during OEO days was located in Knox County, Kentucky. This article describes differential perceptions--ranging from most to least favorable views--of the impact of the program on the conditions of the rural poor.

65
A DIRECTORY OF RURAL ORGANIZATIONS
Washington, D.C.: National Rural Center, undated.

This is a directory of major national organizations involved in various aspects of rural development and policies.

66
ECONOMIC DEVELOPMENT: PANACEA OR PERPLEXITY FOR RURAL AREAS
Smith, Courtland, Thomas C. Hogg, and Michael J. Reagen
Rural Sociology, 36(2): 173-186, 1971.

An economic development project near Sweet Home, Oregon did not result in the hoped-for economic growth, and left the community bearing the costs of improved services.

67
THE ECONOMIC IMPACT OF A BUSINESS AND INDUSTRIAL GUARANTEED LOAN IN A RURAL COMMUNITY
Seaton, Kendell L.
Washington, D.C.: American University, Institute for Applied Public Financial Management, July 1977, 93 pp. NTIS/SHR-0001979.

The Business and Industrial loan guarantee program is a result of the passage and implementation of the Rural Development Act of 1972. Its primary purpose is to revitalize rural areas. This study attempts to improve understanding of how development proceeds in a rural area, emphasizing the economic benefits and the problems encountered with industrialization.

68

EDUCATION MATERIALS FOR COMMUNITY RESOURCE DEVELOPMENT: AN ANNOTATED
BIBLIOGRAPHY FOR EXTENSION PROFESSIONALS
Reeves, John S., ed.
Ithaca, New York: Cornell University, Northeast Regional Center in
Rural Development.

This annotated bibliography is indexed into the following categories:
General and Miscellaneous, Growth and Development, Local Government,
Community Services, Housing, Land Use, National Resources, and Community
Development Processes and Strategies.

69

THE EFFECTS OF INDUSTRIALIZATION ON A RURAL COUNTY: COMPARISON OF
SOCIAL CHANGE IN MONROE AND NOBLE COUNTIES OF OHIO
Andrews, Wade H. and Ward W. Bauder
Wooster: Ohio Agri-Research and Development Center, Department Series
A.E. 507, 1968.

Case study of two counties analyzing the social changes and effects of
industrialization of rural areas.

70

EMERGING TECHNOLOGY AND PROCESSES IN COMMUNITY DEVELOPMENT
Gamm, Larry and Hyman Drew, eds.
1977, 251 pp.

Content includes the proceedings of a symposium on: urban-rural transitions,
community health improvement, new energy potentials, community development, preserving agricultural lands, the national community development
scene, citizen participation and water and waste management.

71

ETHICAL ISSUES IN DEVELOPMENT
Goulet, D. A.
Review of Social Economy, 26(2): 97-117, 1968.

Considers ethics of development on a world scale; many questions regarding
the models of development of the West and the Soviets are raised,
particularly in terms of the effects on the world's poor.

72

AN EVALUATION OF THE EFFECTIVENESS OF A LEADERSHIP DEVELOPMENT PROGRAM
FOR RURAL LAY LEADERS IN LAWRENCE COUNTY, ALABAMA
Dawson, J. I.
Normal, Alabama: Alabama A&M University, Cooperative State Research
Service. Research Bulletin No. 1, 1975.

The purpose of the study was to measure the effectiveness of a leadership development program for rural lay leaders on promoting community improvement in Lawrence County, Alabama. During the leadership development program, emphasis was placed on developing specific leadership skills to enhance the leader's roles in community development.

73
EVALUATION IN EXTENSION
Byrn, Darcie, et al.
ERIC: ED161885.

This is a manual to aid rural community workers to be better able to understand and apply the principles and methods of evaluation. Although the manual is directed toward extension workers, it is very practical and applicable to social work practitioners in rural community settings.

74
EVALUATION OF RURAL REGIONAL COORDINATION DEMONSTRATION PROJECTS:
EXECUTIVE SUMMARY
Cruze, Alvin M.
Washington, D.C.: Community Services Administration, March 1976, 42 pp.
NTIS/PB-255 166/1ST.

Recognizing the need to include the rural poor and minorities in the development and planning process and to develop the capability of rural institutions to be responsive to the needs of the total community, the Community Services Administration funded two demonstration projects, one in South Carolina and the other in Tennessee, that are actively involved in the rural development process. The purpose of these projects was to articulate the needs of the poor and minorities within a comprehensive multi-county approach to regional development and to, thereby, increase the incomes, satisfactions, and general living conditions of the rural poor.

75
AN EVALUATION OF THE SPECIAL IMPACT PROGRAM. VOLUME 1.
Cambridge, Mass.: Abt Associates Inc., December 1973, 30 pp.
NTIS/PB-238/411/3ST.

Volume 1 is the summary of a four volume report of an evaluation of the Special Impact Program which is designed to channel Federal assistance to comprehensive development efforts in depressed urban and rural areas. The principal vehicle of the program at the local level is the Community Development Corporation (CDC), a unique institution that blends elements of community control and participation with principles of individual entrepreneurship.

76
EXPERIMENTS IN RURAL TOWN PLANNING
Sargent, Frederic O.
Journal of the Community Development Society, 4(1): 29-36, 1973.

Article analyzes the reasons why rural town planning has failed in meeting the needs of rural town residents. Cites major reason as rural planning done by urban planners who were often lacking insight into the problems and characteristics of rural areas. Author then explores alternative methods of rural planning and describes seven projects in rural planning occurring in New England.

77

THE EXTENSION SERVICE AS A RESOURCE IN PLANNING AT THE LOCAL LEVEL
Wynn, Eddie and Nelson Jacob
In Human Services in the Rural Environment Reader. David Bast, ed.
Madison: University of Wisconsin - Extension, Center for Social Service, 84-92, June 1976-May 1977.

The purpose of this paper is to briefly review Clemson University's goals and objectives in relation to the Title V program in South Carolina and to describe how the research and Extension components have been effectively integrated in responding to a request for assistance in verifying the feasibility of and planning for the establishment of a human services complex in a rural South Carolina county.

78

EXTENSION'S EXPANDING ROLE IN SOCIAL DEVELOPMENT
Bast, David and Edward Buxton
In Human Services in the Rural Environment Reader. David Bast, ed.
Madison: University of Wisconsin - Extension, Center for Social Service, 99-105, June 1976-May 1977.

This paper focuses upon an innovative attempt of the University of Wisconsin--Extension (UWEX) to more effectively expand its problem-solving capacities in the areas of social development through the creation of a new type of agent position.

79

FACTORS INHIBITING APPALACHIAN REGIONAL DEVELOPMENT
Hale, Carl W.
The American Journal of Economics and Sociology, 30(2): 133-158, 1971.

The author concludes that the major problem in Appalachia regional development is one of attitudes, not resources. These attitudes have prevented the development of a "growth" psychology in the area.

80

FARMER COOPERATIVES
Jorgerson, Randall
In The American Academy of Political and Social Science, F. Clemente, ed.
Vol. 429, 91-102, January 1977.

Farmers cooperatives are voluntary rural business organizations controlled by their member patrons and operated by and for them on a nonprofit or cost basis. Growth in their use, as a dimension of market structure, has been

limited by the prevailaing school of thought on cooperation in the U.S.
The ultimate measure of cooperative success is performance in enhancing
the economic well-being of members and rural communities.

81
FEDERAL ASSISTANCE AND NONDISCRIMINATION: IDENTIFYING ELIGIBLE PARTICIPANTS
IN USDA PROGRAMS
Hammill, Anne and Percy R. Luney
Rural Sociology, 37(1): 98-102, 1972.

All USDA administered farm programs are subject to Title VI of the Civil
Rights Act of 1964. In response to the many problems in identifying
eligible populations, the authors present guidelines for reducing identification problems.

82
A FIELD-THEORY PERSPECTIVE FOR COMMUNITY DEVELOPMENT RESEARCH
Wilkinson, Kenneth P.
Rural Sociology, 37(1): 43-52, 1972.

This article provides a conceptualization of community development within
the general framework of social field theory and indicates critical areas
of needed research as viewed from that perspective.

83
FOREST SERVICE INFORM AND INVOLVE HANDBOOK (draft)
Lake, Robert M.
Washington, D.C.: U.S. Department of Agriculture, Forest Service, 1977.

Designed to supplement Forest Service Manual 1626, Inform and Involve
Program, this draft handbook is a basic "how to" resource for forest
service personnel. It provides detailed information on the public involvement requirements which impinge upon U.S. Forest Service operations and
detailed presentations of a wide range of appropriate techniques. It also
relates specific techniques to specific objectives and situations in the
decision-making and planning process of the Forest Service, both in prose
and in matrix or chart form. Each of the fifty-seven techniques presented
is discussed in terms of its specific objectives, its procedures, its
costs, its advantages, and its disadvantages. Although the document is
designed specifically for the Forest Service, planners of all kinds find
the thoroughness of detail useful.

84
GRASSROOTS ADMINISTRATION
Clifton, Robert L. and Alan M. Dahms
Monterey, California: Brooks/Cole Publishing Co., 1980.

This book is designed to provide information on a broad range of functions
that are important to the effective administration of small community-
based social service programs. General topics include: planning, funding,
and evaluating programs; communications, volunteer support systems; the
internal and external politics of agency survival; staff and leadership
development.

85
A GUIDE FOR COMMUNITY DEVELOPMENT
Ferrise, Anthony
Morgantown: West Virginia University, Cooperative Extension Service,
Center for Extension and Continuing Education, Publication No. 701, May 1972.

The purpose of this publication is to provide information to extension
workers and others with ideas on community development.

86
HOW PEOPLE GET POWER: ORGANIZING OPPRESSED COMMUNITIES FOR ACTION
Kahn, Si
New York: McGraw-Hill Book Company, 1970.

This book is a practical text written for community organizers working in
rural areas.

87
HUSTLERS ON THE RANGE
Henderson, James
Washington Monthly, Vol. 6, 23-24, 1974.

The Northeast Oklahoma Community Development Corporation was set up by OEO
in 1969 to combat rural poverty.

88
IDENTIFYING THE STRUCTURE OF COMMUNITY POWER - SOME SUGGESTIONS FOR
RURAL SOCIAL WORKERS
Colliver, Mac
In 2nd National Institute On Social Work In Rural Areas Reader. Edward B.
Buxton, ed.
Madison: University of Wisconsin--Extension, Center for Social Service,
35-53, 1978.

This paper examines three aspects of community power: 1) the need for
community power structure information on the part of rural social workers
based upon the emerging rural social work literature; 2) the different forms
or structure of community power; and 3) information on the different
approaches the rural social worker could use to identify those key community influentials who could provide vital support for the community's
social delivery system.

89
IDEOLOGY AND DEVELOPMENT: THE RURAL SMALL COMMUNITY
Youngberg, Garth
Cape Girardeau: Southeast Missouri State University, undated.

It is the contention of this paper that ideology remains central to the
developmental process, and that it is essential that present day policy makers
understand and appreciate the idealogical landscape of the rural small
community.

90

THE IMPACT OF ALTERED ECONOMIC CONDITIONS ON RURAL COMMUNITY DEVELOPMENT
Deaton, Brady J.
In Social Work in Rural Areas: Preparation and Practice. R. K. Green and
S. A. Webster, eds.
Knoxville: The University of Tennessee, School of Social Work, 24-35, 1978.

An examination of conditions generated by agricultural transformation and
recent rural industrialization are considered in this paper. Implications
for policy and community developers are discussed briefly.

91

THE IMPACT OF SMALL INDUSTRY ON AN INDIAN COMMUNITY
Ritzenthaler, Robert E.
American Anthropologist, 55(1): 143-148, 1953.

This article is about the effects of the Simpson Electric Company's decision to locate at Lac Du Flambeau, Wisconsin, an Indian community. This
article discusses the initial problems and the effects of the industry on
the community and the individual in terms of the material and change in
habit patterns.

92

IMPLICATIONS OF ENERGY STRATEGIES ON RURAL DEVELOPMENT
Gibbons, John H.
In Social Work in Rural Areas: Preparation and Practice. R. K. Green and
S. A. Webster, eds.
Knoxville: The University of Tennessee, School of Social Work, 45-53, 1978.

This paper reviews the energy situation and discusses related strategies
and implications for rural development practice.

93

THE IMPORTANCE OF COMMUNITY PLANNING, ORGANIZATION AND RESEARCH IN RURAL
BOOM TOWNS
Jirovec, Ronald L.
In Social Work in Rural Areas: Issues and Opportunities. Joseph Davenport,
III, Judith A. Davenport and James R. Wiebler, eds.
Laramie: The University of Wyoming, Department of Social Work, 1980.

Boom towns face the problem of uncontrolled rapid growth. This paper proposes that controlled rapid growth is possible through non-metropolitan
community planning, rural community organization, and research.

94

INCOME DISTRIBUTION CONSEQUENCES OF RURAL INDUSTRIALIZATION
West, Jerry and Roselee Maier
American Journal of Agricultural Economics 57(5): 974, 1975.

Income distribution consequences of various types of industrialization are
examined. Extent of poverty, unemployment, and two measures of income
inequality are used to assess the consequences of growth in employment in
manufacturing, mining, and recreation.

95

INDIAN INDUSTRIAL DEVELOPMENT MANUAL: FOR AND BY NATIVE AMERICANS
Preston, Richard, ed.
Wenham, Massachusetts: American Industrial Development Council,
Educational Foundation, 1975.

Book dealing with industrial development issues: includes sites, financing, prospects, and industrial development organization as related to
Native American problems and situations.

96

INDIGENOUS ART DEVELOPMENT AS A TACTIC IN LOCALITY DEVELOPMENT
Schneider, Gregory S. and Victor L. Schneider
In Effective Models for the Delivery of Services in Rural Areas:
Implications for Practice and Social Work Education. Proceedings of the
Third Annual National Institute on Social Work in Rural Areas.
Barry L. Locke and Roger A. Lohmann, eds.
Morgantown: West Virginia University, August 7-10, 1978. 247 pp.

This paper addresses two intimately related issues. First, it examines
some of the societal bases for local citizen apathy and low identification
with the community. Second, it proposes a new tactic in locality development for dealing with that problem.

97

INDIGENOUS PARAPROFESSIONALS IN COMMUNITY DEVELOPMENT: AN ANNOTATED
BIBLIOGRAPHY
Korsching, Peter F. and Mary Lehman
Lexington: University of Kentucky, Council of Planning Librarians
Exchange Bibliography No. 999, 1976.

The citations included in this bibliography were chosen in connection with
a community development program in the Appalachian section of Kentucky.
Therefore, only sources relevant to the use of paraprofessionals in community development are included.

98

INDUSTRIAL DEVELOPMENT IN RURAL COLORADO
Davis, M. Leroy, Donald Sorenson and Forrest Walters
Journal of the Community Development Society, 6(2): 57-63, 1975.

Article discusses the attitudes of business management in Colorado towards
locating firms in rural areas of Colorado and the concerns of communities
regarding economic development. Results suggest that small rural towns
will have difficulty in attracting industry because manufacturers need
quality labor and adequate transportation, which many small towns cannot
provide. Also highlighted is the role of business inertia; cites tendency
to adapt to present location and to avoid risks inherent in relocation.

99

INDUSTRIALIZATION: THE KEY FACTOR IN CHANGING RURAL COMMUNITIES
Deaton, Brady J.
ERIC: ED152457.

Examines the impact of industrialization on rural communities in terms of
changes in four traditional qualities of agrarian life: control and
self-sufficiency, homogeneity of interests, naturalness, and creativity.
Concludes that future public policy toward industrial development in
rural America must encourage human resource development as well as natural
resource conservation.

100

INDUSTRIALIZATION OF THE MEXICAN BORDER REGION
Taylor, James R.
New Mexico Business 26(3): 3-9, 1973.

In this article, the nature and growth record of Mexico's Border Industrialization Program are described, as well as the future developmental
implications of the program.

101

INDUSTRIALIZATION OF RURAL AREAS
Mississippi State: Southern Rural Development Center, Rural Development
Series No. 1, June 1978, 36 pp. ($1.00).

The purpose of this monograph is to review available research literature
on rural industrialization in order to help improve the cost-effectiveness
of public policies and programs at local, state, and national levels as
well as private action by voluntary community organizations in their quest
for manufacturing employment opportunities.

102

LARGE INDUSTRIES IN SMALL TOWNS: WHO BENEFITS?
Clemente, Frank and Gene F. Summers
Madison: University of Wisconsin, Center for Applied Sociology,
Department of Rural Sociology, Working Paper Series RID 73.9. Feb. 1973.

Concludes that industrialization puts elderly at a relative disadvantage;
elderly and female heads of household usually received little benefit from
underutilization.

103

LEADERSHIP FOR ACTION IN RURAL COMMUNITIES
Kreitlow, B. W., E.W. Aiton and A. P. Torrence
Danville, Illinois: Interstate Publishers, Inc., 1965.

Discusses the various roles and functions which can be performed by community
leaders. The first two sections deal with leadership as it affects community
development and principles and practices of leadership.

104

LIMITED ACCESS: A REPORT OF THE COMMUNITY DEVELOPMENT BLOCK GRANT PROGRAM
IN NONMETROPOLITAN AREAS
Washington, D.C.: Rural America, Inc., December 1977, 412 pp.
NTIS/PB-275 817/5ST.

The report presents a summary of a one-year monitoring study of the
operation of the community development block grant program in nonmetropolitan areas. Findings show that the smallest and poorest communities
have the most trouble in finding out about applying for funds of this
program.

105

A LONGITUDINAL ANALYSIS OF SATISFACTION WITH SELECTED COMMUNITY SERVICES
IN A NONMETROPOLITAN AREA
Molnar, Joseph
Rural Sociology, 44(2): 401-419, 1979.

This study examines changes in rating of satisfaction with selected
community services in three nonmetropolitan Alabama counties.

106

MAKING FEDERALISM WORK
Sundquist, James L. and David W. Davis
Washington, D.C.: Brookings Institution, February 1969, 353 pp.
NTIS/COM-74-11444/8.

The study examines the problems of coordination experienced by regional,
state and local agencies in their efforts to cooperate in the implementation of several federal programs legislated during the 1960's for the
purpose of assisting community economic planning and development. The
review includes an examination of programs in rural areas.

107

MANAGING THE SOCIOECONOMIC IMPACTS OF ENERGY DEVELOPMENT: A GUIDE FOR
THE SMALL COMMUNITY
Armbrust, Roberta
Washington, D.C.: Energy Research and Development Administration,
September 1977, 84 pp.

Decisions concerning large-scale energy development projects near small
communities or in predominantly rural areas are usually complex. This
handbook advises local officials on how they should organize to most
effectively participate with developers, government officials, and consultants in assessing, planning, and managing energy development and how
to insure that information is collected and analyzed to reflect local
priorities and future planning needs.

108

MANIFEST AND LATENT PARTICIPANTS IN A RURAL COMMUNITY ACTION PROGRAM
Young, James N. and Selz C. Mayo
Social Forces, 38(2): 140-145, 1959.

This study determines the relationships between varying levels of participation in a community development program and the following three sets
of variables: (1) social and economic characteristics of the community
residents, (2) their knowledge and understanding of the structure and
function of the organization, and (3) their attitudes toward the community
program.

109

MICROPOLITAN DEVELOPMENT: THEORY AND PRACTICE OF GREATER-RURAL ECONOMIC
DEVELOPMENT
Tweeten, Luther and George L. Brinkman
Ames: The Iowa State University Press, 1977.

The problems and promise of micropolitan (non-metropolitan) areas are
examined comprehensively. The text contains an up-to-date appraisal of
such subjects as human resource development, community services, job
creation, planning, financing, and promoting community involvement.

110

MIGRANT RESPONSE TO INDUSTRIALIZATION IN FOUR RURAL AREAS, 1965-1970
Olsen, Duane A. and John A. Kuehn
Washington, D.C.: U.S. Department of Agriculture, Economic Research
Service, Agricultural Economic Report 270, 1974.

Study of four multi-county areas in Arizona, Mississippi, Central Ozarks,
and Arkansas. Found that 78 percent of jobs created by industrial growth
were filled by the local residents; 22 percent were filled by in-migrants,
despite a high employment rate. Concludes that rural industrialization
programs are likely to experience some leakage of jobs to in-migrants.
However, because in-migrants are younger and better educated, this may
have salutory indirect effects on declining rural areas. Also, new jobs
have slowed the exodus of the young.

111

MOBILIZING RURAL COMMUNITY RESOURCES
Peacock, Stanley
In 2nd National Institute on Social Work In Rural Areas Reader. Edward B.
Buxton, ed.
Madison: University of Wisconsin--Extension Center for Social Service, 1978.

The purpose of this paper is to provide the rural social work practitioner
with some ideas and examples of how to coordinate and utilize rural
community resources to facilitate community follow-up and treatment of
medical and psychiatric clients who have returned to the rural community
after hospitalization.

112
MUSIC AND THE HUMAN CONDITION: UTILIZING LOCALITY ORIENTED MUSIC IN
COMMUNITY ANALYSES
Jankovic, Joanne and Richard Edwards
In Social Work in Rural Areas: Issues and Opportunities. Joseph Davenport,
III, Judith A. Davenport and James R. Wiebler.
Laramie: The University of Wyoming, Department of Social Work, 1980.

The purpose of this paper is to suggest that one way to get beyond stereotypes and to identify issues related to the real needs of rural residents,
particularly those of Appalachia and rural South, is through an exploration
on noncommercial, locality-oriented music.

113
NEW STRATEGIES FOR APPALACHIA
Kahn, Si
New South 25, 59-64, Summer 1970.

The author argues that assisting mountain people in gaining political
power can only be effective by not trying to channel resource energy
through existing organizations in Appalachia. New organizations are
needed, for existing organizations (having been ineffective in the past)
have discredited themselves in the eyes of most mountain people.

114
NONGOVERNMENTAL SOCIAL PLANNING IN RURAL AREAS OF THE UNITED STATES
Leadley, Samuel M. and Joan S. Thomson
Paper presented at the Third World Congress for Rural Sociology.
Baton Rouge, Louisiana: August 23, 1972, 12 pp. ERIC: ED070956.

The purpose of this experimental project conducted in Pennsylvania was
to compare public and private sector approaches to social planning in
rural areas. Preliminary conclusions were: (1) the introduction of nongovernmental social planners into rural areas can be accomplished in
approximately six months less time than introducing the same social role
through a public agency; (2) the selection of personnel for private planning role is more critical to program effectiveness than in a more highly
structured public project; and (3) the review of proposed community development projects by nongovernmental social planners, while inhibited by
their lack of formal structural ties with the public planning commission,
is possible through the establishment of informal relationships within
the rural community settings.

115
NONMETROPOLITAN SOCIAL PLANNING
Wylie, Mary L.
In Social Work in Rural Communities. Leon H. Ginsberg, ed.
New York: Council on Social Work Education, 48-61, 1976.

Most social planning is urban-oriented. The author of this article
describes some of the problems of rural social planning, and how
social planning technology can be applied to nonmetropolitan communities.

116
ORGANIZATIONS SERVING COOPERATIVES
Washington, D.C.: U.S. Department of Agriculture, 1978, 26 pp.

Includes national cooperatives, trade and farm services, federal
agencies and state cooperative councils and associations.

117
PARAPROFESSIONALS IN AN APPALACHIAN COMMUNITY DEVELOPMENT PROGRAM
Korsching, Peter F. and Paul D. Warner
Community Development Journal, 10(3): 183-188, 1975.

This paper explores issues which arise in the use of paraprofessionals
in the roles of developer and researcher in community development programs. These issues include possible conflict in research and extension
tasks, adequate and effective supervision, the paraprofessional's status
in the community and employee turnover.

118
PARAPROFESSIONALS AND PROFESSORS: ACTION RESEARCH AND COMMUNITY DEVELOPMENT
IN THE APPALACHIAN HIGHLANDS
Korsching, Peter F., Paul D. Warner, and C. Milton Coughenour
Lexington: University of Kentucky, Department of Sociology, 1975.

This paper outlines the conceptual frame of reference of a program established under Title V of the Rural Development Act of 1972 to use paraprofessionals in community development. It describes characteristics of
the people and the area, the strategy for community development and a preliminary evaluation of the project.

119
PERCEIVED ADEQUACY OF COMMUNITY SERVICES: A METRO-NONMETRO COMPARISON
Burdge, Rabel and Paul D. Warner
Rural Sociology, 44 (2): 392-400, 1979.

This article addressed the question: If adequacy of community services
varies by place of residence, do persons perceive these differences?
Furthermore, do personal characteristics explain variations?

120
PLANNED CHANGE AND SYSTEMIC LINKAGE IN A FIVE-YEAR EXTENSION PROGRAM WITH
WITH PART-TIME FARM FAMILIES
Hardee, J. Gilbert
Rural Sociology, 30(1): 23-32, 1965.

In this study an attempt is made to test empirically a body of theory
related to linkage of social systems in explaining sociocultural agencies.
Data for the paper are based on a longitudinal study of an extension
educational program with a sample of part-time farm families in one North
Carolina county, 1955-1960.

121
PLANNERS AND CITIZEN BOARDS: SOME APPLICATIONS OF SOCIAL THEORY TO THE
PROBLEM OF PLAN IMPLEMENTATION
Clavel, Pierre
Journal of the American Institute of Planners 34(2): 130-139, 1968.

Discusses the problem of relationships between citizen boards and expert
planners. Suggests that in rural areas citizen boards lack the economic
resources, administrative resources, time, and experience to use the
expert's advice. The result is the continuation of traditional rural
institutions by the citizen boards; these institutions often prohibit
and/or inhibit needed change.

122
PLANNING AND MANAGING COMMUNITY PROGRAMS: A PROCESS APPROACH
Matejic, Denise, M. W. Huang, and N. Gaston
New Brunswick, N.J.: Rutgers University, Cooperative Extension Service.

A useful manual as an educational tool in needs assessment and objective
setting, project planning and development, project implementation, and
evaluation.

123
PLANNING IN RURAL AREAS
Hahn, Alan J.
American Institute of Planners Journal, 36: 44-49, 1970.

Rural planning can be very difficult and often unsuccessful because plans
do not consider the social organization, attitudes, and perceptions of
rural residents.

124
PLANNING IN RURAL ENVIRONMENTS
Lassey, William R.
New York: McGraw-Hill Book Company, 1977, 257 pp.

Providing comprehensive treatment of major topics and issues in rural
planning, this book offers a body of basic concepts, research based
information, planning procedures, and management tools which can help
to strengthen the capability and effectiveness of planning units with
responsibility for rural regions.

125
THE POVERTY OF PUBLIC SERVICES IN THE LAND OF PLENTY: AN ANALYSIS AND
INTERPRETATION
Lupsha, Peter and Siembieda Lupsha
In the Rise of the Sunbelt Cities.
Beverly Hills: Sage Publications, 1977.

In this paper the disparities in the provision and delivery of public
services between the southern and northern regions of the United States

are discussed. It is the thesis that the present gap in the aggregate and particular levels of public services between these regions cannot be eliminated simply by bringing the Sunbelt up to economic and demographic part with the North.

126
THE PRACTICE OF COMMUNITY AND RURAL DEVELOPMENT
Athens: University of Georgia, Cooperative Extension Service, Special Bulletin No. 5, 1977, 35 pp.

Guide for CD professionals intended to be used with local volunteer groups in explaining what CD is not and how CD works at the community level. Focuses on principles, assumptions, approaches and values which guide the methods and procedures used in the field.

127
THE PROCESS AND THE PRODUCT: COMMUNITY DEVELOPMENT IN MISSOURI
Columbia: University of Missouri, Extension Division, June 1975.

This brochure briefly describes the goals and processes of Extension Community Development work in Missouri.

128
A PROGRAM OF TECHNICAL ASSISTANCE TO INDUSTRY IN TWENTY-SIX MISSISSIPPI COUNTIES AND THE CHOCTAW INDIAN RESERVATION
Jackson: Mississippi Research and Development Center, Management and Technical Services Division, Final Report, October 1969, 155 pp.

This report describes the activities of the Mississippi Research and Development Center directed toward comprehensive economic development. Comprehensive development is defined as the process of identifying, evaluating, and effectively mobilizing all of the natural, physical, economic and human resources of community or area, thereby creating an environment conducive to the orderly expansion of investment and employment opportunities to the end that balanced community growth and individual welfare is enhanced.

129
PUBLIC FINANCING OF HEALTH SERVICES: MEDICARE AND MEDICAID
Washington, D.C.: Rural America, Inc., December 1977, 28 pp.

Explains how the Medicare and Medicaid programs function and suggests ways of making these programs more effective in rural areas.

130
PUBLIC INVOLVEMENT AND THE FOREST SERVICE: EXPERIENCE, EFFECTIVENESS AND SUGGESTED DIRECTIONS
Hendee, John C., et al.
Washington, D.C.: U.S. Department of Agriculture, Forest Service, 1973.

This study is based upon recent Forest Service experience in public involvement and offers recommendations to improve the effectiveness of public involvement programs. While the study advocates public involvement, it does not necessarily represent Forest Service policy. The study was performed by an eight-man team of social scientists and forest managers. Current procedures were investigated by collecting information from three forests and nine administrative regions. The study covers techniques, methods of analysis, and evaluation.

131
REGIONAL DEVELOPMENT AND THE RURAL POOR
Hansen, Niles M.
Journal of Human Resources, 4(2): 204-214, 1969.

The paper is a critique of the regional policy of the President's National Advisory Commission on Rural Poverty. The author quotes the Commission, in substance, as recommending that the rural poor have delivered to them the socio-economic amenities of urban living. He then raises the question of whether the Commission is realistic in its recommendations.

132
RENEWAL PLANS: A GENERAL SYSTEMS ANALYSIS OF RURAL TOWNSHIPS
Harp, John and Richard Gagen
Rural Sociology, 33(4): 460-473, 1968.

A general systems approach using concepts such as information accessibility and availability is shown to have utility in predicting participation by New York rural townships. Controlling for the presence of an urban center within the township, the major factors representing accessibility of renewal information and predicting a renewal plan for rural townships are population size, income, distance from metropolitan areas, and age of housing.

133
RENEWED GROWTH IN RURAL COMMUNITIES
Beale, Calvin L.
The Futurist, 196-202, August 1975.

Factors contributing to the migration of people from urban to rural areas are examined.

134
RESEARCH AND COMMUNITY DEVELOPMENT: A PRACTITIONER'S VIEWPOINT
Yoak, Margaret O'Neill
Journal of the Community Development Society, 10(1): 39-47, 1979.

Practitioners in community development depend on research results as a theoretical foundation and for support in practice. In order to meet research needs, there must be a clarification of the concept of research both by practitioners and social scientists. Broad types of research include case studies, methodological guides, and theoretically based research of practical value. Topical areas of research may be classified as: community structures, dynamics and reactions; human behavior research;

methodology, process, teaching and training; and evaluation of community development effectiveness. Obstacles to meeting research needs may be overcome through increased communication and understanding between researchers and practitioners; clarification and sharing of roles and through the creation of new roles to help bridge the gap between research and practice.

135
RESEARCH AND DEVELOPMENT PROJECTS
Washington, D.C.: U.S. Department of Labor, Employment and Training Administration, 1978.

This annual edition summarizes the projects funded by the Office of Research and Development of the Employment and Training Administration between July 1, 1975 and September 30, 1978.

136
A RESEARCH REPORT ON DEVELOPING A COMMUNITY LEVEL NATURAL RESOURCE INVENTORY SYSTEM
Burlington, Vermont: Center for Studies in Food Self-Sufficiency, August 1977, 54 pp.

The document reports on the development of a computer mapping system and on its application to land and resource planning at a local level. The paper reviews existing systems, describes the program developed, and explains how the program was used in two Vermont towns.

137
RESOURCE GUIDE FOR RURAL DEVELOPMENT
Washington, D.C.: National Rural Center, undated.

The guide provides information about public and private funding sources for rural development.

138
RESOURCES IN EVALUATION FOR RURAL DEVELOPMENT
Mississippi State: Southern Rural Development Center, Rural Development Bibliography Series No. 2, April 1977, 90 pp. ($3.00).

This partially annotated bibliography is an excellent resource guide to materials on evaluative research and rural development.

139
RESOURCES FOR RURAL DEVELOPMENT: HOW TO WRITE PROPOSALS FOR STATE, FEDERAL AND PRIVATE FUNDS
Marshall, Terry
Ithaca: Cornell University, Northeast Regional Center for Rural Development, Handbook No. 2, May 1977.

A handbook for writing proposals for rural development funds.

140
RESOURCES FOR RURAL DEVELOPMENT SERIES: HANDBOOK #1 - HOW TO GATHER
INFORMATION ABOUT COMMUNITY NEEDS AND FUNDING SOURCES: #2 - HOW TO WRITE
PROPOSALS FOR STATE, FEDERAL AND PRIVATE FUNDS: #3 - HOW TO FINANCE AND
ADMINISTER RURAL DEVELOPMENT PROGRAMS
Ithaca, New York: Northeast Regional Center for Rural Development,
Department of Rural Sociology, 1976-1977.

This handbook is one of a series to aid community leaders, Cooperative
Extension agents, local government officials, change agents and others in
their efforts to gain external resource needs to support local efforts in
rural development.

141
THE ROLE OF THE UNIVERSITY IN COMMUNITY DEVELOPMENT
Pulver, Glen, Daniel Schler and Lee Cary
Three papers presented at the Mid-Continent Conference,
Columbia: University of Missouri, January 12-14, 1969.

This monograph contains three papers presented at the conference. The
titles are: The Role of the University in Community Development: An
Urban Experience; The Role of the University in Community Development:
An Examination of Three Concepts; and The Role of the University in
Community Development: A Commitment to Participation with the Community.

142
RURAL COMMUNITY ACTION: STATUS AND RECOMMENDATIONS
Zimmerman, Stanley
Washington, D.C.: National Demonstration Water Project, 137 pp.
NTIS/PB-275 811/8ST.

The report is an evaluation of the Community Action Program in rural
America. The report describes the conditions and problems of the poor
in rural areas, and gives recommendations for future directions.

143
RURAL COMMUNITY ACTION THROUGH ECONOMIC DEVELOPMENT
Office of Economic Opportunity
Washington, D.C.: U.S. Government Printing Office, Executive Office of
the President, 1969.

Purpose of report is to suggest some of the ways community action agencies
can aid the 16 million poor people in rural America. Methods include:
self-help via self-employment; attraction of business and industry; and
increased local manpower availability through training and/or education.
Report serves to establish guidelines and patterns for community action
agencies.

144
RURAL COMMUNITY DEVELOPMENT: A NATIONAL NECESSITY
Pearson, James B.
Kansas Business Review, 23(11): 3-6, 1970.

The author discusses the growing interest in rural community development
as one of the more significant events in the past decade.

145
RURAL COMMUNITY ORGANIZATION
Sanderson, Dwight and Robert A. Polson
New York: John Wiley and Sons, Inc., 1939.

Many of the basic principles, concepts, and practice methods of rural
community organization were first brought together in this book. Much
of it is based on twenty years or more of experience prior to and during
the Great Depression.

146
RURAL DEVELOPMENT: AN EMERGING SOCIAL, ECONOMIC AND DEMOGRAPHIC IMPERATIVE
Leagons, Paul J.
Social Sciences: Education, No. 2, 1-18, June 1974.

The author examines how the rural development process has become separated
from the agricultural development process. Considered are the implications
for land-grant universities, government agencies, and business enterprises
for broader roles in public service.

147
RURAL DEVELOPMENT FROM A DECISION-MAKING PERSPECTIVE
Brown, David W.
International Development Review, 17(2): 12-16, 1975.

Rural development has the dual purpose of stimulating economic growth and
helping certain disadvantaged groups. The decision-maker is confronted
with a difficult task, since these two aims are sometimes at odds with
each other.

148
RURAL DEVELOPMENT IN A LAND USE PERSPECTIVE
Soil Conservation Society of America, Iowa, 29(1): 1974, 40 pp.

Series of articles assembled to create an awareness among natural resource
managers of problems related to rural development. Includes the following
topics: conservation, equity and efficiency, public institutions, natural
resource dimensions, human resources and leadership, population and settlement perspectives, planning and implementation and providing public services.

149
RURAL DEVELOPMENT LITERATURE 1976-1977: AN UPDATED ANNOTATED BIBLIOGRAPHY
Buzzard, Shirley
Columbia: University of Missouri, Cooperative Extension Service,
1976, 81 pp.

Designed for Extension CRD staff, researchers and state rural development
committees. Provides references on seven key rural development area
community services, manpower training and vocational educational, recreational facilities, local government structure and housing.

150
RURAL DEVELOPMENT PARTICIPATION: CONCEPTS AND MEASURES FOR PROJECT DESIGN
IMPLEMENTATION AND EVALUATION
Cohen, John M. and Norman T. Uphoff
Ithaca, New York: Rural Development Committee, Center for International
Studies ($5.00).

This monograph is a very useful handbook for workers attempting to facilitate greater popular participation in community development activities.

151
THE RURAL HOUSING AND COMMUNITY DEVELOPMENT DELIVERY SYSTEM
Washington, D.C.: Rural America, Inc., December 1977, 11 pp. (55¢).

Reviews the present rural housing delivery systems, recent efforts to
improve systems in cooperation with state governments, and suggests
future improvements.

152
THE RURAL IMPACT OF ENERGY DEVELOPMENT: IMPLICATIONS FOR SOCIAL WORK
PRACTICE
Bates, V. Edward
In Social Work in Rural Areas: Preparation and Practice. R. G. Green and
S. A. Webster, eds.
Knoxville: The University of Tennessee, School of Social Work, 54-72, 1978.

The author argues that there is a crisis of unprecedented magnitude for
the people in rural areas coping with strip-mining operation, new coal
conversion plants, or similarly related construction activities. The
author presents a structural model to compartmentalize the kinds of
problems, specific tasks, and interventive roles the rural social work
practitioner should consider in the chaos of boom-town changes.

153
RURAL INDUSTRIALIZATION AND COMMUNITY ACTION: NEW PLANT LOCATIONS
AMONG MISSOURI'S SMALL TOWNS
Kuehn, John A., C. Braschler, and J. S. Slonkwiler
Journal of the Community Development Society, 10(1): 95-107, 1979.

Small communities in Missouri can influence their attractiveness for new
manufacturing plants, according to this study of new plant locations

during 1972 through 1974 among Missouri towns of less than 5,000 population. Major location factors subject to community control include sewer capacity, zoning, general aviation airports, vocational-technical schools, fire protection, and an active industrial development organization.

154
RURAL INDUSTRIALIZATION: PROBLEMS AND POTENTIALS
North Central Regional Center for Rural Development
Ames: The Iowa State University Press, 1976.

This book reviews and explores the need for and methods of attracting industry to rural areas as well as the social and economic benefits and liabilities that exist after industrialization occurs.

155
RURAL INDUSTRIALIZATION: PROSPECTS, PROBLEMS, IMPACTS, AND METHODS
Baker, John A.
Washington, D.C.: U.S. Senate Committee on Agriculture and Forestry,
April 19, 1974, 151 pp. ERIC: ED108841.

The nine papers in this compilation on rural industrial development cover several areas. Some of the more relevant ones include the demographic, economic, and social impacts of a large industry in a rural area, and community planning and decision-making to attract industry.

156
RURAL JOBS FROM RURAL PUBLIC WORKS
Godwin, Lamond, et al.
Washington, D.C.: The National Rural Center, 1977.

This is the first-phase report of an experimental demonstration project in rural counties in the South where the Corps of Engineers is constructing a waterway. The project "is an attempt to develop a model which will ensure that indigenous rural people, and particularly minorities, have equitable access to jobs created by federal construction projects."

157
RURAL ORIENTED RESEARCH AND DEVELOPMENT PROJECTS: A REVIEW AND SYNTHESIS
Washington, D.C.: U.S. Department of Labor, Employment and Training,
R&D Monograph 50, 1977.

This document is intended primarily for use by researchers, planners and operators of employment and training programs in rural areas. It provides suggestions and techniques for carrying out planning and program operation responsibilities; identifies potential research opportunities; and surveys a number of reports on previous projects.

158
RURAL PLANNING SPECIALIST: A UNIQUE APPROACH TO THE PROBLEMS OF POVERTY
IN RURAL AMERICA
Harrisburg: Pennsylvania Department of Consumer Affairs, 1973, 127 pp.
NTIS/SHR-0001182.

Guidelines are presented for the implementation of rural planning
specialist (RPS) projects to assist rural communities in developing their
human and organizational resources. Six generalized steps in the RPS
process--introduction and inventory, initial project, working with the
community, defining a problem situation, working toward change, and
leaving the community--are defined, based on the experiences and comments
of Pennsylvania RPS.

159
RURAL PRACTICE MODELS: COMMUNITY DEVELOPMENT
Omer, Salema
In Social Work in Rural Areas: Preparation and Practice. R. G. Green and
S. A. Webster, eds.
Knoxville: The University of Tennessee, School of Social Work, 107-137,
1978.

This paper discussed community development as a rural practice model for
the development of human resources. The author traces the history of
community development and relates theoretical concepts to the rural
practice model.

160
RURAL PUBLIC TRANSPORTATION
Burkhardt, Jon, et al.
Washington, D.C.: Transportation Research Board, 1978, 96 pp.

This book includes an overview of problems and prospects in rural passenger
transportation, state role in rural public transportation, and rural
development policy.

161
RURAL RESOURCE DEVELOPMENT
Campbell, Paul
Human Services in the Rural Environment, 1(2): 7, 1979.

The author discusses the challenge of developing rural resources. He
examines influence as a resolace, rural program advantages and disadvantages, attributes of a successful rural program, and planning and
resource development.

162
RURAL SOCIAL PROBLEMS, HUMAN SERVICES, AND SOCIAL POLICIES
Derr, Jim
Working Paper 2: Economic Development Center for Social Research and
Development, Denver Research Institute, 1973.
Denver: University of Denver ($1.00).

In this paper, programs, proposals and related efforts in rural economic development are discussed. The results of policies and programs have not had particular significance, except that all do some good by virtue of providing some needed attention and funds to rural areas.

163
RURAL SOCIAL PROBLEMS, HUMAN SERVICES, AND SOCIAL POLICIES
Derr, Jim
Working Paper 5, Transportation and Communication. Economic Development Center for Social Research and Development, Denver Research Institute, 1973.
Denver: University of Denver.

Transportation and communication networks are vital in any large-scale strategy to solve rural economic problems because the physical distances and population densities in rural areas have dramatic impact on the patterns of daily rural life, especially the life of the rural poor.

164
ST. FRANCOIS SANITARY LANDFILL, PUBLIC PROBLEM SOLVING THROUGH UNIVERSITY-WIDE EXTENSION: A CASE STUDY
Boesch, Donald M. and John B. Heagler
Journal of Community Development Society, 4(1): 40-47, 1973.

This case study presents the details as to how a community development specialist and an Extension Civil Engineer assisted local people in bridging the gap between awareness of a public problem and solving of the problem.

165
SEX STRATIFICATION IN COMMUNITY POLITICS AND DECISION MAKING
Stuart, Nina G.
Illinois Agricultural Economics Staff Paper, 1977, 15 pp.

Paper argues that institutional barriers exist which effectively exclude women from entry into community politics and decision making and that the exclusion may result from women's socialization into their "proper" roles with consequent self-elimination from high status positions, as well as through barriers that are external to the person.

166
SKILLS HANDBOOK: 4-H IN COMMUNITY RESOURCE DEVELOPMENT
Manhattan: Kansas State University, Cooperative Extension Service, June, 1974.

This is a handbook to be used by anyone needing answers to the problems in carrying out a community service, community resource development, ecology, conservation, anti-pollution, or environmental protection activities.

167
THE SOCIAL AND ECONOMIC CONSEQUENCES OF INDUSTRY: AN ANNOTATED BIBLIOGRAPHY
Harvey, Prentice
Lexington: University of Kentucky, Department of Sociology, 1976.

A partially annotated bibliography on the consequences, both economic and
social, of industrial growth. Citations deal principally with results of
development of rural industry.

168
SOCIAL POWER IN A RURAL COMMUNITY
Ferrell, Mary Zey, O. C. Ferrill and Quentin Jenkins
Growth and Change, 4(2): 3-6, 1973.

This article explores the nature of social power relationships at the community level, with particular focus upon the distribution of power through
the utilization of the monomorphic-polymorphic perspective and upon the
kinds of relationships which tend to produce power in a particular
community.

169
SOCIAL STRATIFICATION AND RURAL ECONOMIC DEVELOPMENT: LESSONS FROM THE
ANTI-POVERTY PROGRAMS IN THE U.S.
Bould-Vantil, Sally
Paper presented at the World Congress of Rural Sociology.
Torun, Poland: August 1976, 25 pp. ERIC: ED131972.

Four kinds of U.S. anti-poverty programs were analyzed in terms of their
impact upon the rural poor. Examination of 13 rural community development corporations in terms of prior and present poverty of non-manager
employees indicated the effect of these programs was one of merely changing the source of income rather than the stratification system, since the
unemployed simply became employed in low skill, low wage jobs.

170
SOCIO-CULTURAL FACTORS AND ENERGY RESOURCE DEVELOPMENT IN RURAL AREAS
IN THE WEST
Albrecht, Stan L.
Paper presented at the Annual Meeting of the Rural Sociological Society,
New York, New York: August 1976, 39 pp. ERIC: ED129526.

This study relies on the use of a model to predict the impacts of energy
development on the Rocky Mountain West on three socio-cultural dimensions:
(1) interpersonal, family, and community social problems; (2) growing
pressures on public services; and (3) the quality of environmental life.

171
A STUDY OF ECONOMIC DEVELOPMENT ACTIVITIES IN RURAL COMMUNITY ACTION
AGENCIES
Yankelovich, Daniel
New York: Yankelovich, Inc., August 1969, 108 pp. NTIS/PB-185 957.

The report describes the roles played by ten rural community action agencies (CAAs) and considers how participation of the poor is affected by the participation of the CAA in economic development activities and how relationships between OEO and CAA affected the agencies' participation in such activities.

172
A STUDY OF RURAL COOPERATIVES: AN ANALYSIS
Hamilton, William L.
Cambridge, Mass.: Abt Associates, February 1973, 279 pp. NTIS/PB-220 526/8.

The study is designed to answer questions dealing with developing and structuring programs of support to cooperatives. Examined are coop goals, strategies, effectiveness, internal/external factors, type and level of support.

173
SYSTEMS PLANNING OF ECONOMIC DEVELOPMENT IN EASTERN OKLAHOMA
Nelson, James and Luther Tweeten
American Journal of Agricultural Economics, 57(3): 480-489, 1975.

Simulation of economic development in a seven-county area in the Eastern Oklahoma Development District. Evaluates several development strategies for a simulated 15-year period based on two criteria: (1) poverty amelioration; and (2) efficiency in generating income in the study area. Concludes that public assistance and job development programs are necessary components of successful development strategies. However, alone, neither of these activities is adequate to alleviate poverty efficiently.

174
THE THEORY AND PRACTICE OF COMMUNITY DEVELOPMENT
Littrell, Donald W.
Columbia: University of Missouri, Extension Division, September 1977.

This publication is a very concise and practical guide to the theory and practice of community development.

175
THEY'LL CUT OFF YOUR PROJECT
Perry, Huey
New York: Praeger, 1972.

This is a narrative account of community organization efforts with poor people during early OEO days. The successes and failures of efforts in Mingo County, West Virginia are discussed within the context of political resistence.

176
THROUGH HUMAN EYES: A NEW APPROACH TO THE PROBLEM OF WORK FORCES IN REMOTE AREAS
Simmonds, W.
Ottawa: National Research Council of Canada, April 1975, 19 pp.

The often unstable workforce in remote areas can be strengthened by
stabilizing adjacent human settlements with community design which works
from the inside out to emphasize the human, social, cultural, and environmental aspects of the settlement.

177
TOP-DOWN PLANNING: ANALYSIS OF OBSTACLES TO COMMUNITY DEVELOPMENT IN AN
ECONOMICALLY POOR REGION OF THE SOUTHWESTERN UNITED STATES
Jacobs, Sue-Ellen
Human Organization, 37(3): 246-256, 1978.

Argues that an anthropologist or other social scientist or planner, who
can serve as an advisor to both agency and community, can help prevent many
types of community development problems in a culturally diverse area. The
paper is based on a social impact assessment made for the Bureau of Reclam-
ation and community members in the Espanola Valley of New Mexico.

178
UTAH COMMUNITY PROGRESS
Utah Community Progress Steering Committee
Logan: Utah State University Press, Cooperative Extension Service, 1973.

A workbook presentation of the processes involved in successfully developing local communities. The publication is a series of questions which,
when answered, depict the areas needing improvement and/or availability
of the required services. Analyzes human relations, cultural enrichment,
economic development, physical environment, services, community attitudes,
and organization and planning.

179
WHAT IS COMMUNITY RESOURCE DEVELOPMENT?
Myers, Galen S. and George H. Breiding
Morgantown: West Virginia University, Cooperative Extension Service,
Misc. Pub. 403, 5 pp. undated.

Provides a brief description of the dimensions and problems of community
resource development.

180
WORKING WITH PEOPLE IN COMMUNITY ACTION, AN INTERNATIONAL CASEBOOK FOR
TRAINED COMMUNITY WORKERS AND VOLUNTEER COMMUNITY LEADERS
King, Clarence
New York: The Association Press, 190 pp.

This casebook stresses cooperation with community workers and leaders.
Separate sections deal with means of developing rapport with host communities, assessing felt needs, initiating community action, planning and
conducting committees, organizing and using community and neighborhood
councils, providing field work and discussion-oriented training for new
community workers, and meeting various psychological and sociocultural
problems in community action.

CHAPTER 6

HEALTH

General Topics

Alcoholism   Health Manpower Development

Child Abuse/Neglect   Health Planning

Consumer Participation   Health Services

Delivery Systems   Home Health Care

Folk Medicine   Indian Medicine

Health Care and Cultural Influences   Migrant Health Care

Health Maintenance Organizations   Nutrition

1
ADVOCACY FOR THE ABUSED RURAL CHILD
Leistyna, Joseph
Children Today, 7(3): 26 pp., 1978.

The author discusses his experiences as an only practicing pediatrician in a Virginia County. The author discusses the need to direct attention to rural children and their distressed families.

2
ALCOHOLISM, ILLNESS, AND SOCIAL PATHOLOGY AMONG AMERICAN INDIANS IN TRANSITION
Littman, Gerard
American Journal of Public Health, 60(9): 1,769-1,787, 1970.

Based upon several years experience at a center for American Indians in Chicago. The author analyzes the problem of alcoholism and the possibilities of treatment, rehabilitation, and control.

3
AMERICAN INDIAN ELDERS: NEEDS AND ASPIRATIONS IN INSTITUTIONAL AND HOME HEALTH CARE
Red Horse, John G.
Prepared for the Seventh National Institute on Minority Aging.
Tempe: Arizona State University, School of Social Work.

This paper examines needs and aspirations of American Indian elders pertinent to institutional and home care facilities. A guiding principle is that service delivery systems must revitalize the "life space" of elders.

4
AMERICAN INDIAN INFLUENCE ON MEDICINE AND PHARMACOLOGY
Vogel, Virgil J.
The Indian Historian, 1(1): 12-15, 1967.

This article discusses the Indian influence on American medicine. It is intended to shed light on the acculturation process which takes place when two cultures come in contact with each other.

5
AMERICAN INDIAN MEDICINE
Vogel, Virgil J.
Norman, Oklahoma: University of Oklahoma Press, Publishing Division of the University, 1970.

To American Indians the term medicine embraces much more than the cure of disease and the healing of injuries. The focus of this book is on these aspects and particularly those that we have borrowed.

6

ANNUAL MEDICAL REPORT OF THE COASTAL BOARD MIGRANT COUNCIL HEALTH PROJECT,
SAN PATRICIO MIGRANT HEALTH CENTER, TEXAS, 1973-1974.
Krebethe, William F.
Washington, D.C.: Department of Health, Education and Welfare,
Migrant Health Service, 1974.

This publication explores the health services provided to migrant and
seasonal farmworkers. Various medical services and logistics for providing
these services are discussed.

7

AN APPLIED ANALYSIS OF NORTH AMERICAN INDIAN DRINKING PATTERNS
Price, John A.
Human Organization, 34(1): 16-17, 1975.

Some American Indian societies have had alcoholic beverages and recognized
the problems related to excessive drinking since aboriginal times, while
others have acquired these problems with the historic introduction of
alcohol. These problems have become extremely serious with the breakdown
of traditional cultural controls in a context or racial discrimination,
frustrations related to low economic success, peer group pressure to
drink socially, and the spread of patterns of drinking to complete drunkenness. Simple legal solutions, such as the external imposition of prohibi-
tions and arrest for public drunkenness, have been ineffective as well as
unjust, but there is evidence of the kinds of practical things that can be
done to improve the situation. There is particularly a need to enhance
existing social controls with Indian societies on self-destructive
drunken comportment.

8

AN APPROACH TO MATERNAL AND CHILD HEALTH SERVICES IN A RURAL SETTING
Millington, Marie
In 2nd Annual Northern Wisconsin Symposium on Human Services in the
Rural Environment Reader, David Bast and Julie Schmidt, eds.
Madison: University of Wisconsin-Extension, Center for Social Science,
90-94, 1977.

A successful pilot project in the development of maternal and child health
services in Wisconsin Rapids, Wisconsin is described. The effort was
initiated through group prenatal education for prospective parents.

9

CHILD NEGLECT IN A RURAL COMMUNITY
Polansky, Norman, et al.
Social Casework, 49(8): 467-474, 1968.

This article is a report of a pilot study of mothers in rural Southern
Appalachia.

10
COMMUNITY ACTION KIT: NATIONAL RURAL HEALTH WEEK
Chicago: American Medical Association, 1976

A kit containing publications on programming and resources including information on rural health services, facility loans, medical and dental
practices program suggestions, and a bibliography.

11
COMMUNITY HEALTH CENTER PROGRAMS
Washington, D.C.: Rural America, Inc., December 1978, 8 pp.

Brief description of HEW's community health center program.

12
CONSUMER PARTICIPATION IN HEALTH CARE: HOW IT'S WORKING
Danaceau, Paul
Prepared for the U.S. Department of Health, Education and Welfare by
Human Services Institute for Children and Families, Inc., Arlington, Va.
Springfield, Virginia: National Technical Information Service, 1975.

This study involved four case studies of consumer involvement in health
care planning and health care delivery. The objectives of the study were
to determine what the objectives of consumer participation were, how
consumer representatives were selected, who was selected to represent
consumers, what relationships were established between consumer representatives and health professionals, how extensively consumer representatives
participated in decision making, and how both consumer representatives and
health professionals assessed consumer participation. In general, the
assessment was positive, although consumer representatives were more
enthusiastic about their participation than were health professionals.

13
CONSUMER PARTICIPATION IN HEALTH PLANNING
Strauss, Marvin D.
Cincinnati, Ohio: Cincinnati University, Department of Community Health
Organization.

This item was published by the Society for Public Health Education, and
it treats the most significant issues involved in citizen or consumer
involvement in health planning. It is designed primarily for agency staff
persons. There are articles on a broad range of issues relating to citizen
involvement in health. A bibliography on consumer participation and health
education is included.

14
CONTINUING EDUCATION FOR RURAL HOSPITAL NURSES
Packard, Myrna and Nancy Burns
Nursing Outlook, 27(6): 416-419, 1978.

This article discusses a plan to provide nurses practicing in rural areas
with an opportunity to update their nursing knowledge.

15

THE COST OF MATERNITY CARE IN RURAL HOSPITALS
Journal of American Medical Association, 240(3), 2051-2052, 1978.

Commentary. Suggests federal health planners support the development of
regional systems of perinatal care and education to contain obstetric
service cost rather than to enforce large scale consolidation. Time and
distance to hospitals were factors cited. Supports service care that is
close to the patient's home.

16

CRITICAL HEALTH MANPOWER SHORTAGE AREAS: THEIR IMPACT ON RURAL HEALTH
PLANNING
Fitzwilliams, Jeannette
Washington, D.C.: U.S. Department of Agriculture, 1977, 17 pp.

Report describing the 673 critical health manpower shortage areas listed
by the Federal Register for 1975 in relation to the Comprehensive Health
Planning areas. Describes how the program is designed to cope with
shortage problems and how this program is related to the work of health
service agencies.

17

CULTURAL DIFFERENCES AND MEDICAL CARE
Saunders, L.
New York: Russel Sage Foundation, 1954.

This book explores the difficulties inherent in supplying "Anglo" health
care and medical services to Spanish-speaking people in the American
Southwest. This book describes some of the healing ways historically and
currently used by Spanish-speaking people.

18

DELIVERY OF RURAL COMMUNITY SERVICES: SOME IMPLICATIONS AND PROBLEMS
Carruthers, Garrey E., et al.
Las Cruces, New Mexico: New Mexico State University, July 1975, 49 pp.

Summarizing research conducted under the Western Regional Research Project
on the delivery of rural community services, this report presents explications of the following generalizations which have been supported by
research: (1) many rural service institutions need reorganization and
renewal; (2) regionalization increases organizations' ability to provide
some rural community services; (3) rural development depends directly on
citizen participation and representation of various population segments;
(4) effective leaders view development as a community process, not a personal
one; (5) public leaders seem to be drawn primarily from certain community
segments; (6) even with fewer and less adequate services, rural residents
prefer rural life; (7) availability of health-care services affects their
use; (8) rural people want innovative health care practices; (9) mechanisms are needed for using results from rural community service research.

19

DELIVERY OF SOCIAL SERVICES IN HEALTH CARE: A RURAL PERSPECTIVE
Johnson, Louise C.
In Social Work in Rural Areas: Issues and Opportunities.   Joseph Davenport,
III, Judith A. Davenport and James R. Wiebler, eds.
Laramie: The University of Wyoming, Department of Social Work, 1980.

The social work program and the Division of Allied Health Sciences at the
University of South Dakota became aware that there was a need to develop
an educational program for persons desiring to practice social work in
health settings in the state.   This paper discusses a study conducted to
determine the state of social work in health settings in the state.

20

DETERMINANTS OF GENOCIDE FEAR IN A RURAL TEXAS COMMUNITY: A RESEARCH NOTE
Farrell, Walter C., Jr. and Marvin P. Dawkins
American Journal of Public Health, 69(6): 605-607, 1979.

This article explores the relative importance of social background factors
as predictors of genocide fear among blacks in a rural Texas community.

21

DIFFERENTIAL UTILIZATION OF THE HEALTH CARE DELIVERY SYSTEM BY NUMBERS OF
ETHNIC MINORITIES
Brown, Patricia A.
Journal of Sociology and Social Welfare, 3(5): 516-523, 1976.

Patterns of utilization and variables associated with levels of utilization
of the health care delivery system by members of ethnic minorities are
examined in this article.   With respect to Native Americans, the author
suggests that improvement in their basic living conditions, not the utilization of the health care delivery system, is the key to their improved
health status.

22

DISCHARGE PLANNING IN THE SMALL RURAL HOSPITAL: PROBLEMS AND ISSUES
Gunter, P. L. and Anita Rosen
In Social Work in Rural Areas: Issues and Opportunities.   Joseph Davenport,
III, Judith A. Davenport and James R. Wiebler, eds.
Laramie: The University of Wyoming, Department of Social Work, 1980.

The purpose of this study was to gain some knowledge of discharge planning
in the small, rural hospital.   Since little information about rural hospital
discharge planning exists, the authors undertook the study in order to
gain information and possibly provide a view of pertinent issues.

23

DIVERSITY OF RURAL SOCIETY AND HEALTH NEEDS
Copp, James H.
In Rural Health Services: Organization, Delivery and Use.
Ames: The Iowa State University, Press, 26-37, 1976.

The health needs of rural America and its subpopulations are discussed in this paper. The author's review of available information leads him to conclude that useful data in the subject are almost totally lacking.

24
ESTABLISHING A RURAL CHILD ABUSE/NEGLECT TREATMENT PROGRAM
Sefcik, Thomas R. and Nancy J. Ormsby
Child Welfare, 57(3): 187-195, 1978.

Project Children is a rural child abuse/neglect program in south central Indiana. This article relates the methods employed in the program to various issues. In an environment with limited resources, one of the most significant factors in program success was learning to work with people, both professional and lay, in a manner nonthreatening to the small community.

25
ESTABLISHING A SOCIAL SERVICE DEPARTMENT IN A RURAL HOSPITAL
Schlosser, Fred J., Jr.
Hospital Progress, 51(1): 44-45, 1970.

Steps taken and problems encountered in establishing a social service department in a rural Illinois hospital are described briefly in this article.

26
THE ESTABLISHMENT OF SOCIAL WORKER PARTICIPATION IN RURAL PRIMARY HEALTH CARE
Hookey, Peter
In 2nd Annual Northern Wisconsin Symposium on Human Services in the Rural Environment Reader. David Bast and Julie Schmidt, eds.
Madison: University of Wisconsin-Extension, Center for Social Science, 95-109, 1977.

Two programs utilizing social workers in rural primary health care are described and compared in this paper.

27
EVALUATION OF DISTRICT V HEALTH AND SOCIAL SERVICES INTEGRATION PROJECT THROUGH JUNE 1974
Cedar City, Utah: Five County Association of Governments, September 1974, 167 pp.

The project, undertaken to demonstrate innovative approaches to services integration in an area which incorporates isolated, rural communities, uses the Five County Association as the general purpose government integrator and management authority. An evaluation of the project is presented in this report.

28
AN EVALUATION OF RURAL HEALTH CARE RESEARCH
Kane, Robert, Marilyn Dean and Marian Soloman
Evaluation Quarterly, 139-189, May 1979.

This paper directs attention toward ongoing research, examines unanswered
questions and unresolved issues, and suggests a framework for future coordination of research and evaluation efforts in the field.

29
FACTORS AFFECTING THE USE OF PHYSICIAN SERVICES IN A RURAL COMMUNITY
Luft, Harold S., John C. Hershey, and Joan Morrell
American Journal of Public Health, 66(9): 865-871, 1976.

Socioeconomic, demographic, attitudinal, and health status factors are
examined for predicting physician utilization in a rural community.

30
FEDERAL HEALTH CARE (WITH RESERVATIONS)
Kane, Robert L. and Rosalie A. Kane
New York: Springer Publishing Co., Inc., 1972

This is a study of the Indian Health Service, a multimillion-dollar
federal health care system serving a deprived population. Successes, failures and recommendations for change in the Indian Health Service are examined.

31
FEDERAL HEALTH POLICIES IN RURAL AREAS
Appendix to Hearings, 93rd Congress, 2nd Session, October 1-3, 1974.
Washington, D.C.: U.S. Government Printing Office, 1974, 174 pp.

This report was prepared by the Congressional Research Service for the
sub-committee for hearings "to review health needs and problems, to
determine how these needs are being met, what services are available, how
the government programs are being implemented and what actions need to be
taken to improve health services to the non-metropolitan areas."
The greatest need in rural areas is the acquisition of physicians and
dentists and using new personnel in efficient health programs. The low
income status of many rural people is an important impediment to attracting
and retaining rural practitioners, since their ability to pay for services
is low. Efforts to improve this situation are outlined and supported by
available data.

32
THE FEDERAL INITIATVE IN RURAL HEALTH
Martin, Edward D.
Public Health Reports, 90(4): 291-297, 1975.

The article reviews the programs designed to provide better health care.
Some of the programs and the impact they have had include: The Public
Health Service, the Indian Health Service, the National Health Service
Corps, and the Emergency Medical Services Systems Act. The impact of a
National Health Insurance program is discussed.

33
FROM FARM TO MEDICAL SCHOOL
Brownlee, W. Elliot
In Women in the Economy
New Haven: Yale University Press, 131-143, 1976.

Chapter illustrates the potential of Victorian women and the general
conditions of the rural areas where they lived. Story of Bethinia Angelina
Owens-Adair (1840-1926) who was a prominent medical practitioner.

34
HEALTH CARE IN APPALACHIA: ATTITUDES TOWARD NURSE PRACTITIONERS
Sebastian, Margaret and Eileen Payne
In Effective Models for the Delivery of Services In Rural Areas:
Implications for Practice and Social Work Education. Barry L. Locke and
Roger A. Lohmann, eds.
Morgantown: West Virginia University, August 7-10, 1978, 247 pp.

At present in the Appalachia area there is a shortage of primary health
care facilities and primary care providers. This article is a study of
the attitudes of the older Appalachian woman about nurse practitioners
providing primary health care services.

35
HEALTH CARE DELIVERY: REACHING OUT TO RURAL COMMUNITIES - PART I AND
PART II
Phillips, Donald
Hospitals, Vol. 46, June 1972.

These papers are based on panel discussions at the Conference on Hospitals
and Rural Health Services sponsored by the American Hospital Association
in 1971.

36
HEALTH CARE DELIVERY IN RURAL AREAS
Chicago, Illinois: American Medical Association, 1972, 41 pp.
ERIC: ED076287.

A review of the problems of rural health delivery is presented in this
booklet with selected plans and models for delivery of services in certain
rural areas of the nation.

37
HEALTH CARE IN RURAL AMERICA
Ahern, Mary C.
Economic, Statistics, and Cooperative Services
Washington, D.C.: U.S. Department of Agriculture, July 1979, 43 pp.

Neometropolitan and totally rural areas have greater unmet health needs and
fewer health resources than urban areas. This report compares four factors
indicative of the continuation of the health care system in both areas and
shows that rural areas' lower incomes, larger aged populations, hazardous
occupations, and lower educational levels contribute to poorer health care
conditions.

38
HEALTH MAINTENANCE ORGANIZATIONS
Washington, D.C.:   Rural America, Inc., 12 pp.

Tells how HEW's HMO program works and the problems it faces in serving
rural needs.

39
HEALTH MANPOWER DEVELOPMENT AND RURAL SERVICES
Federson, D.A.
Journal of the American Medical Association, 225(13): 1627-1631, 1973.

Review of federal programs having direct bearing on rural health care
and manpower needs with recommendations for the future.

40
HEALTH SERVICES: AN ESSENTIAL COMPONENT OF RURAL DEVELOPMENT
Chicago, Ill.:   American Medical Association, Council on Rural Health,
1973, 4 pp.

The Council on Rural Health of the American Medical Association is a professional advisory group to the AMA's Rural Health Department.   This booklet emphasizes the importance of cooperation with rural development programs for improving effectiveness of rural health care services.

41
HEALTH SERVICES IN RURAL AMERICA
Matthews, Tresa H.
Washington, D.C.:   U.S. Department of Agriculture, Economic Research
Service, Bulletin No. 3, 1974, 40 pp.

Health care needs and services in rural areas are compared with those in
urban areas.   Federal health legislation and its effect on rural areas are
discussed.   Examples of successful public and private experimental health
delivery programs are given.

42
HEALTH STATUS IN RURAL AMERICA
Washington, D.C.:   Rural America, Inc., December 1977.   (75¢)

Describes health conditions of rural people, distribution of health
resources, federal recognition of rural health problems.

43
IMPACT OF A RURAL PREVENTIVE CARE OUTREACH PROGRAM ON CHILDREN'S HEALTH
Cowen, David, et al.
American Journal of Public Health, 68(5): 471-476, 1978.

The purpose of this study was to determine the effectiveness of preventive
health outreach services, delivered in conjunction with pediatric outpatient care, in preventing or arresting certain common childhood diseases
as compared to pediatrics outpatient care alone.

44
IMPROVED PUBLIC HEALTH PRACTICES IN A DISADVANTAGED RURAL COMMUNITY
Gould, Judith, William Groff and Donald Francis
A project funded by Title V, Rural Development Act of 1972.
Storrs, Connecticut: University of Connecticut, College of Agriculture
and Natural Resources, 26 pp.

This report presents a Connecticut study of a community development model
for improving public health in a disadvantaged rural area.

45
INDIAN HEALTH CARE IMPROVEMENT ACT: REPORT
U.S. Congress. Senate Committee on Interior and Insular Affairs,
94th Congress, First Session, Senate Report No. 94-133, May 13, 1975.

Reports on The Indian Health Care Improvement Act which was later signed
into law (P.L.94-437) by President Ford.

46
INDIAN HEALTH SERVICE
Washington, D.C.: Rural America, Inc., December 1977, 9 pp. (75¢).

Tells the history of HEW's Indian Health Service and summarizes 1976 Task
Force recommendations for improvement. Also summarizes 1976 Indian Health
Care Improvement Act.

47
INNOVATIVE, RATIONAL APPROACH TO RURAL HEALTH CARE
Kirsch, M. H.
Medical Hypothesis, 4(4): 262-266, 1978.

An answer to the problem of physician shortage in rural areas is proposed and
modeled on an innovative proposal affecting southern Illinois.

48
INTEGRATION OF FAMILY PLANNING AND MATERNAL-CHILD HEALTH PROGRAMS IN
RURAL AREAS
Lapham, Robert J.
Revised version of a paper prepared for the Third World Congress for
Rural Sociology.
Baton Rouge, Louisiana: August, 1972, 24 pp. ERIC: ED069448.

The functional integration of maternal and child health (MCH) services with
family planning programs in rural areas is discussed and suggestions for
the successful implementation of research demonstration projects are
provided.

49

INTERDISCIPLINARY COLLABORATION ESSENTIAL TO PROVIDE HEALTH SERVICES TO
THE RURAL POPULATION
Guerin, Dorris
In Social Work in Rural Areas: Preparation and Practice.
Knoxville: The University of Tennessee, School of Social Work, 321-327, 1978 .

Manpower shortages in rural health care require interdisciplinary collaboration among professionals in rural communities.

50

MEETING THE HEALTH CARE NEEDS OF RURAL FAMILIES
Small, Linda and Thomas Whitfield
Children Today, 2-6, November-December 1977.

Based on Children's Health Program of Great Barrington, Massachusetts.
Important services include home visits, outreach and utilization of community leaders in services. Rural persons accept preventative health care
and education more readily when it is based on the community's inherent
strengths.

51

MIGRANT HEALTH PROGRAM
Washington, D.C.: Rural America, Inc., December 1977, 14 pp. (75¢)

Describes the functions of farm worker health centers and suggests how
centers can be made more effective. An HEW program.

52

MIGRANT WORKERS (A BIBLIOGRAPHY OF ABSTRACTS)
Kenton, Edith
Springfield, Va.: National Technical Information Service, July 1979, 86 pp.
NTIS/PS-79/0664/7ST.

Needs and problems of the migrant worker are reviewed. Aspects include
medical and health care, housing, employment, education needs, and the
interaction of the migrant and the community. This updated bibliography
contains 78 abstracts.

53

NATIONAL HEALTH SERVICE CORPS
Washington, D.C.: Rural America, Inc., December 1977, 12 pp. (70¢)

Gives a history of the National Health Service Corps and suggests how the
program can be made more effective in rural areas.

54

NATIONAL HEALTH SERVICE CORPS AND PRIMARY CARE TRAINING
Pollner, Phillip and Jerrold J. Parris
Journal of the American Medical Association, 228(11): 1405-1407, 1974.

This communication points out that after three years since the National
Health Service Corps became funded, only a small fraction of underserved

areas received any benefits from the program. The note offers several factors contributing to this poor goal achievement. The establishment of a primary care training program for medical students is discussed as a means of stimulating students to practice in rural areas.

55
NATIONAL NUTRITION POLICY STUDY - 1974
United States Senate
Hearings before the Select Committee on Nutrition and Human Needs of the United States Senate, 93rd Congress, 2nd Session - Part 3.
Washington, D.C.: June 19, 1974. ERIC: ED103532.

This report focuses on the testimony of witnesses to this Senate Select Committee. The topics include nutritional problems of various populations and programs designed to meet these needs.

56
NATIONAL NUTRITIONAL POLICY STUDY - 1974
United States Senate
Hearings before the Select Committee on Nutrition and Human Needs of the United States Senate, 93rd Congress, 2nd Session - Part 3A.
Appendix to Nutrition and Special Groups.
Washington, D.C.: June 20, 1974. ERIC: ED103533.

This report of these hearings covers 11 topics related to nutrition and human needs. Various nutrition problems and programs designed to meet these needs were reported and discussed.

57
THE NATIVE AMERICAN
Bullough, Bonnie and Verna Bullough
In Poverty, Ethnic Identity and Health Care.
Appleton Century-Crafts, Merian Corporation, 89-108, 1972.

The article discusses Indian and Health services. The inadequacies of the health system are discussed from an Indian perspective.

58
NAVAJO HEALTH AND WELFARE AIDES: A FIELD STUDY
Halpern, Katherine Spencer
Social Science Review, 45(1): 37-52, 1971.

Prior to the current interest in paraprofessional workers, health and welfare agencies had developed positions for Navajo aide-interpreters to meet the special needs of their service programs. An interview study shows how the original conception of the aides' roles has been extended from linguistic and cultural interpreting to other mediating functions, the satisfactions that the aides see in their jobs, and how their contributions are valued by their supervisors. Implications for generic aide roles and careers in "human services" for Navajos and for other developing communities are discussed.

59

NAVAJO MEDICINE AND PSYCHOANALYSIS

Bergman, Robert L.

Human Behavior, Vol. 2, 8-15, July 1973.

A psychiatrist for the Indian Health Service in Window Rock, Arizona found that the wisdom of Navajo medicine men who blend healing and worship life together may point the way for medicine in the future.

60

ORGANIZATION OF HEALTH SERVICES FOR RURAL AREAS

Crawford, Charles O.

In Rural Health Services: Organization, Delivery and Use.

Ames: The Iowa State University Press, 121-136, 1976.

The health service delivery systems for meeting primary, secondary, and tertiary care in rural areas are examined.

61

PATHWAYS OF RURAL PEOPLE TO HEALTH SERVICES

Hassinger, Edward W.

In Rural Health Services: Organization, Delivery and Use.

Ames: The Iowa State Press, 164-187, 1976.

In order to shed light on understanding rural health consumer behavior, the author examines the characteristics of rural society, the health care system, and the patterned behavior of people in seeking health care.

62

PEDIATRIC PRACTICE IN A RURAL SOUTHWESTERN COMMUNITY HEALTH CLINIC

Boldstein, Mark A.

Clinical Pediatrics, Vol. 17, 363-379, April 1978.

Report finds 56.8% patients were female, 50% over 18 years of age. Suggests that pediatricians revise age limit to include up to thirty years of age. Early pre-natal and birth control among added services. Gallup, New Mexico study site.

63

PERCEIVED HEALTH NEEDS AND CONCERNS IN OREGON DISTRICT NO. 8

Meinke, Cindy

Medford, Oregon: Jackson-Josephine Comprehensive Health Planning

Council, Inc., 1974, 64 pp. NTIS/HRP-0003926/3ST.

A survey of residents in Jackson and Josephine Counties (Oregon) was conducted to determine perceived health needs and concerns. A copy of the survey instrument and descriptions of survey procedures and random sampling techniques are included along with the findings of the survey.

64

PLANNING AND DEVELOPING COMMUNITY HEALTH SERVICES
University Park: Pennsylvania State University, Cooperative Extension
Service, 1977, 185 pp.

A correspondence course describing educational programs on planning and
developing community health services. Designed for individuals interested or involved in community health decision making.

65

PLANNING AND DEVELOPING COMMUNITY HEALTH SERVICES: A PILOT EDUCATIONAL
PROJECT OF THE COOPERATIVE EXTENSION SERVICE
Fiddick, Carol C., Sam M. Cordes and Charles O. Crawford
University Park: Pennsylvania State University, Cooperative Extension
Service, 1977, 50 pp.

A nine lesson correspondence course about community health services
directed to individuals or groups interested or involved in community
development work. The goal is to increase skills in identifying and
resolving community health problems.

66

A PRIMARY CARE MEDICAL CENTER: ONE COUNTY'S ANSWER TO RURAL HEALTH CARE
NEEDS
University Park: Pennsylvania State University, Cooperative Extension
Service, 1977, 9 pp.

An approach to rural health care resulting in a community owned and operated primary care medical center is described. Outlines leadership needs
formulating a plan choosing a type of center, services, staffing and
financing.

67

THE PROFESSIONAL HEALTH EDUCATOR AS CHANGE AGENT IN A RURAL COMMUNITY
Weiss, Nancy
In Human Services in the Rural Environment Reader. David Bast, ed.
Madison: University of Wisconsin-Extension, Center for Social Service,
93-98, 1976-77.

The role of the health educator as a change agent in a rural community of
northeastern Connecticut is described. Her activities with community
organizations, particularly the Extension Service, are discussed.

68

A PROFILE OF U.S. COMPREHENSIVE HEALTH PLANNING AREAS
Fitzwilliams, Jeannette
Washington, D.C.: U.S. Department of Agriculture, Agricultural Economic
Report No. 339, 1977, 37 pp.

A report describing the Comprehensive Health Planning Program with its
multi-county approach. It helps equip rural populations to identify
needs and methods to influence plans to solve health problems.

69

PROMOTING COMMUNITY HEALTH - 1976
Washington, D.C.: Government Printing Office, Order No. 017-026-00050-0,
1976.

Developments in community health are reported in this booklet describing
the programs, activities, grants, and contracts of the Bureau of Community
Health Services (BCHS), DHEW. Summaries are presented of BCHS programs,
such as migrant health and rural health initiatives.

70

PSYCHIATRIC AND MEDICAL PROBLEMS IN RURAL COMMUNITIES IN SOCIAL WORK IN ...
Neff, James Alan, Begar A. Husaini and James McCorkel
In Social Work in Rural Areas: Issues and Opportunities. Joseph Davenport,
III, Judith A. Davenport and James R. Wiebler, eds.
Laramie: The University of Wyoming, Department of Social Work, 103-110,1980.

In this paper the authors report that chronic physical ailments and psychiatric impairment are often found in the same person in rural areas. They
conclude that health and mental health manpower should diagnose and treat
the person in a coordinated manner.

71

PUBLIC FINANCING OF HEALTH SERVICES: MEDICARE AND MEDICAID
Washington, D.C.: Rural America, Inc., December 1977, 28 pp.   (75¢).

Explains how the Medicare and Medicaid programs function and suggests ways
of making these programs more effective in rural areas.

72

PUBLIC POLICY OF RURAL HEALTH
Swanson, Bert E. and Edith Swanson
In Rural Health Services: Organizations, Delivery and Use.
Ames: The Iowa State University Press, 137-163, 1976.

Contemporary health policy issues as they relate to rural America are
discussed in this article.

73

THE QUALITY OF PERINATAL CARE IN SMALL RURAL HOSPITALS
Hein, Herman A.
Journal of American Medical Association, Vol. 240, 2070-2072, November 1978.

Study based on Iowa birth and mortality statistics. Small hospitals with
fewer than 500 deliveries per year have acceptable perinatal care, provided that referrals of high-risk pregnancy cases are made. Offers
suggestions to health planners.

74

THE RELIGIOUS COMPONENT IN SOUTHERN FOLK MEDICINE

Snow, L. F.

In Traditional Healing: New Science or New Colonialism (Essays in
Critique of Medical Anthropology), P. Singer, ed.
Owerri, New York: London: Conch Magazine Limited, 1977.

Many of the rural and urban poor belong to churches of a fundamentalist
and pentecostal nature in which the religious experience is intense and
passionate. When health problems occur, the illness referral system is
affected by religious belief. The author questions why the social system
allows so many people to exist under conditions where God seems to be the
only listener.

75

REMOTE AREA HEALTH SERVICES: SOUTHWEST NEW MEXICO

Anderson, James G.

University Park, N.M.: New Mexico State University, Physical Science
Laboratory, Volume I, Design, Development and Accomplishments: Volume II,
Implementation: Volume III, Evaluation. Report No. HSRDI-71-41.
May 1970, 341 pp.

There is a severe overall national shortage of physicians and trained
health personnel in rural areas. The object of the project was to study
the feasibility of installing a system of health services delivery for
rural populations through uses of N.A.S.A. technology and innovative manpower and transportation systems. Volume I - An assessment of needs -
essentially a bibliography with comment. Dual Volume II and III -
Describes implementation planning of first phase, measures need, presents
design and development of a new health care system purported to meet needs.

76

RURAL HEALTH CARE

Roemer, Milton I.

St. Louis: The C. V. Mosby Company, 1976.

This volume presents five papers analyzing the problem of rural health
services along several dimensions. These papers are divided into the
following chapters: historical perspective on rural health services
in America; development of public health services in a rural county;
organized health services in a rural county; health needs and services
of the rural poor; and rural health care solutions attempted around the
world.

77

RURAL HEALTH CARE IN THE SOUTH

Davis, Karen and Ray Marshall

Summary report prepared for the Task Force on Southern Rural Development
and presented at the meeting of the Task Force in Atlanta, Georgia on
October 10-11, 1975.
Washington, D.C.: The Brookings Institution.

This report summarizes the state of rural health care in the South. The authors have reviewed the uniqueness of rural health, (obstacles-approaches) and made recommendations for changing several facets of rural health care delivery-training, content, minorities and financing.

78
RURAL HEALTH CARE SYSTEMS
Wilson, Vernon W.
Journal of the American Medical Association, 216(10): 1623-1626, 1971.

Discussion of federal proposals for improving rural health through health maintenance organizations, family health center, extension of medical facilities construction, promoting health manpower production, and expanding data collection.

79
RURAL HEALTH COUNCIL
Washington, D.C.: Rural America, Inc., 1978, 3 pp.

Gives the background of the newly formed Rural Health Council.

80
THE RURAL HEALTH INITIATIVE - PRIMARY CARE RESEARCH AND DEMONSTRATION
Rural Health Systems, U.S. Dept. of Health, Education, and Welfare,
1979, 30 pp.

This bulletin describes how a variety of local projects are pursuing five of the principal themes reflected throughout the Rural Health Initiative effort. These are: 1) coordination of resources, 2) community involvement, 3) comprehensive care, 4), response to need, and 5) quality care.

81
RURAL HEALTH SERVICES (A BIBLIOGRAPHY WITH ABSTRACTS)
Harrison, Elizabeth A.
Springfield, Virginia: National Technical Information Service,
February-November, 1977, 312 pp. NTIS/PS-77/1086/6ST.

Primary health care, health planning, health care delivery systems, health resources, health care facilities, legislation, costs, and manpower are the subjects covered. Also included are studies of mental health care.

82
RURAL HEALTH SERVICES: ORGANIZATION, DELIVERY, AND USE
North Central Regional Center for Rural Development
Ames: The Iowa State University Press, 1976.

This book covers the highly diverse concerns of rural health: transportation and communications, health needs, physicians, history, financing, and public policy.

83

RURAL HEALTH SERVICES: VOL. I AND II. (BIBLIOGRAPHIES WITH ABSTRACTS)
Harrison, Elizabeth A.
Springfield, Virginia: National Technical Information Service,
November and December, 1977, 103 pp. NTIS/PS-78/1211/8ST.

Primary health care, health planning, health care delivery systems, health
resources, health care facilities, legislation, costs, and manpower are
the subjects discussed in these bibliographies. (Volume I contains 307
abstracts, none of which are new entries to the previous edition.)

84

RURAL NURSE PRACTITIONERS - A CHALLENGE AND A RESPONSE
Sullivan, Judith, et al.
American Journal of Public Health, 68(10): 972-976, 1978.

The use of nurse practitioners to resolve rural health manpower shortages
was evaluated in a survey of 85 nurses in rural settings.

85

RURAL SOCIAL PROBLEMS, HUMAN SERVICES, AND SOCIAL POLICIES, WORKING PAPER
8: HEALTH
Derr, Janet Morton
Denver, Colorado: University of Denver, Center for Social Research and
Development, September, 1973. NTIS/HRP-0007590/3ST.

The findings of a review of literature pertaining to health status and
resources of rural populations are reported.

86

RURAL SOCIAL PROBLEMS, HUMAN SERVICES, AND SOCIAL POLICIES, WORKING PAPER
11: NUTRITION
Derr, Janet Morton
Denver, Colorado: University of Denver, Center for Social Research
and Development, September 1973. NTIS/HRP-0007592/9ST.

This review is presented as one in a series of 13 working papers on the
problems, services, and policies affecting the well-being of rural populations. Of five identified high-risk population subgroups with regard
to malnutrition, four are rural. The five groups are: the unemployed
or partly employed rural poor, migrant workers, reservation Indians,
the poor in large cities, and Alaska Indians and Eskimos.

87

SOCIAL AND CULTURAL FACTORS IN THE RESPONSE OF MEXICAN-AMERICANS TO
MEDICAL TREATMENT
Nall, Frank and Joseph Speilberg
Journal of Health and Social Behavior, 8(4): 299-308, 1967.

This paper explores the cultural and social factors related to the acceptance or rejection of a modern medical treatment by Mexican-Americans. The research reported here deals with the responses of a sample of Mexican-Americans, from the lower Rio Grande Valley of Texas, to a recommended medical regime for treatment of tuberculosis. The findings suggest a "milieu effect" rather than a set of specific and isolable factors inhibiting acceptance of the treatment regime.

88
SOCIAL WORK IN A RURAL FOUNDATION HEALTH MAINTENANCE ORGANIZATION: THE BOOTHEEL PROJECT
Hookey, Peter
Paper presented at the 1975 Annual Meeting of the American Public Health Association, November, 1975, 21 pp. NTIS/HRP-0006790/0ST.

This paper reports that professional social work services have become an important and integral part of a foundation-type, family-oriented health maintenance organization (HMO) serving the Missouri Bootheel, a six-county, low income area. The project social worker has provided a wide range of ambulatory care services: one-to-one psychosocial, preventive, educational, and resource-finding services; and community organization support services for self-help groups and several other human service organizations. The project has developed strategies for the interpretation of social work roles to physicians and osteopaths who can make a major contribution to patient referral.

89
A STRATEGY FOR HEALTH MANPOWER--REFLECTIONS ON AN EXPERIENCE CALLED MEDEX
Smith, Richard, et al.
Journal of the American Medical Association, 217(10): 1362-1367, 1971.

Medex is a program creating a new class of medical professionals who work with physicians in providing medical care. It is one answer to the rural community with a shortage of health manpower.

90
A STUDY OF CONSUMER PARTICIPATION IN THE ADMINISTRATIVE PROCESSES IN VARIOUS LEVELS OF HSMSA'S SERVICE PROJECTS, FINAL REPORT
Sausalito, California: Community Change, Inc. and Public Sector, Inc., June 1972.

This study was done for the U.S. Dept. of Health, Education and Welfare (Contract HSM 110-71-135) in order to provide the basis for future policy regarding citizen participation in health programs. It analyzes participation at the local project level, as well as at various administrative levels. Eight different HEW programs were examined. The study provides extensive detail on how citizen participation is working out, from the points of view of both providers and consumers, and develops guidelines for future citizen participation policy in the health field.

91
TOWARD A RURAL HEALTH PLATFORM
Washington, D.C.: Rural America, Inc., June 1978, 28 pp. ($2.00).

Report on the findings and recommendations of the National Rural Health
Conference, December 1977, and policy statement adopted by the Rural Health
Council of Rural America.

92
URBAN-ORIENTED METHODS: FAILURE TO SOLVE RURAL EMERGENCY CARE PROBLEMS
Waller, Julian A.
Journal of the American Medical Association, 226(12): 1441-1446, 1973.

Inadequate available skills and dollars often result in inadequate medical
emergency services for rural areas. Personnel may not gain needed experience. A proposed plan to alleviate these problems is presented with
reference to resource materials.

93
USE AND ADEQUACY OF HEALTH-CARE SERVICES IN NEW MEXICO
Eastman, Clyde, et al.
Las Cruces: New Mexico State University, Agricultural Experiment Station
Report No. NMAES - 320, 14 pp. ERIC: ED127059.

Patterns of health care in New Mexico were examined to determine whether
income, education, occupation, or socio-economic characteristics were
associated with use of the service. Some findings were: variation in
household use of health care services was not consistently related to
ethnicity, education, occupation, income or age; rural people rated travel
time and distance as their biggest difficulty; and more Spanish Americans
used home remedies and were more inclined to gather their own while Anglos
looked to commercial sources.

94
USE OF EXPENDITURES FOR MEDICAL SERVICES BY RURAL FAMILIES OF ARKANSAS
Charlton, J. L.
Fayetteville: University of Arkansas, Division of Agriculture,
Agricultural Experiment Station, Bulletin 812, November 1976.

This study determines the relationships of costs and use of medical services
to income of the households, to advancement in the family life cycle, and
to the method of financing services. The linkage of income and several
social measures, and the mutual and complementary association of these with
expenditure, were analyzed.

95
VOLUNTARY PARTICIPATION IN HEALTH PLANNING: A STUDY OF HEALTH CONSUMER
AND PROVIDER PARTICIPATION IN COMPREHENSIVE HEALTH PLANNING IN SELECTED
AREAS OF PENNSYLVANIA
Parkum, Kurt H. and Virginia C. Parkum
Harrisburg, Pennsylvania: Pennsylvania Dept. of Health, 1973.

This paper reports on an analysis of a random sample of volunteer participants in three of the six health planning agencies operating in Pennsylvania
at the time the study was done. One item of concern was the extent of
consumer involvement in planning, since Pennsylvania guidelines required
at least 51 percent of the advisory board members to be consumers. In
fact, even 21 percent of the "consumers" had health related professions.
The study also analyzed reasons for participation, the socio-economic
characteristics of voluntary participants, and the history of their
involvement.

CHAPTER 7

MENTAL HEALTH

General Topics

Aftercare   "CURANDERISMO"

Alcoholism   Deinstitutionalization

Clinical Practice   Ethnocultural Factors

Community Involvement   Indigenous Mental Health Workers

Community Mental Health   Natural Helping

Community Psychiatry   Outpatient Services

Consultation and Education   Prevention

Counseling   Social Pathology

Crisis Intervention   Suicide

1
ADOLESCENT SUICIDE AT AN INDIAN RESERVATION
Dizmang, Larry H., et al.
American Journal of Orthopsychiatry, 44(1): 43-49, 1974.

The backgrounds of ten American Indians who committed suicide before the
age of twenty-five are compared statistically with a matched control
group from the same tribe. The contrast is significant in at least six
variables that point to the greater individual and familial disruption
experienced by the suicidal youths. Suggestions for treatment and prevention based on the experiences of this tribe are offered.

2
ALASKA NATIVE REGIONAL CORPORATIONS IN COMMUNITY MENTAL HEALTH
Bloom, J. D. and W. W. Richards
Psychiatric Annals, 4(9): 67-75, 1974.

The native population of Alaska, which is composed of about 55,000
ethnically diverse people, is enumerated and described in this report.
The resources and potential for mental health program development of
several of the regional health corporations are discussed.

3
ALCOHOLISM, ILLNESS, AND SOCIAL PATHOLOGY AMONG AMERICAN INDIANS IN
TRANSITION
Littman, Gerard
American Journal of Public Health, 60(9): 1769-1787, 1970.

Based upon several years' experience at a center for American Indians in
Chicago, the author analyzes the problem of alcoholism and the possibilities of treatment, rehabilitation, and control.

4
AMERICAN INDIAN MYTHS
Locklear, H. H.
Social Work, 17(3): 72-80, 1972.

Discusses the many ways in which Indian myths, customs and attitudes have
been consistently misinterpreted. The author refutes the myths and offers
some suggestions fof constructive change. Attention is also given to how
American Indian centers are helping Indian people in adjusting to urban
life.

5
ANATOMY OF PSYCHIATRIC CONSULTATION TO RURAL INDIANS
Kinzie, J. D., J. H. Shore, and E. M. Pattison
Community Mental Health Journal, 8(3): 196-207, 1972.

This article describes four progressive steps in the development of a community mental health consultation program to an Indian population geographically isolated and with minimal community resources.

6

ANOMIA AND COMMUNICATION BEHAVIOR: THE RELATIONSHIP BETWEEN ANOMIA AND UTILIZATION OF THREE PUBLIC BUREAUCRACIES
March, C. Paul, Robert H. Dolan, and William L. Riddick
Rural Sociology, 32(4): 435-445, 1967.

The research reported here was concerned with the degree of anomia exhibited by individuals and the consequence of anomia for communication behavior. A specific objective was to test the hypothesis: the level of anomia is inversely associated with the utilization of the Employment Security Commission, the Agricultural Extension Service, and area vocational schools.

7

APPALACHIAN PUBLIC HEALTH NURSING: MENTAL HEALTH COMPONENT IN EASTERN KENTUCKY
Looff, D. H.
Community Mental Health Journal, 5(4): 295-303, 1969.

This report describes the Manchester Project and its attendant public health nursing activity as a unique mental health program in Kentucky. By focusing upon the intrinsic mental health component of public health work, the project demonstrates an effective way of meeting community mental health needs in impoverished rural areas.

8

APPALACHIA'S CHILDREN: THE CHALLENGE OF MENTAL HEALTH
Looff, David H.
Lexington, Ky.: The University Press of Kentucky, 1971.

Mental disorders in children and failure of family structure in eastern Kentucky are examined in this book.

9

ASSESSING MENTAL HEALTH NEEDS OF CHILDREN
Lund, D. A. and S. L. Josephson
American Journal of Orthopsychiatry, 45(2): 207-208, 1975.

At the fifty-second annual meeting of the American Orthopsychiatric Association, a 253 item questionnaire designed to assess physical and mental health needs, to identify service utilization patterns, and to identify natural care givers serving children within two rural counties was discussed.

10

A BASIC PHILOSOPHY IN DEVELOPING A RURAL MENTAL HEALTH PROGRAM
Ramage, James W.
Public Welfare, 475-477, Fall, 1971.

The author outlines eight simple rules to govern the philosophy of a comprehensive community mental health center.

11
BEYOND THE CITIES
Witt, J.
Mental Health, Vol. 60, 4-6, Winter 1977.

This article addresses the increased interest in rural mental health care. The Rural Initiative and Health Underserved Rural Areas programs are briefly summarized. Several examples of innovative rural mental health programs are described.

12
THE CHALLENGE IN RURAL MENTAL HEALTH SERVICES
Hollister, W. G.
Keynote presentation of the 1973 Summer Study Program in Rural Mental Health Services.
Madison, Wisconsin: University of Wisconsin, Cooperative Extension Service.

Based on his experiences reported in depth and in detail in his nine-volume series, the author provides a discussion of some of the assumptions and challenges from that project.

13
CITIZEN PARTICIPATION AND INTERAGENCY RELATIONS: ISSUES AND PROGRAM IMPLICATION FOR COMMUNITY MENTAL HEALTH CENTERS
Holton, Wilfred E., Peter Kong-Ming New, and Richard M. Hessler
Boston, Mass.: Tufts University, School of Medicine, December 1971, 192 pp.
NTIS/PB-210 093.

This report is of a study exploring issues related to citizen participation and interagency relations in poverty areas, and methods for improving the utilization of community input.

14
A CLINICAL MODEL FOR RURAL PRACTICE
Nooe, Roger M.
In Social Work in Rural Areas: Preparation and Practice.
Ronald K. Green and Stephen A. Webster, eds.
Knoxville: The University of Tennessee, School of Social Work, 347-360, 1978.

This paper describes a short-term psycho-therapeutic approach which is applicable in rural settings.

15
COLLABORATION FOR COMMUNITY MENTAL HEALTH
Muhlberger, E. V.
Social Work, 20(6): 445-447, 1975.

Implementation of a collaborative approach by a small, new community mental health center in a rural community is reported. Results suggest that collaboration is a more feasible goal than consultation for small centers in both rural and urban settings.

16

COMBINING INDIVIDUAL AND CONJOINT SESSIONS IN MARITAL THERAPY
Kugel, L.
Hospital and Community Psychiatry, 25(12): 795-798, 1974.

The author discusses her approach to seeing troubled marital partners individually and together for a total of three sessions per week over a limited period of time. The approach resulted in improved relationships in most cases.

17

COMMUNITY CHANGE IN RURAL AREAS: IMPLICATIONS FOR MENTAL HEALTH SERVICES
Morris, Lynne Clemmons and Judson Henry Morris, Jr.
In Effective Models for the Delivery of Services in Rural Areas:
Implications for Practice and Social Work Education. Barry L. Locke and Roger A. Lohmann, eds.
Morgantown: West Virginia University, 1978.

The purpose of this paper is the identification of social impacts: particular stresses and conflicts which are accompanying population growth, industrialization, and agribusiness expansion in a small rural community in eastern Oregon.

18

COMMUNITY CONTROL AND THE DETERMINATION OF PROFESSIONAL ROLE IN RURAL MENTAL HEALTH
Mermelstein, Joanne and Paul Sundet
In Human Services in the Rural Environment Reader. David Bast, ed.
Madison: University of Wisconsin-Extension, Center for Social Services, 29-43, 1976-1977.

The central theme of this paper is that professional role in rural community mental health should be determined by the phenomena addressed and not by pre-existing and imposed methodology and/or disciplinary training Emphasis is placed on the dynamic configuration of community as consumer, community control, mental health as enhancement, and professional role as generalist.

19

COMMUNITY HEALTH AND MENTAL HEALTH CARE DELIVERY FOR NORTH AMERICAN INDIANS
New York: MSS Information Corporation, 655 Madison Ave., New York, N.Y. 10021.

Studies dealing with mental health issues in American Indian populations are presented, along with an overview of health services for Indians.

20

COMMUNITY INVOLVEMENT IN THE PLANNING OF A RURAL MENTAL HEALTH CENTER
Jones, M.
In The Community Mental Health Center. A. Beigel and A. Levenson, eds.
New York: Basic Books, 1972.

This article describes the development of the Prairie View Mental Health
Center. The author offers 19 principles and observations about rural
community mental health center planning.

21

COMMUNITY MENTAL HEALTH CENTER ACCESSIBILITY: A SURVEY OF THE RURAL POOR
Lee, Soong H., Daniel T. Gianturco and Carl Eisdorfer
Archives of General Psychiatry, 31(3): 335-339, 1974.

The results of a survey undertaken to evaluate the accessibility of a
community mental health center in a rural poverty area and to identify
barriers to increasing the center's accessibility to the people it
serves are reported. Findings suggest that long-term community education,
indigenous workers, and backup services to local physicians would facilitate mental health service to the community.

22

A COMMUNITY MENTAL HEALTH CENTER PROGRAM TO PROVIDE EMERGENCY INPATIENT
SERVICES IN A RURAL AREA
Nunley, B.
In The Community Mental Health Center. A. Beigel and A. Levenson, eds.
New York: Basic Books, 1972.

Emergency inpatient services are provided to a rural area through arrangements with local hospitals. A case example is used for illustrations.

23

COMMUNITY MENTAL HEALTH CENTER: STRATEGIES AND PROGRAMS
Beigel, Allan and Alan I. Levenson
New York: Basic Books, Inc., 1972.

Problems related to community mental health center planning, organization,
and programming are presented in this collection of papers. The volume
is focused on the practical strategies being used by many community
mental health centers to implement the services mandated by the Community
Mental Health Centers Act. Centers in both rural and urban settings are
discussed.

24

COMMUNITY MENTAL HEALTH CENTERS IN RURAL AREAS: VARIATIONS ON A THEME
Mahoney, S. C. and A. Hodges
Mental Hygiene, 53(3): 484-487, 1969.

This is a conceptual overview of the community mental health center model
in rural settings. The center's theme provides for wide variation to meet
local needs and resources.

25

COMMUNITY MENTAL HEALTH IDEOLOGY--A PROBLEMATIC MODEL FOR RURAL AREAS
Berry, Bonnie and Ann E. Davis
American Journal of Orthopsychiatry, 48(4): 673-679, 1978.

An examination of the realities of rural community mental health services
is provided. It is pointed out that clinics located in rural areas have
problems that are different from those of urban clinics. Problems related
to education and urban-born and trained mental health problems are cited.
The desirability of using indigenous workers is emphasized.

26

COMMUNITY MENTAL HEALTH AND MENTAL HEALTH CARE DELIVERY FOR NORTH
AMERICAN INDIANS, 1974
New York: MSS Information Corporation, 655 Madison Ave., New York, N.Y.
10021.

Studies dealing with mental health issues in American Indian populations
are presented, along with an overview of health services for Indians.

27

COMMUNITY MENTAL HEALTH MOVEMENT SUCCESSES: A RURAL CENTER
Dyck, G. and E. Ediger
In An Assessment of the Community Mental Health Movement. W. E. Bartson and
C. J. Sanborn, eds.
Lexington, Mass.: Lexington Books, 1977.

Describes the development of Prairie View Mental Health Center, its
organizational structure, its financial arrangements, its relationship
with medicine. Prairie View continually examines the limits of its responsibilities as a mental health center and expands them beyond the
traditional boundaries, always involving indigenous support.

28

COMMUNITY MENTAL HEALTH - NEW APPROACHES FOR RURAL AREAS USING
PSYCHIATRIC SOCIAL WORKERS
Guillozet, Noel
Medical Care, 13(1): 59-67, 1975.

The development of accessible and effective mental health services for
rural communities is addressed, and one approach that has met with success
in an isolated community in California is described. Problems in the
development of accessible rural mental health services are considered to
include community perception of need, availability of funds from State
and Federal sources, and feasibility of exploiting traditionally urban-
centered health and social services for rural areas.

29

COMMUNITY MENTAL HEALTH SERVICES IN RURAL AREAS--SOME PRACTICAL ISSUES
Jeffrey, Michael J. and Ronald E. Reeve
Community Mental Health Journal, 14(1): 54-62, 1978.

This study analyzes the special problems, from a systems point of view, faced by new mental health centers in the social and professional structure of rural communities.

30
COMMUNITY PSYCHIATRY: SCOTT COUNTY EVALUATION
Bowden, C. L. and A. E. Reeb
Journal of the Kentucky Medical Association, 106-108, February 1972.

The authors describe the community psychiatry program in Scott County, Kentucky, and the evaluation of this program. Treatment was aimed toward dealing with acute symptoms and role dysfunction, with prompt evaluation and supplementation by consultation and educational services.

31
COMMUNITY PSYCHIATRY - SOME SPECIAL FACTORS IN PROVIDING COMPREHENSIVE MENTAL HEALTH CARE IN THE NONURBAN SETTING
Corney, R. T.
Psychosomatics, 9 (3): 140-144, 1968.

This report presents a plan for initiating comprehensive mental health care in a nonurban setting. Under the aegis of community psychiatry, activities are suggested which conform to a medical model of diagnosis and treatment, and to a public health model with the aim of correcting social and psychological problems of the community.

32
COMMUNITY STRUCTURE AND ACCEPTANCE OF PSYCHIATRIC AID
Raphael, Edna
American Journal of Sociology, 69(4): 340-358, 1964.

Ecological distribution of cases examined at a child guidance clinic is atypical when compared to distribution of indexes of personal and social disorganization. The hypothesis that this distribution is related to diffusion of psychological and psychiatric explanations of conduct is sustained when variation in rates among areas is observed to correspond closely with indicators of community acceptance of psychological and psychiatric explanations.

33
COMPARATIVE EFFECTS OF TWO COUNSELING APPROACHES ON INTENSITY OF DEPRESSION AMONG RURAL WOMEN OF LOW SOCIOECONOMIC STATUS
Padfield, Marianne N.
Journal of Counseling Psychology, Vol. 23, 209-214, May 1976.

Study conducted with women, ages 21-56,(N=24). Women of lowest socio-economic status made the most improvement regardless of treatment model. Income below the poverty level seemed detrimental to level of depression. Concludes that a life supporting income is necessary to maintain good mental health.

34
COMPONENTS AND CORRELATES OF MENTAL WELL-BEING
Beiser, M.
Journal of Health and Social Behavior, 15(4): 320-327, 1974.

This reports on a six year study of 112 rural Canadian residents which
examined the formulation of the process through which psychological well-
being is maintained.

35
CONCEPTS OF PREVENTION IN RURAL MENTAL HEALTH SERVICES
Mazer, M.
Presented at the Summer Study Program on Rural Mental Health Services,
Madison, Wisconsin, 1974.
Madison, Wisconsin: University of Wisconsin Extension, Mental Health
Sciences.

The author presents a discussion of preventive mental health services in
rural areas, such of which is contained in his book, People and Predic-
aments. This includes an extensive discussion of a conceptual basis for
the presentation of psychiatric disorder and the causes of disorder.

36
CONSULTATION AND EDUCATION IN RURAL COMMUNITY MENTAL HEALTH CENTERS
Perlmutter, Felice D.
Community Mental Health Journal, 15(1): 58-68, 1979.

This paper reports on the status of consultation and education in the
rural community mental health center. Programs and their characteristics
are described and compared with nonrural programs.

37
CONSULTATION MODELS IN RURAL MENTAL HEALTH CENTERS
Hunter, W. F.
Presented at the Rural Mental Health Seminar.
Madison: University of Wisconsin, Cooperative Extension Service, 1973.

This presentation is an effort to synthesize the current literature on
various mental health consultation models and to view them from the
perspective of the practitioner in a rural mental health setting.

38
COUNSELING THE INDIAN
Sprang, A.
Journal of American Indian Education, 5(1): 10-15, 1965.

It is the thesis of this paper that a counselor's philosophy of counseling
and use of scientific techniques must undergo some modifications when
counseling Indian students.

39
CRISIS INTERVENTION IN RURAL COMMUNITY DISASTERS
Borgman, Robert D.
Social Casework, 562-567, November 1977.

This article describes the professional response of social workers and
social service agencies in small towns and rural communities to recurrent
natural disasters and mass tragedies.

40
A CRISIS TELEPHONE SERVICE IN A NON-METROPOLITAN AREA
Greene, R. J. and F. G. Mullen
Hospital and Community Psychiatry, 24(2): 94-97, 1973.

The authors discuss the special problems of establishing and operating a
telephone crisis service in a nonmetropolitan area, including a lower
volume of calls, less sophisticated telephone routing equipment, and
greater difficulties with confidentiality.

41
CULTURAL FACTORS IN CASEWORK TREATMENT OF A NAVAJO MENTAL PATIENT
Tyler, I. M. and Sophie Thompson
In Differential Diagnosis and Treatment in Social Work. F. J. Turner, ed.
New York: Macmillan Publishing Co., Inc., 503-511, 1976.

Planning aftercare service for a non-English-speaking Navajo Indian who
has been a long-term mental patient presents the social worker with specific
kinds of problems. The case discussed in this article illustrates the
importance of the worker's understanding the Navajo's language and culture.

42
CULTURE CHANGE, MENTAL HEALTH AND POVERTY
Finney, J. C., ed.
Lexington: University of Kentucky Press, 1969.

A collection of essays from a symposium on ethnopsychology and crosscultural
psychiatry at the University of Kentucky as part of its centennial. The
theme of the conference was the psychosocial aspects of poverty and social
change.

43
CURANDERISMO
Kier, A.
New York: Free Press, 1968.

This book is the result of a study on Mexican-American folk psychiatry in
San Antonio, Texas. It seeks to determine the nature of a folk healer's
sensitivity to the nuances and subtleties of psychopathology among this
group.

44
CURANDEROS: CLINICAL ASPECTS
Martinez, Cervando, Jr.
Journal of Operational Psychiatry, 8(2): 35-38, 1977.

Describes what "curanderos" (healers) do and how they fit into the mental
health system in the Southwest. The author also presents some case
reports of how "curanderos" and "curanderismo" occur in clinical practice.

45
A DECADE IN RURAL PSYCHIATRY
Gurian, H.
Hospital and Community Psychiatry, 22(2): 56-58, 1971.

The author recounts his ten years of experience in rural psychiatry. The
author describes his experience on entry to the rural setting and the
development of professional loneliness. His is one of the few programs
offering psychiatric training in the rural setting.

46
DEINSTITUTIONALIZATION OF MENTAL HEALTH SERVICES IN RURAL AREAS
Bachrach, L. L.
Hospital and Community Psychiatry, 28(9): 669-672, 1977.

While the deinstitutionalization movement in both urban and rural areas has
been plagued by problems, the author feels that they are exaggerated in
rural communities and complicated by such factors as the essentially
urban nature of the deinstitutional model, the unique demographic conditions
of rural America, and the lack of anonymity in rural communities.

47
DELIVERING MENTAL HEALTH SERVICES TO A RURAL INDIAN POPULATION
Taylor, B., et al.
Presented at the 1973 Summer Study Program in Rural Mental Health Services,
Madison: University of Wisconsin, Cooperative Extension Service, 1973.

Alcoholism, depression, and family problems are common among Navajo
Indians living in San Juan County, Utah. The Four Corners Comprehensive
Mental Health Center has developed a mental health delivery system attempting to solve these problems. The staff integrate traditional Navajo ideas
or practices into standard western therapy ideas and programs.

48
DEMOGRAPHIC FACTORS AND RESPONSES TO STRESS AMONG RURAL PEOPLE
Edgerton, J. W., et al.
American Journal of Public Health, 60(6): 1065-1071, 1970.

The authors used the Health Opinion Survey to help assess the demographic
factors and responses of rural populations to stress. Comparing this study
to similar ones conducted in North Carolina and Virginia, emotional disorders were found to be significant with age, race, rural lifestyle,
marital status, education, occupation and income.

49

DEVELOPING A COMMUNITY MENTAL HEALTH CLINIC ON AN INDIAN RESERVATION
Kahn, M.   and J. Delk
International Journal of Social Psychiatry, Vol. 19, 299-306, 1974.

This study describes the development of a psychological services clinic
on a Papago Indian Reservation. It was found that a community consultation
model employing indigenous mental health workers was operationally effective.

50

DEVELOPING A MANAGEMENT INFORMATION SYSTEM IN A RURAL COMMUNITY MENTAL
HEALTH CENTER
Maypole, Donald E.
Administration in Mental Health, 6(1): 69-80, 1978.

This paper describes how one rural community mental health center developed
a management information system and responded to the pressures for accountability from funding bodies and collateral agencies in the community.

51

DEVELOPMENT OF AN AFTERCARE PROGRAM IN A NONMETROPOLITAN AREA
Kantor, L. E., D. F. Kausch, and L. L. Smith
Community Mental Health Journal, 14(1):46-53, 1978.

This article describes the development of a nontraditional aftercare program
set in a predominantly rural area. The planning format as conceived by
representatives of this board is outlined, and the steps involved in oper-
ationalizing specific services and a research program are described.

52

DISTRIBUTION OF MENTAL HEALTH MANPOWER IN FACILITIES IN THE UNITED STATES
WITH RURAL-URBAN COMPARISONS
Tweed, Dan, Mildren Konan, and James W. Longest
College Park: University of Maryland. Agricultural Experiment Station.
June 1978. 83 pp. NTIS/PB-292 940/4ST.

This report examines manpower statistics in relation to six basic factors:
the type of mental health service structure present in the catchment area,
the level of need for mental health services, the level of poverty in the
catchment area, the rural-urban status of the catchment area, and state
and regional location.

53

AN ECONOMICAL RURAL MENTAL HEALTH CONSUMER SATISFACTION EVALUATION
Gilligan, J. F. and R. Wilderman
Community Mental Health Journal, 13(1): 31-36, 1977.

An economical direct and indirect consumer satisfaction evaluation was
conducted in a rural community mental health center. Adjective generation technique scores indicated that consumers felt significantly better
after a psychotherapy session.

54

EFFECTS OF DISTANCE ON USE OF OUTPATIENT SERVICES IN A RURAL MENTAL
HEALTH CENTER
Cohen, J.
Hospital and Community Psychiatry, 23(3): 27-28, 1972.

The effects of distance on the use of outpatient services in a rural mental
health center were investigated. Results indicated that at distances of
30 miles or more from the center, utilization rates for outpatient services
were likely to drop from 50 percent to almost 80 percent.

55

AN EMPIRICAL STUDY OF THE IMPACT OF FEDERALLY FUNDED COMMUNITY MENTAL
HEALTH CENTERS ON STATE MENTAL HOSPITAL UTILIZATION
Scully, Diana and Charles Windle
Rockville, Maryland: National Institute of Mental Health, Report No. NIMH-
73-38. November 1, 1973. 164 pp. NTIS/PB-259 365/5ST.

The purpose of the study was to determine the extent to which the Centers
program was achieving its goal of reducing the use of state mental
hospitals. The results of the study apply mainly to more rural areas.

56

AN EPIDEMIOLOGICAL STUDY OF SUICIDE AND ATTEMPTED SUICIDE AMONG THE
PAPAGO INDIANS
Conrad, Rex D. and M. H. Kahn
American Journal of Psychiatry, 131(1): 69-72, 1974.

An epidemiological study of suicide among the Papago Indians of the desert
Southwest was conducted over a three-year period. Data gathered from
several sources showed that this tribe's suicide rate exceeded that for
the nation but was not as high as rates reported for other tribes. Most
of the suicide victims were young men who had problems with alcohol.
Papagos who lived on the reservation were found to complete suicide less
often than their urban counterparts.

57

THE ETHNO-CULTURAL FACTOR IN MENTAL HEALTH: A LITERATURE REVIEW AND
BIBLIOGRAPHY.
Giordano, Joseph and Grace P. Giordano
New York: Institute on Pluralism and Group Identity of the American
Jewish Committee, 1977.

Excellent review of ethnic factors in the prevalence of mental illness
and cultural barriers in treatment and the utilization of services.
Many of the ideas are transferable to ethnic populations in rural areas.

58

AN EVALUATION OF PSYCHOTHERAPY AT A COMMUNITY MENTAL HEALTH CENTER
Beatty, F. S. and J. M. Beatty
Journal of Psychology, 76(1): 45-55. 1970.

An improvement rate of 63 percent was found among 148 patients undergoing psychotherapy from psychologists and psychiatric social workers at a non-urban community mental health center.

59

EVALUATION OF A RURAL COMMUNITY MENTAL HEALTH PROGRAM
Thomson, C. A. and N. W. Bell
Archives of General Psychiatry, 20(4): 448-456, 1969.

This report considers the advantage of two evaluation approaches used in a developing rural community mental health service with a staff of four. It is concluded that mental illness should be treated locally and that a small rural program with clear goals and accessible services can be very effective.

60

AN EVALUATION STUDY OF A GROUP THERAPY PROCEDURE FOR RESERVATION ADOLESCENT INDIANS
Kahn, M. W., J. Lewis, and R. Galves
Psychotherapy: Theory, Research, and Practice, 11(3): 239-242, 1974.

This study concerns an effort to develop means for mental health intervention with high school Indian youths on the Papago Indian Reservation. The therapeutic techniques outlined in this paper were seen to be effective in reducing delinquent behavior.

61

EXPECTATIONS FOR THE COMPREHENSIVE MENTAL HEALTH CENTER: THE COMMUNITY
Hodges, A. and S. C. Mahoney
Community Mental Health Journal, 6(1): 75-77, 1970.

This report describes the process of developing community support for a comprehensive mental health center in a rural and an urban setting. In his efforts to obtain community commitment, the mental health professional must be aware that idiosyncratic expectations of what the center will accomplish are held by the sponsoring agencies.

62

EXPERIENCES IN RURAL MENTAL HEALTH I: SURVEYS (9 Vols.)
Bentz, W. K., et al.
Chapel Hill: North Carolina University, 1973

This booklet is the first in a series of nine and deals with methods of gathering preliminary information. Basically, this booklet presents information gathering techniques, and applications; reports on findings of the after survey; and discusses sources of information for detecting community needs.

63

EXPERIENCES IN RURAL MENTAL HEALTH III: DEVELOPING CITIZEN PARTICIPATION
Hollister, W., et al.
Chapel Hill: North Carolina University, 1973.

This guide deals with promotion of citizen participation in rural mental health. Describing both program successes and failures, this booklet presents the major communication bridges employed by the mental health programs developed in Vance and Franklin counties.

64
EXPERIENCES IN RURAL MENTAL HEALTH IV: STRENGTHENING EXISTING RESOURCES - HELPING THE HELPERS
Hollister, W. G., et al.
Chapel Hill: North Carolina University, 1973.

This guide deals with strengthening and coordinating the existing services. Divided into three sections, this booklet details the successes and failures of program efforts in Vance and Franklin counties.

65
EXPERIENCES IN RURAL MENTAL HEALTH V: CREATING ALTERNATIVES TO CLINICAL CARE
Hollister, W. G., et al.
Chapel Hill: North Carolina University, 1973.

This booklet deals with the process of creating alternatives to clinical care in Vance and Franklin counties. Included are discussions of a ministerial counseling network, personal enrichment classes, and developing rural mental retardation services.

66
EXPERIENCES IN RURAL MENTAL HEALTH VI: PROGRAMMING SCHOOL MENTAL HEALTH
Hollister, W. G., et al.
Chapel Hill: North Carolina University, 1973.

This guide deals with programming school mental health in Vance and Franklin counties. Detailing both successes and failures, this booklet presents ten program activities.

67
EXPERIENCES IN RURAL MENTAL HEALTH VII: PROMOTING SELF-HELP WITH EDUCATIONAL PROGRAMS
Hollister, W. G., et al.
Chapel Hill: North Carolina University, 1973.

This guide deals with promoting self-help via educational programs in Vance and Franklin counties. Emphasizing both cognitive and affective experiences, this booklet details four program activities.

68
EXPERIENCES IN RURAL MENTAL HEALTH VIII: PROGRAMMING AND ADMINISTRATIVE PROBLEMS
Hollister, W. G., et al.
Chapel Hill: North Carolina University, 1973.

This guide deals with programming and administrative problems in Vance and Franklin counties. Describing those problems believed to be most likely to occur in rural areas, this booklet details five areas.

69
EXPERIENCES IN RURAL MENTAL HEALTH IX: MEASURING AND MONITORING STRESS IN COMMUNITIES
Hollister, William G.
Chapel Hill: North Carolina University, 1973.

Based on a North Carolina feasibility study (1967-73) which focused on development of a pattern for providing comprehensive mental health services to rural people, this guide deals with measuring and monitoring stress in the community.

70
FACTORS CONTRIBUTING TO THE SUCCESSFUL USE OF INDIGENOUS MENTAL HEALTH WORKERS
Herbert, G. K., M. C. Chevaliet, and C. L. Meyers
Hospital and Community Psychiatry, 25(5): 308-310, 1974.

This report presents details of a rural community mental health center in Harlinger, Texas, which uses indigenous mental health workers in a treatment program initiated in 1969.

71
THE FACTORY: SITE FOR COMMUNITY MENTAL HEALTH PRACTICE
Blanco, Antonio and Sheila Akabas
American Journal of Orthopsychiatry, 38(3): 532-552, 1968.

Utilizing a functionally directed approach during factory visits, a community mental health professional succeeded in engaging and treating emotionally ill blue collar patients. The results suggest that flexible approaches may offer new opportunities for establishing contact between mental health professionals and the community. The employees of the factory selected for this study were largely Italian immigrants and Spanish-speaking workers who came originally from Puerto Rico and various Central and South American countries.

72
GOLD AWARD: A RURAL MENTAL HEALTH DELIVERY SYSTEM, FOUR CORNERS COMMUNITY MENTAL HEALTH CENTER - PRICE, UTAH
Hospital and Community Psychiatry, 26(10): 671-674, 1975.

The establishment and first three years of operation of a community mental health service center serving the residents of four sparsely populated rural counties in southeastern Utah are described. The services provided by the Center are summarized and special problems encountered in attempting to provide mental health services to the Native American population are discussed.

73

GROUP PRACTICE APPROACH TO RURAL COMMUNITY MENTAL HEALTH
Guillozet, N.
Western Journal of Medicine, 121(3): 249-253, 1974.

The integration of psychiatric social workers into private medical group
practice in a remote rural community in California is examined as a means
to attain mental health services in communities where isolation and in-
sufficient finances prevent the development of comprehensive mental health
care.

74

GROUP RELATIONS AND THE EXPRESSION OF AGGRESSION AMONG AMERICAN INDIAN
TRIBES
Alderfer, Clayton P., et al.
Phoenix, Arizona: Phoenix Indian Medical Center, 4212 N. 16th St.,
Phoenix, Arizona 85016.

Using an open-systems model of human behavior which attends to intra-
psychic, intragroup and intergroup components of human behavior, the
authors examined American Indian aggression at the dominant white
American society. The classic psychoanalytic formulation of the depres-
sive illness as internalized aggression is expanded to include a syndrome
called "cultural depression." The authors suggest that any work in re-
directing such anger must, to insure the highest probability of success,
simultaneously involve the individual and the group as a whole.

75

A HAZARD TO MENTAL HEALTH: INDIAN BOARDING SCHOOLS
Beiser, Morton
American Journal of Psychiatry, 131(3): 305-306, 1974.

In this editorial the author argues that in spite of volumes of testimony
before congressional committees little or no improvement in the conditions
of Indian boarding schools has taken place. Even when model programs are
successful, they are usually terminated, with the overall system continuing
as it did before.

76

HISPANIC CULTURE AND HEALTH CARE
Martinez, R. A., ed.
St. Louis: C. V. Mosby, 1978.

This book contains a collection of 19 articles dealing with Hispanic
culture as it relates to perception of disease, utilization of folk
practitioners and reaction to the health care delivery system.

77
IMPLEMENTATION AND EVALUATION OF A CLERGY IN-SERVICE TRAINING PROGRAM
IN PERSONAL COUNSELING
Dworkin, E. P.
Journal of Community Psychology, 2(3): 232-237, 1974.

The implementation and evaluation of a clergy in-service training program
in a rural midwestern county are reported. Seventeen clergy, religious
educators, and social workers participated in a series of ten biweekly,
three-hour sessions concerning theory, practice, and application of
counseling skills.

78
INCEST PROJECT
Shultz, LeRoy G.
In Effective Models for the Delivery of Services in Rural Areas:
Implications for Practice and Social Work Education. Barry L. Locke and
Roger A. Lohmann, eds.
Morgantown: West Virginia University, 1978.

This paper deals with the social problem of incest, current attitudes and
values, current approaches to intervention or the lack thereof, and some
recommendations for the future.

79
AN INDIAN CONTROLLED MENTAL HEALTH PROGRAM
Ostendorf, D. and C. A. Hammerschlag
Hospital and Community Psychiatry, 28(9): 682-685, 1977.

In 1971, the Apaches began operating a community mental health center on a
reservation in northeastern Arizona. The authors discuss sociocultural
factors that influenced the centers development and give several reasons
for the center's problems.

80
THE INDIAN HEALTH PROGRAM OF THE U.S. PUBLIC HEALTH SERVICE, 1969.
U.S. Health Services and Mental Health Administration
Washington, D.C.: U.S. Public Heatlh Service, Publication No. 1026.

As reported in this publication, about 410,000 Alaskan Indians, Eskimos,
and Aleuts receive a full range of curative, preventive, and rehabili-
tative health services. In providing these services, geographic and
cultural isolation problems, communication, and religion are encountered.

81
INDIAN SELF-DETERMINATION: A DILEMMA FOR SOCIAL WORK PRACTICE
Brown, E. F.
In Mental Health Services and Social Work Education with Native Americans.
F. J. Pierce, ed.
Norman: University of Oklahoma, School of Social Work, 1977.

The goals of several national policies and social service delivery
systems often conflict with the goal of Indian self-determination.
Schools of social work must train professionals to reflect the perspectives of American Indians with commitment to the self-determination of
Indian communities.

82
THE INDIGENOUS AMERICAN INDIAN MENTAL HEALTH WORKER: EVOLUTION OF A JOB
AND A CONCEPT
Roehl, C. A.
In the Community Mental Health Center. A. Beigel and A. Levenson, eds.
New York: Basic Books, 1972.

The recruitment of an indigenous Indian mental health worker is described.
A native to the area and a person familiar with the subgroup is more
effective in communicating with the people for case finding and in offering direct counseling and advice.

83
INITIATING COMMUNITY CONSULTATION IN RURAL AREAS
Halpern, H. and R. W. Love
Hospital and Community Psychiatry, 22(9): 274-277, 1971.

This article describes the conceptual basis and the development of a satellite clinic and community consultation program in Nebraska. The authors
became "convinced that community mental health concepts can be applied
more usefully in small rural communities than in complex, sprawling
metropolitan areas."

84
INNOVATIVE PROGRAMS IN MENTAL HEALTH
Columbus, Ohio: Ohio Department of Mental Health and Mental
Retardation, 1976, 68 pp. NTIS/HRP-0013131/8ST.

The digest is intended as a report on the progress on Ohio mental health
projects for fiscal year 1976. Each summary states the problem to which
the project is addressed, the goals and objectives of the project, and
briefly, implementation and evaluation methodologies. Rural projects
included rural clergy as mental health associates, volunteers in the rural
community, and mental health outreach in a low-income rural area.

85
IOWA PROGRAM FOR RURAL MENTAL HEALTH PRACTICE
Jacobsen, G. Michael and Cheryl Purgett
In Social Work in Rural Areas: Issues and Opportunities. Joseph Davenport,
III, Judith A. Davenport and James R. Wiebler, eds.
Laramie: University of Wyoming, Department of Social Work, 94-103, 1980.

Discusses a conceptual framework for development of a holistic approach
to mental health services in rural areas and a training program for
rural mental health practice.

86
ISSUES IN THE DELIVERY OF RURAL MENTAL HEALTH SERVICES
Clayton, T.
Hospital and Community Psychiatry, 28(9): 673-676, 1978.

This reports on a rural mental health conference held May, 1977. Reports
on problems encountered in the rural areas including the size of rural
catchment areas, communication difficulties, funding problems, and the
difficulties in obtaining medicare and medicaid coverage.

87
LATINO MENTAL HEALTH: BIBLIOGRAPHY AND ABSTRACTS
Padilla, A. M. and P. Aranda
Rockville, Md.: National Institute of Mental Health, 1974.

A citation and abstract of literature on Latino mental health from
psychological, psychiatric, anthropolitical, sociological, and social work
sources.

88
LATINO MENTAL HEALTH: A REVIEW OF THE LITERATURE
Padilla, A. M. and R. A. Ruiz
Rockville, Md.: National Institute of Mental Health, 1972.

This book contains a review of literature dealing with Latino mental
health. The book is broken down into eight substantive areas while noting
the difficulties of generalizations.

89
THE MENTAL HEALTH CONSULTANT AS SEEN BY HIS CONSULTEES
Eisdorfer, C. and L. Batton
Community Mental Health Journal, 8(2): 171-177, 1972.

In this study, the reactions of a group of public health nurse consultees
to their former consultants has been described and an initial effort made
at proposing a "consultuary" of consultant types. The paper discusses an
attempt to explore the response to mental health consultation by a group
of professionals who have received consultations from ten consultants
during an eleven-year period.

90
MENTAL HEALTH COURSES AS A FACILITATOR FOR CHANGE IN A RURAL COMMUNITY
Naftulen, Donald H., Frank A. Donnelly, and Patricia B. O'Halloran
Community Mental Health Journal, 10(3): 359-365, 1974.

This article presents the findings of a study of a University effort to
assist a rural community in developing a mental health educational program for primary interveners within the community.

91

MENTAL HEALTH FACTORS IN AN INDIAN BOARDING SCHOOL
Krush, Thaddeus and John Bjork
Mental Health, Vol. 49, 94-103, 1969.

The article describes a mental health project at a boarding school in
South Dakota in which efforts were made to elicit factors pertinent to
the mental health of Indian students by a series of cultural, behavioral
and physical studies.

92

MENTAL HEALTH PROGRAM DEVELOPMENTS IN RURAL ALASKA - CHANGING ROLES OF
PUBLIC AND PRIVATE PSYCHIATRISTS
Bloom, J. D. and W. Richards
Alaska Medicine, 18(3): 25-28, 1976.

Improved transportation and communication, plus major state and federal
legislation are aiding the development of the rural mental health program
in Alaska. A shift toward the private sector is apparent in psychiatrists
who are looking for work in rural areas.

93

MENTAL HEALTH AND RURAL AMERICA: AN OVERVIEW AND ANNOTATED BIBLIOGRAPHY
Washington, D.C.: National Institute of Mental Health, U.S. Department
of Health, Education, and Welfare, 1979. 216 pp.

This document constitutes one facet of NIMH's ongoing efforts to address
the mental health problems of rural America. The first section of the
book places the mental health problems and programs of rural areas in
a broad conceptual perspective. The second part consists of an annotated bibliography that is based on an extensive review of the literature
in medicine and psychiatry, psychology, nursing, sociology, and social
work.

94

MENTAL HEALTH OF RURAL AMERICA: THE RURAL PROGRAMS OF THE NATIONAL
INSTITUTE OF MENTAL HEALTH
Segal, Julius, ed.
Washington, D.C.: U.S. Government Printing Office, August 1973.
Order Number 1724-00297.

The problems of supplying mental health services to rural areas in the
U.S. and the involvement of the National Institute of Mental Health
(NIMH) in the solution of these problems are reported. The text is
composed of studies of rural life and mental health which include demographic and epidemiological studies; approaches to service based on
hospital and community resources; a discussion of community mental health
centers in rural U.S.; five case histories of rural mental health centers;
programs for State hospitals with rural patients; and programs for supplying the manpower to meet rural needs.

95
MENTAL HEALTH IN THE RURAL COMMUNITY
Held, Harold M.
In Human Services in the Rural Environment Reader. David Bast, ed.
Madison: University of Wisconsin-Extension, Center for Social Service,
46-58, 1976-1977.

This paper examines factors which tend to retard the entry of a mental
health program in a rural community. Specific strategic steps which
must be taken to facilitate its entry are examined also.

96
MENTAL HEALTH SERVICES FOR AMERICAN INDIANS AND ESKIMOS
Torrey, D. F.
Community Mental Health Journal, 6(6): 455-463, 1970.

Past and present mental health services for American Indians and Eskimos
are surveyed and found to be inadequate. A plan is outlined for the
development of such services based upon a cooperative rather than a
paternalistic venture with these minority groups.

97
MENTAL HEALTH SERVICES TO SPARSELY POPULATED AREAS
Gould, L. H.
Rocky Mountain Medical Journal, 31-36, March 1969.

The development and operation of an innovative mental health system for
a rural Sierra-Nevada community in California are provided in this
article.

98
MENTAL HEALTH AND SOCIAL WORK IN RURAL AREAS
Hargrove, David Scott
In Social Work in Rural Areas: Issues and Opportunities. Joseph
Davenport, III, Judith A. Davenport and James R. Wiebler, eds.
Laramie: University of Wyoming, Department of Social Work, 1980.

This paper is the closing remarks to the fourth national conference on
social work in rural areas. The author discusses the rural mental health
perspective and the challenge of practice in rural areas.

99
MEXICAN AMERICAN INTERACTION WITH SOCIAL SYSTEMS
Sotomayor, Marta
Social Caseowrk, 52(5): 316-322, 1971.

Among other things, this article examines the structure of Mexican-American
families and the sole use of the psychoanalytical model in determining
pathology.

100

MEXICAN AMERICAN MENTAL HEALTH SERVICE UTILIZATION: A CRITICAL EXAMINATION
OF SOME PROPOSED VARIABLES
Barrera, M.
Community Mental Health Journal, 14(1): 34-44, 1978.

Although a number of factors have been proposed to account for the underutilization of mental health services by Mexican-Americans, none of the
factors has been adequately supported by existing research. Variables
associated with the responsiveness and quality of mental health services
are advocated as the most relevant areas for future research.

101

MODERN INDIAN PSYCHOLOGY
Bryde, J. F.
Vermillion, South Dakota: The University of South Dakota, Institute of
Indian Studies, 1971.

Considers many of the cultural factors of Native American life that affect
modern Indian psychology.

102

THE NAVAJO INDIAN: A DESCRIPTIVE STUDY OF THE PSYCHIATRIC POPULATION
Schoenfeld, Lawrence and S. I. Miller
The International Journal of Social Psychiatry, Vol. 19, 31-37,
Spring/Summer, 1973.

This is a descriptive study of 348 new cases coming to the attention of
the Mental Health team serving the Navajo Indian. Tribal affiliation,
sex, marital status, age, type of schooling, religion, referral source,
deposition, and primary diagnosis are presented and discussed.

103

NAVAJO MEDICINE AND PSYCHOANALYSIS
Bergman, Robert L.
Human Behavior, Vol. 2, 8-15, July 1973.

A psychiatrist for the Indian Health Service in Window Rock, Arizona found
that the wisdom of Navajo medicine men who blend healing and worship life
together may point the way for medicine in the future.

104

A NEW TYPE OF MILIEU THERAPY
Nell, R.
Journal of Contemporary Psychotherapy,1(1): 37-42, 1968.

The author describes a type of milieu therapy which works in an isolated
rural home with borderline schizophrenics in an attempt to bring them
back to a state of mental health in which they can live constructively.

105

1975 DIRECTORY OF FEDERALLY FUNDED COMMUNITY MENTAL HEALTH CENTERS
Washington, D.C.: U.S. Government Printing Office, National Institute
of Mental Health, DHEW Publication No. 75-258, 1975.

This is a listing of all community mental health centers in 1975 accompanied by a legislative history of the community mental health center movement.

106
OBSERVATIONS ON SUICIDAL BEHAVIOR AMONG AMERICAN INDIANS
Resnik, H. L. P. and Larry H. Dizmang
American Journal of Psychiatry, 127(7): 882-887, 1971.

The author discusses the sociocultural factors that have provided suicide rates on some Indian reservations that are significantly higher than the national average.

107
AN OPERATIONAL FRAMEWORK FOR WORKING WITH RURAL FAMILIES IN CRISIS
Anderson, D.B.
Journal of Marriage and Family Counseling, 2(2): 145-154, 1976.

This article presents a variation of short-term family crisis treatment adapted to the specific needs of rural families in northern New Hampshire. It is suggested that crisis intervention may be the treatment of choice in a rural setting.

108
AN OUTPUT VALUE ANALYSIS OF A COMPREHENSIVE MENTAL HEALTH SYSTEM
Binner, P. R., et al.
Denver, Colorado: U.S. Department of Health, Education and Welfare.

Aim of this project is to develop a method for measuring the output of a mental health system. With this output measure and some previously developed measures of input and process, a series of studies examining the relationship among these components of a mental health system will be performed.

109
OVERVIEW OF MENTAL HEALTH SERVICES FOR WOMEN IN CRAIG, COLORADO
Angerman, A.
Presented at the Summer Study Program on Rural Mental Health Services, Madison, Wisconsin, 1976.
Madison: University of Wisconsin, Cooperative Extension Service.

In a small, isolated rural town, women, especially those with academic degrees, with the absence of day care services, and with "male chauvinism" so prevalent as a rural value, became scared or depressed. The author started a women's therapy group from referrals which came from welfare and included women of lower socioeconomic classes. The development of this group is described.

110
PERCEPTIONS OF MENTAL ILLNESS AMONG PEOPLE IN A RURAL AREA
Bentz, W. K., J. Edgerton, and M. Kherlopian
Mental Hygiene, 53(3): 457-465, 1969.

A random sample of 1,045 rural North Carolina residents was used to examine their opinions, perceptions, and knowledge of mental illness. Results were compared to data from previously conducted studies in 1950 and 1955.

111
PERSPECTIVES ON THE MENTAL HEALTH OF RURAL BLACKS RELATED TO SOCIAL WORK
EDUCATION
Icard, Larry
Paper presented at the Council on Social Work Education, Annual
Program Meeting. Boston, Massachusetts, March 1979.

This paper attempts to describe selected socio-cultural and socio-structural
conditions evidencing being endemic to rural Blacks. The selected conditions are addressed as being significant for the mental health and
"possible" mental health care needs of this sub-group.

112
PHYSICIANS'S VIEW OF MEDICAL PRACTICE IN NONMETROPOLITAN COMMUNITIES
Bible, Bond L.
Paper prepared for the Southern Agricultural Workers Association.
Richmond, Virginia: February 14-16, 1972, 7 pp. ERIC: ED092290.

The distribution and availability of physicians and other medical professionals for rural areas were studied during 1967. Findings indicated
that (1) a significant relationship exists between size of place where
physician was raised; and (2) particular individual characteristics,
situational factors, best opening when ready to practice, geographic
preference, family, suggestions of friends, nearness of an internship
place, state assistance, and American Medical Association physician's
placement services.

113
PROBLEMS ASSOCIATED WITH THE INTRODUCTION OF A PSYCHIATRIC UNIT INTO A
RURAL GENERAL HOSPITAL
Bloomberg, S.
American Journal of Psychiatry, 130(1): 28-31, 1973.

The establishment of a psychiatric unit in a rural general hospital in
Massachusetts and some of the problems that arose in the first two years
are described.

114
PROBLEMS AND ISSUES IN RURAL COMMUNITY MENTAL HEALTH: A REVIEW
Solomon, Gary
A monograph published by Mental Health Sciences Unit.
Madison: University of Wisconsin Extension.

Rural community mental health is becoming a legitimate area of specialization. A comprehensive review of the literature is presented. Critical
issues and problems are discussed.

115
PROFILE OF THE RURAL COMMUNITY MENTAL HEALTH CENTER
Jones, James D., Morton D. Wagenfeld, and Stanley S. Robin
Community Mental Health Journal, 12(2): 176-181, 1976.

Rural community mental health centers are described and compared with
their counterparts in urban areas.

116
PROGRESS IN COMMUNITY MENTAL HEALTH: VOLUME II
Barten, Harvey H. and Leopold Bellak
New York, N.Y.: Payne Whitney Psychiatric Clinic, 1972.

Key issues in the field of community psychiatry and community mental health
are the focal points of the articles in this volume. The readings explore
ways of meeting the special needs of diverse segments of society, including
the populations of rural areas.

117
PROVIDING LOCAL SERVICES FOR RURAL COUNTIES
Erickson, G. and A. Macht
Hospital and Community Psychiatry, 21(4): 128-129, 1970.

A description of the mental health system in Wisconsin with specific
reference to the development of a plan of care for four counties is
provided. An emphasis on local services and a de-emphasis on state
hospitals is recommended.

118
PSYCHIATRIC CONSULTATION ON TWO INDIAN RESERVATIONS
Robertson, C. G. and M. Baizerman
Hospital and Community Psychiatry, 20(6): 186, 1969.

The authors describe their experiences in developing a psychiatric
service on the Crow and Northern Cheyenne Indian Reservation with a focus
on community education and consultation.

119
PSYCHIATRIC DAY CARE IN A RURAL AREA
Janzen, S. A.
American Journal of Nursing, 73(12): 2216-2217, 1974.

Psychiatric day care provided in a sparsely populated rural area is
reported. The evolution of the program from the initial conceptualization, through program development and cohesion, to its expansion are
detailed.

120
PSYCHIATRIC IMPAIRMENT IN RURAL COMMUNITIES
Neff, James Allen and Robert H. Stone
Journal of Community Psychology, 7(2): 137-146, 1979.

This household survey of 713 adults in nine rural middle Tennessee counties
found the prevalence of psychiatric impairment to be highest among females,
the divorced, widowed, or separated, and those in the lower socioeconomic
strata.

121
PSYCHIATRIC AND MEDICAL PROBLEMS IN RURAL COMMUNITIES
Neff, James Alan, Begar A. Husaini and James McCorkel
In Social Work in Rural Areas: Issues and Opportunities.
Joseph Davenport, III, Judith A. Davenport and James R. Wiebler, eds.
Laramie: University of Wyoming, Department of Social Work, 103-110, 1980.

In this paper the authors report that chronic physical ailments and
psychiatric impairment are often found in the same person in rural areas.
They conclude that health and mental health manpower should diagnose and
treat the person in a coordinated manner.

122
PSYCHIATRIC RESIDENTS PROVIDE EXTRA MANPOWER FOR RURAL COMMUNITY AGENCIES
Withersty, David J.
Hospital and Community Psychiatry, 26(5): 270-271, 1975.

The author describes his experience as a psychiatric resident at the
West Virginia University Medical Center in providing manpower for rural
community agencies. Activities such as psychiatric evaluations, medi-
cation checks, psychotherapy cases, teaching, and consultation were
performed.

123
PSYCHIATRIST BY TELEPHONE PROVES SUCCESSFUL: "THIS IS YOUR THERAPIST
CALLING"
Medical World News, 11(15): 30, 1970.

Therapy by telephone may be an acceptable alternative for patients who
cannot participate in an adequate follow-up program after having been
discharged from an institution.

124
PSYCHIATRY IN A SMALL TOWN
Pentlarge, V. H.
Massachusetts Journal of Mental Health, 5(2): 14-17, 1975.

The role of the psychiatrist in a small town or rural area is examined.
Comparisons are made between rural and urban practices.

125

PSYCHOTHERAPEUTIC AGENTS: NEW ROLES FOR NON-PROFESSIONALS, PARENTS, AND
TEACHERS
Guerney, B. G., ed.
New York: Holt, Rinehart, and Winston, 1969.

This collection of readings focuses on a strategy of using nonprofessionals
for meeting mental health needs. Such a strategy is particularly useful
in rural areas where mental health professionals are frequently too few
in number.

126

RACE AND MENTAL ILLNESS: AN EPIDEMIOLOGICAL UPDATE
Warheit, G. J., C. E. Holzer and S. A. Arey
Journal of Health and Social Behavior, 16(3): 243-257, 1975.

This paper presents findings on the relationship between race and mental
health extracted from a five-year epidemiologic study conducted in southeastern United States. Mental health scores on five psychiatric scales
are compared for blacks and whites. The authors conclude that there is
no evidence that race alone is a primary etiologic factor in accounting
for differences in the rates of mental illness between blacks and whites.

127

REALITY THERAPY AS APPLIED TO FLOOD COUNSELING IN A RURAL APPALACHIAN
SETTING
Kelly, John S.
In Effective Models for the Delivery of Services in Rural Areas:
Implications for Practice and Social Work Education. Barry L. Locke and
Roger A. Lohmann, eds.
Morgantown: West Virginia University, 1978.

This paper explores the practices of reality therapy in short term
counseling with flood victims and is based on experience with People
Reaching Out Program, a service of Logan-Minto Area Mental Health, Inc.,
Williamson, West Virginia.

128

RELATIVES' PERCEPTIONS OF RURAL AND URBAN DAY CARE CENTER PATIENTS
Michaux, Mary H., et al.
Psychiatry, 36(2): 203-212, 1973.

The authors found that tolerance of deviant behavior tends to be higher in
rural than urban areas. This finding may have implications for hospitalization or community treatment programming, depending on residence of the
psychiatric client.

129
RESEARCH IN A COMMUNITY MENTAL HEALTH CENTER: A FRAMEWORK FOR ACTION
Hinkle, J. E., C. W. Cole, and E. R. Oetting
Community Mental Health Journal, 4(2): 129-133, 1968.

Research and evaluation are a central part of the program of the Southwest
Wyoming Mental Health Center. Benefits include refined programming,
increased staff effectiveness, and improved feedback to the community.

130
RESEARCH DIRECTIONS FOR RURAL MENTAL HEALTH
Cedar, Toby and John Salasin
In collaboration with the National Institute of Mental Health, July 1979.
McLean, Virginia: The MITRE Corporation, Metrek Division.

This paper identifies research and development efforts that could contribute
solutions to some problems in delivering mental health services in rural
areas. This work is part of ongoing collaborative research between the
MITRE Corporation and the National Institute of Mental Health. This
research is focused on developing approaches to improve the management
of research and development programs.

131
RESIDENCE, SOCIAL CLASS, AND SCHIZOPHRENIA
Eaton, W. W.
Journal of Health and Social Behavior, 15(4): 289-299, 1974.

Rates of first hospitalization for schizophrenia in rural, suburban, and
urban areas of Maryland are presented. The hypothesis that social class
interacts with area of residence in affecting rates of schizophrenia is
tested.

132
THE ROLE OF MENTAL HEALTH PROGRAMS IN RURAL AREAS
Fink, Richard L.
In Social Work in Rural Areas: Preparation and Practice. Steven Webster
and Ronald Green, eds.
Knoxville: The University of Tennessee, School of Social Work,
328-340, 1978.

The author appraises the community mental health movement, critiques that
part of the movement in rural areas, and provides some guidelines for a
model redefining and relating rural mental health needs to design and
implementation of programs.

133
ROOTS OF FUTILITY
Polansky, N. A., R. D. Borgman, and C. Desaix
San Francisco, California: Josey Bass, 1972.

In a study of the apathy and sense of hopefulness that immobilize mothers and children in some Appalachian regions, families in rural Georgia and North Carolina were interviewed.

134
RURAL COMMUNITY MENTAL HEALTH CENTER USES DECISION MAKING MODEL
Gibson, K. D.
Evaluation, 3(1-2): 27-28, 1976.

A decision theoretic model used in planning and evaluating research and programs at a national level has been successfully used as a decision making model by a rural community mental health center. Benefits of this program are enumerated.

135
RURAL FAMILY COUNSELING
Veverka, J. F. and J. Goldman
Journal of the Iowa Medical Society, 63(8): 395-398, 1973.

A feasibility study of family counseling in a rural setting was made. It is concluded that rural people will accept and use counseling services, especially if they are provided in their own community.

136
RURAL MENTAL HEALTH CENTERS--ARE THEY DIFFERENT?
Jones, James D., Stanley S. Robin, and Morton Wagenfeld
International Journal of Mental Health, 3(2-3): 77-92, 1974.

Data from a national study of community mental health centers were used to study the extent to which rural community mental health centers are inclined toward involvement and outreach, staff perspectives of the rural centers, and the extent to which staff of the rural centers are committed to the ideology of community mental health.

137
RURAL MENTAL HEALTH DELIVERY SYSTEM: FOUR CORNERS COMMUNITY MENTAL HEALTH CENTER - PRICE, UTAH
Hospital and Community Psychiatry, 26(10): 671-674, 1975.

The establishment and first three years of operation of a community mental health center serving the residents of four sparsely populated rural counties in Utah are described. The Center serves persons living in small towns or on isolated farms, ranches, or Indian reservations through central offices and satellite centers. The services provided by the Center are summarized, and special problems encountered in attempting to provide mental health services to the Native American population are discussed.

138
RURAL MODELS
Huessy, H. R.
In Progress in Community Mental Health. H. Barton and L. Bellak, eds.
New York: Grune and Stratton, 1972.

This is an extensive review of rural mental health problems and approaches
to their solutions. Included is a discussion of the distinguished characteristics of rural mental health problems and the advantages of the
rural area.

139
THE RURAL POOR AND MENTAL HEALTH
Cowan, Sylvia Cavalier
In Human Services in the Rural Environment, 1(2): 9, 1979.

The author describes the problem of the rural poor and mental health,
discusses the federal government involvement, and offers recommendations
for rural mental health service delivery.

140
RURAL PROGRAM DEVELOPMENT
Tranel, N.
In The Practice of Community Mental Health. H. Grunebaum, ed.
Boston: Little, Brown, 1970.

The author presents a model for the provision of mental health services
to rural areas especially applicable to the Rocky Mountain West based on
development and operation of a mental health center program in northern
Wyoming.

141
RURAL SETTINGS: A NEW FRONTIER IN MENTAL HEALTH
Bischoff, H. G. W.
Presented at Summer Study Program on Rural Mental Health Services.
Madison, Wisconsin, 1976.
Madison: University of Wisconsin, Cooperative Extension Service.

This paper describes four relationships that the mental health professional
must attend to in the transition from urban to rural practice.

142
RURAL SOCIAL PROBLEMS, HUMAN SERVICES, AND SOCIAL POLICIES. WORKING
PAPER 10: MENTAL HEALTH AND MENTAL RETARDATION
Derr, Janet Morton
Denver: University of Colorado, Center for Social Research and
Development, September 1973. NTIS/HRP-0007591/1ST.

Findings of a literature review with regard to mental health and mental
retardation in rural communities are presented. Lack of community
resources, physical and social isolation, and individual poverty combine

to create obstacles to solving mental health problems as well as conditions which increase the probability that these problems will exist. Pilot projects in rural mental health are noted.

143
SATELLITE HALFWAY HOUSES IN VERMONT
Huessy, H. R.
Hospital and Community Psychiatry, 20(5): 147-149, 1969.

The author provides a detailed description of Spring Lake Ranch, Vermont's first halfway house located in a rural community. The author feels that many kinds of halfway houses to meet the needs of many kinds of guests are needed and are better provided through private enterprise.

144
SCREENING EMOTIONALLY DISTURBED CHILDREN IN A RURAL SETTING
Schultz, Edward W., A. B. Manton, J. A. Salvia
Exceptional Children, 39(2): 134-137, 1972.

This study was undertaken to ascertain the efficacy of screening procedures in a two-county rural area in east central Illinois.

145
SELF IMAGE OF THE AMERICAN INDIAN: A PRELIMINARY STUDY
Bromberg, Walter and Sarah H. Hutchinson
The International Journal of Social Psychiatry, Vol. 20, 39-44.
Spring/Summer, 1974.

By studying native drawings, the authors found clues to the self-image and psychology of the American Indian.

146
THE SERVICE GUIDE
Hollister, William G.
American Journal of Public Health, 60(3): 428-429, 1970.

This editorial describes a "guide to service" for the non-professional mental health assistant serving rural areas. Obstacles to patient care in rural areas are described and the training of service workers to provide services are presented.

147
SOCIAL FORCES IN RURAL COMMUNITIES OF SPARSELY POPULATED AREAS--FINDINGS AND RECOMMENDATIONS GROWING OUT OF A MENTAL HEALTH STUDY
Kraenzel, C. F. and F. H. MacDonald
Rural Sociology, 37(2): 272-280, 1972.

Kraenzel's and MacDonald's bulletin concerned with the findings and recommendations growing out of a mental health study was reviewed. Included is a discussion of a lack of opportunities for males to develop self-acceptable roles and statuses with particular reference to sparsely populated communities.

148

SOCIAL SCIENCE RESEARCH ON RURAL HEALTH CARE DELIVERY: A COMPILATION OF
RECENT AND ONGOING STUDIES
Cordes, Sam M.
University Park: Pennsylvania State University, Pennsylvania Agricultural
Experiment Station, Rept. No. AE&RS 131, August 1977, 60 pp.   ERIC: ED153777.

Summaries of 89 studies on rural health care (underway or recently completed)
in the U.S. as of December 1976 are reported.

149

THE SOCIAL WORKER IN THE RURAL COMMUNITY MENTAL HEALTH CENTER
Wagenfeld, Morton O. and Stanley S. Robin
In Social Work in Rural Communities. Leon H. Ginsberg, ed.
New York: Council on Social Work, 69-83, 1976.

The themes in this paper include: rural mental health and social problems,
characteristics of rural community mental health centers (CMHCs), characteristics of social workers, social workers as community mental health workers,
and social workers in rural CMHCs.

150

SOME FOLK BELIEFS ABOUT MENTAL ILLNESS: A RECONSIDERATION
Karno, M. and R. B. Edgerton
International Journal of Social Psychiatry, 20(3/4): 292-296, 1974.

The responses to a survey done in east Los Angeles on folk beliefs are
summarized. Findings indicate that Mexican-Americans and those Anglo-
Americans who are of rural and small town background are more likely than
urban Anglo-Americans to identify the symptoms of depression as representing illness, and are more likely to believe the heritability of mental
illness.

151

SOME THOUGHTS ON THE FORMATION OF PERSONALITY DISORDER: STUDY OF AN
INDIAN BOARDING SCHOOL POPULATION
Krush, Thaddeus P., et al.
American Journal of Psychiatry, Vol. 122, 868-876, February 1966.

The authors contend that Indian boarding schools promote "psycho-social
nomadism" and shifting value systems which lead to confusion and disorganization of the Indian child's personality.

152

STAFFING
Levenson, A. I.
In The Practice of Community Mental Health. H. Grunebaum, ed.
Boston: Little, Brown, 1970.

This is an extensive discussion of staffing patterns and guidelines emana-
ting from the basic concepts and philosophy of the community mental health

center program. Because comprehensive care must be provided, the staff
of a community mental health center must possess a wide variety of skills
and consequently be drawn from a number of different professional
disciplines.

153
STRUCTURAL AND PROFESSIONAL CORRELATES OF IDEOLOGIES OF COMMUNITY MENTAL
HEALTH WORKERS
Wagenfeld, M. O., S. S. Robin, and J. D. Jones
Journal of Health and Social Behavior, Vol. 15, 199-210, 1974.

An examination of community mental health ideological variations among
staff from a nationwide sample of mental health centers, their perceptions
of their organization's position on a social service/medical continuum,
and the relationship between ideology and organizational structures indicated highest ideological adherence within rural areas under agency/
board structures, among social workers and psychologists, and among those
closer to social than medical services.

154
A STUDY OF PERSONALITY ASSETS IN A RURAL COMMUNITY
Beiser, M.
Archives of General Psychiatry, 24(3): 244-254, 1971.

This study was conducted on the adult population in a rural county in
maritime Canada to (a) identify personality attributes considered personal
assets, and (b) to determine the relevance of these attitudes to positive
mental health and psychiatric disorder.

155
STUDY PROGRAM ON RURAL MENTAL HEALTH SERVICES, MADISON, WISCONSIN, 1976
Madison: University of Wisconsin, Community Extension Service.

The rural community mental health direct service provider must be an expert
in human relations. This monograph concentrates on the subject of human
relations training, which deals with the development and enhancement of
therapeutic or counseling skills.

156
SUICIDE AMONG THE AMERICAN INDIANS: TWO WORKSHOPS. 1969
Washington, D.C.: U.S. Government Printing Office. Report No. PHSP-1903.
41 pp. (50¢) ERIC: ED054907.

Health problems among the American Indians have been of major concern to
the U.S. Public Health Service for some time. The long history of social
and cultural turmoil that has confronted the American Indian has created
unique problems, and one of the outcomes is an increase in suicide and
other self-destructive behavior.

157
SUICIDE PREVENTION IN A RURAL AREA
Thomsen, C. P.
Bulletin of Suicidology, 49-52, July 1968.

This article describes the Davis Suicide Prevention Answering Service, a
spontaneously generated, self-sustaining, completely voluntary community
service. It is hoped that this service may serve as a model for other
small communities.

158
SUPERVISION AND CONSULTATION IN RURAL MENTAL HEALTH PRACTICE
Munson, Carlton E.
In Social Work in Rural Areas: Issues and Opportunities. Joseph Davenport,
III, Judith A. Davenport and James R. Wiebler, eds.
Laramie: The University of Wyoming, Department of Social Work, 1980.

The major thesis of this paper is that conceptualization of rural practice
cannot be effectively accomplished in comparison or contrast to urban
practice. The arenas of supervision and consultation are discussed to
begin to document rural practice.

159
SURVEY OF RURAL COMMUNITY MENTAL HEALTH NEEDS AND RESOURCES
Gertz, Boris, Jill Meider, and Margaret L. Pluckhan
Hospital and Community Psychiatry, 26(12): 816-819, 1975.

Results are reported of a survey of 215 rural mental health services across
the country to identify the problems and needs of mental health practitioners in rural areas. Ninety-two responses (42%) were received. The
major problem in delivery of services to rural communities was identified
as a lack of adequate resources. Other problems involved geography,
distance, and entry of the mental health system into the community.

160
SUSANVILLE: A COMMUNITY HELPS ITSELF IN MOBILIZATION OF COMMUNITY
RESOURCES FOR SELF-HELP IN MENTAL HEALTH
Beier, Ernst, Peter Robinson, and Gino Micheletti
Journal of Consulting and Clerical Psychology, 36(1): 142-150, 1971.

Adult lay members and high school students were trained to work with
families selected for having problem children in schools or being under
stress. Evaluation of project and community-wide measures applicable for
future efforts are discussed.

161
TACTICS AND TARGETS IN THE RURAL SETTING
Huessy, H.R.
In The Handbook of Community Mental Health. S. E. Golann and C. Eisdorfer,
eds.
Englewood Cliffs, New Jersey: Prentice-Hall, 1972.

In this extensive review of rural mental health, the author addresses the
differences between urban rural settings, the history of rural mental
health care, and the tremendous diversity present in the rural setting.

162
THE THERAPIST IN THE COMMUNITY
Mazer, M.
In The Practice of Community Mental Health. H. Grunebaum, ed.
Boston: Little, Brown, 1970.

This article presents information largely contained in the book by the same
author. This is a balanced and complete description of the problems and
advantages of being a psychiatrist or a psychotherapist in the rural setting.

163
TOWARD A CONCEPTUALIZATION OF NATURAL HELPING
Patterson, Shirley L.
ARETE, 4(3): 161-173, 1977.

This research study demonstrates that informal, unorganized networks exist
in small towns and rural communities. These networks cannot be duplicated;
they should be nurtured and extended, rather than supplanted by professional
practice.

164
TOWARD AN UNDERSTANDING OF THE MENTAL HEALTH AND SUBSTANCE ABUSE ISSUES OF
RURAL AND MIGRANT ETHNIC MINORITIES: A SEARCH FOR COMMON EXPERIENCES
Ryan, Robert A. and Joseph E. Trimble
Paper prepared for the National Conference on Minority Group Alcohol,
Drug Abuse and Mental Health Issues. Denver, Colorado, May 22, 1978, 28 pp.

The type and extent of substance abuse varies among ethnic groups but is
increasing for the rural and ethnic minorities as it is for their urban
counterparts. It is possible to gain a partial understanding of the
likely problems by reviewing studies of the ethnic minorities rural to
urban migration and the coping patterns of rural and migrant communities.

165
TRAINING HELPERS IN RURAL MENTAL HEALTH DELIVERY
Kelley, Verne R., et al.
Social Work, 22(3): 229-232, 1977.

Two training programs in rural Iowa demonstrated that community helpers
can be trained to function effectively in rural mental health service
delivery. These programs are described in this article.

166
TRANSITION FROM URBAN TO RURAL MENTAL HEALTH PRACTICE
Riggs, R. T. and L. F. Kugel
Social Casework, 57(9): 562-567, 1976.

The process of adjustment to the transition from urban to rural mental
health practice includes identifiable stages: euphoria, depression, and
adaptation. The authors report their experiences and those of their staff
in making this transition.

167
USING T-GROUPS TO TRAIN AMERICAN INDIANS AS PHYSICIAN ASSISTANTS
Hammerschlag, C. A.
Hospital and Community Psychiatry, 25(4): 210-211, 1974.

The author describes using a T-group as part of a two-year training program for American Indians who will become physician assistants. This was intended to be a learning experience in group dynamics, leadership, and interpersonal relations that could be used in later work settings.

CHAPTER 8

CHILDREN AND YOUTH

General Topics

Adolescent Suicide	Early Childhood Development
Adoption	Education
Child Abuse/Neglect	Foster Care
Child Protection	Juvenile Delinquency/Juvenile Justice
Day Care	Migrant Children
Drug Abuse	Sexuality

1

ADJUSTMENT TO MODERN SOCIETY BY YOUTHS FROM RURAL AREAS: A LONGITUDINAL
ANALYSIS, 1965-1971
Geurin, Virginia, et al.
Fayetteville: University of Arkansas, Agricultural Experiment Station
Bulletin 280, April 1977.

This report describes the occupational adjustment of a group of Arkansas
males who left a rural area for employment in an urban, technologically
oriented society. Poor correspondence between occupational aspirations
and occupational treatment was found.

2

ADOLESCENT SUICIDE AT AN INDIAN RESERVATION
Dizmang, Larry H., et al.
American Journal of Orthopsychiatry, 44(1): 43-49, 1974.

The backgrounds of ten American Indians who committed suicide before the
age of twenty-five are compared statistically with a matched control
group from the same tribe. The contrast is significant in at least six
variables that point to the greater individual and familial disruption
experienced by the suicidal youths. Suggestions for treatment and prevention based on the experiences of this tribe are offered.

3

ADOPTIVE PLACEMENT OF AMERICAN INDIAN CHILDREN WITH NON-INDIAN FAMILIES -
PART II
Davis, Mary
Child Welfare, 40(6): 12-15, 1961.

The article reports on the role of an adoption agency in a demonstration
project. Also presented are the agency's impressions of the Indian child
and his adaptability as well as some evaluative factors involved in the
selection of adoptive families for Indian children.

4

ADVOCACY FOR THE ABUSED RURAL CHILD
Leistyna, Joseph
Children Today, 7(3): 26+, 1978.

The author discusses his experience as an only practicing pediatrician in
a Virginia county. He underscores the need to direct attention to a
rural children and their distressed families.

5

AFFECT STRUCTURE AND ACHIEVEMENT IN A SELECT SAMPLE OF RURAL NEGRO CHILDREN
Powell, Evan R. and William F. Whyte
The Journal of Negro Education, 41(1): 53-56, 1972.

This study examines cognitive and affective relationships among a select sample of rural black children who were economically deprived.

6

AGE OF TRANSITION, RURAL YOUTH IN A CHANGING SOCIETY
Johnson, Helen W.
Washington, D.C.: U.S. Dept. of Agriculture, Report No. USDA-AGR-HB-347, October 1967, 96 pp. ERIC: ED013696.

Extensive comparisons of rural and urban youth are graphically and verbally presented in the following areas in this booklet: 1) the world we live in, 2) preparing for life, 3) making a living, 4) health and welfare, 5) the quality of rural life, and 6) the world of tomorrow.

7

AMERICAN INDIAN AND ANGLO CONSIDERATIONS FOR EARLY CHILDHOOD DEVELOPMENT
Milner, John G.
Paper presented at the All-Indian Foster Parent Conference held in Phoenix, Arizona, March 29, 1977.

Differences between American Indian and Anglo early childhood development are discussed. In addition, the author points out how one-sided trans-acculturation between Indians and Anglos has been.

8

AMERICAN INDIANS AND WELFARE: THE PROBLEM OF CHILD ADOPTION
Byler, W., S. Deloria and Alan Gurwitt
Current, Vol. 158, 30-37, 1974.

Discusses the problems and policies pertaining to the removal of Indian children from their homes for placement in adoptive or foster homes.

9

ANALYSIS OF COGNITIVE ABILITY IN RURAL WHITE CULTURALLY DIFFERENT CHILDREN
Vance, Hubert B. and Norman Hankins
The Journal of Psychology, 98(1): 15-21, 1978.

The functional and operational intellectual capacity of rural mountain culturally different white children was examined in this study.

10

APPALACHIA'S CHILDREN: THE CHALLENGE OF MENTAL HEALTH
Looff, David H.
Lexington: The University of Kentucky Press, 1971.

Mental disorders in children and failure of family structure in eastern Kentucky are examined in this book.

11
AN APPROACH TO MATERNAL AND CHILD HEALTH SERVICES IN A RURAL SETTING
Millington, Marie
In 2nd Annual Northern Wisconsin Symposium on Human Services in the
Rural Environment Reader. David Bast and Julie Schmidt, eds.
Madison: University of Wisconsin-Extension, Center for Social Science,
90-94, 1977.

A successful pilot project in the development of maternal and child health
services in Wisconsin Rapids, Wisconsin is described. The effort was
initiated through group prenatal education for prospective parents.

12
ASPIRATIONS AND CAPABILITIES OF RURAL YOUTH
Jordan, Max F., J. F. Golden, and L. D. Bender
Fayetteville: University of Arkansas, Agriculture Experiment Station,
Bulletin 722, May 1967.

This study determined the aspirations and capabilities of rural youth in
selected low-income counties in Arkansas. The study also related aspirations and capabilities to personal background and youth occupational plans
to present and projected labor market requirements.

13
ASSESSING THE COSTS OF FOSTER FAMILY CARE IN RURAL AREAS: MYTHS AND
REALITIES
Settles, Barabara, et al.
Revision of paper presented at the Annual Meeting of the Rural Sociological
Society, New York, New York, August 1976, 30 pp. ERIC: ED1542562.

This study examined the history and connection of foster care to rural
areas in the U.S., the current situation for foster care in rural America,
and the adaptations necessary to use current data in estimating the costs
of foster care in rural areas.

14
CAREER DESIDERATA OF RURAL YOUTH AND THE STRUCTURING OF AMBITION: A
COMPARATIVE PERSPECTIVE
Schwarzweller, Harry K.
International Journal of Comparative Sociology, 19(3-4): 185-202, 1978.

This paper reports and discusses findings from a study that explores the
patterning of occupational career desiderata among rural youth in Norway
and the United States.

15
CHILD ABUSE IN A RURAL SETTING
Lloyd-Still, J. C. and B. Martin
Pennsylvania Medicine, 79(3); 56-60, 1976.

Data from the Milton S. Hershey Medical Center concerning child abuse and
neglect in a semirural area of central Pennsylvania are presented and

summarized. Findings reveal many similarities to the experience in other parts of the country in relation to the death rate, rate of mobility, psychiatric problems, incidence of other physical disorders, and history of drug ingestion.

16
CHILD NEGLECT IN A RURAL COMMUNITY
Polansky, Norman A., et al.
Social Casework, 49(8): 467-474, 1968.

This article is a report of a pilot study of mothers in rural Southern Appalachia.

17
CHILD PROTECTION IN A RURAL SETTING
Shepard, Georgianna
In 2nd Annual Northern Wisconsin Symposium on Human Services in the Rural Environment Reader. David Bast and Julie Schmidt, eds.
Madison: University of Wisconsin-Extension, Center for Social Science, 21-26, 1977.

This paper deals with the protection of children, with emphasis upon how the rural context affects the development of a delivery system.

18
CHILDREN OF CRISIS: A STUDY OF COURAGE AND FEAR
Coles, Robert
Boston: Little Brown, 1969.

Working in towns and rural areas of the South, the author examines the problems of negro black and white youth by eliciting intimate histories through personal interviews.

19
CHILDREN AND FARM LABOR
Stockburger, Cassandra
New Generation, 54(3): 12-18, 1972.

The author reviews the history of child farm labor and the development of legal protection for them.

20
COMMUNITY PLANNED PROGRAMS FOR CHILDREN: DO THEY WORK?
Liston, Jennie S. and Andrew H. Van de Ven
A report on Implementation of Demonstration Projects of the Texas Department of Community Affairs, Early Childhood Development Division.
Austin: Texas State Department of Community Affairs, December 1976, 112 pp.

This report describes and evaluates 14 early childhood development demonstration projects which were funded by the Texas Department of Community Affairs but planned and implemented in primarily rural areas.

21
COMMUNITY SERVICES FOR CHILDREN OF MIGRANT FARM WORKERS: A STATUS REPORT
Stockburger, Cassandra
New York, N.Y.:   Ford Foundation, September 1978.   ERIC: ED153750.

This report indicates that although community services for migrant children
have increased over the past 15 years, the status of these services is
questionable.   For instance, services are restricted to special federal
or state legislation, they are fragmented, no real delivery system exists,
and eligibility and definitions of clients create confusion and duplication
of services.   The report concludes that in order to effectively intervene
in the needs of migrant children, basic issues relating to development
and delivery of community services must be addressed.

22
CONFLICTS BETWEEN GENERATIONS MAY BE REASONS FOR JUVENILE DELINQUENCY
Pickett, Elizabeth
Navajo Times, A-2 to A-9, March 22, 1979.

Discusses problems of alienation of Indian generations and how this contributes to juvenile delinquency.

23
CREATIVITY IN RURAL, URBAN, AND INDIAN CHILDREN
Williams, John D., Johanna Teubner, and Steven D. Harlow
The Journal of Psychology, Vol. 83, 111-116, 1973.

"Torrance Tests for Creative Thinking" were administered to test the verbal
and figural creativity of five groups: urban-middle income, urban-lower
income, rural children, Indian-lower income children, and Indian-impoverished children.

24
CREATIVE RESTITUTIONS: AN INNOVATIVE MODEL FOR USE IN RURAL AREAS
Gandy, John R.
In Effective Models for the Delivery of Services in Rural Areas:
Implications for Practice and Social Work Education.   Barry L. Locke and
Roger A. Lohmann, eds.
Morgantown: West Virginia University, 1978.

The social worker involved in the criminal justice system in rural areas
has a preexisting orientation in the community which would be supportive
and conducive to creative restitution.   A brief discussion of restitution
in general is presented, followed by a presentation of creative restitution.

25
CRIMINAL JUSTICE IN RURAL AMERICA
Schultz, LeRoy G.
Social Casework, 51(3): 151-156, 1970.

The author discusses the crime and justice problem of rural America and
reviews alternatives for confronting these problems.

26

A CRITIQUE OF SELECTED NON-JUDICIAL TREATMENT ALTERNATIVES FOR
JUVENILE OFFENDERS
Yegidis, Bonnie L.
In Effective Models for the Delivery of Services in Rural Areas:
Implications for Practice and Social Work Education. Barry L. Locke and
Roger A. Lohmann, eds.
Morgantown: West Virginia University, 1978.

This paper presents a synthesis and critique of the juvenile treatment
programs that seem to hold some promise of success, as documented by preliminary evaluation, and will attempt to define roles and implications
for social work practice.

27

A CULTURAL NETWORK MODEL: PERSPECTIVES FROM AN URBAN-AMERICAN INDIAN
YOUTH PROJECT
Red Horse, John and Yvonne Red Horse
Tempe, Arizona: Arizona State University, School of Social Work.

This article discusses a program designed to overcome dissonance between
an American Indian community and Educational Social Services. The
article proceeds with discussions on conceptual information relevant to
American Indian family structure and cultural pattern maintenance, life
circumstances of Indian adolescent girls that interfere with mainstream
concepts of educational and helping processes, and a staging process
inherent to an innovative cultural network model designed to bridge the
gap between two worlds.

28

CURRICULUM DEVELOPMENT AND TRAINING IN THE MANAGEMENT OF RURAL YOUTH CARE
SERVICES.
St. Paul: University of Minnesota, Center for Youth Development and
Research, 1976, 40 pp. NTIS/SHR-0002828.

The ultimate goal of the project was to enhance the quality of rural
youth care services. Project objectives focused on curriculum development in the management of youth care systems in rural areas; training
efforts in youth care for community caretakers; community service providers, parents, volunteers, adults, and youth; and education planning
and resource development.

29

DAY CARE PROBLEMS AND NEEDS IN RURAL AREAS
Van Zandt, Sally and Susan Bosworth
Public Welfare, 26(3): 219-223, 1968.

Day care centers with well-trained staff are usually available only in
larger cities. This article examines where rural children are kept when
the mother is at work, what need exists for rural child care centers, and
the effect small children have on the labor participation of rural women.

30

THE DELINQUENT IN A RURAL AREA
Dahl, Stephen
In 2nd Annual Northern Wisconsin Symposium on Human Services in the Rural
Environment Reader. David Bast and Julie Schmidt, ed.
Madison: University of Wisconsin-Extension, Center for Social Science,
27-37, 1977.

This paper examines factors contributing to delinquency in rural areas
and roles to be performed by social workers in developing needed systems
of support for the juvenile.

31

A DEMONSTRATION PROJECT IN THE DEVELOPMENT OF RURAL CHILD CARE
67 pp. ERIC: ED016545.

This project was designed for seven eastern Kentucky counties which are
among the most impoverished in the U.S. Three programs were implemented,
including: 1) day care for pre-school children, 2) homemaker service for
families, and 3) casework service with both parents and children.

32

DIFFERENCES IN FAMILY SIZE AND MARRIAGE AGE EXPECTATIONS AND ASPIRATIONS
OF ANGLO, MEXICAN AMERICAN AND NATIVE AMERICAN YOUTH IN NEW MEXICO
Edington, Everett and Leonard Hays
Adolescence, 13(51): 393-400, 1978.

Findings of this study in New Mexico included: a) significant differences
existed between ethnic groups in family size expectations and family size
aspirations; b) significant differences existed between ethnic groups in
age expected and desired for marriage; c) no differences existed between
age groups for expected and aspired age of marriage or number of children;
d) a proportionately larger number of Native Americans were less future
oriented in aspirations and expectations than Anglos.

33

DROP-OUT FROM AN AMERICAN INDIAN RESERVATION SCHOOL: A POSSIBLE
PREVENTION PROGRAM
Delk, J., et al.
Journal of Community Psychology, 2(1): 15-16, 1974.

This study looks at Papago Native Americans' reasons for dropping out of
high school. The findings point to certain home and family patterns as
a primary factor in the background of drop-outs, but not in those of
continuing students.

34
DRUG USE AND DELINQUENT BEHAVIOR OF SMALL TOWN AND RURAL YOUTH
Forslund, Morris A.
Journal of Drug Education, 7(3): 219-224, 1977-1978.

This article reports the results of one of the few studies which examines
the relationship between drug use and involvement in delinquent activities
among small town and rural youth.

35
EARLY CHILDHOOD EDUCATION FOR MIGRANTS: AN EVALUATION OF BEHAVIORAL AND
PHYSICAL CHANGE
Spinks, Nellie J.
Office of Program for the Disadvantaged
Washington, D.C.: Department of Health, Education, and Welfare, Office
of Education, Research Monograph No. 3, 1972. ERIC: ED067190.

The purpose of this publication was to describe a program for migrant
children to maximize their educational potential and to increase the
probability of a successful educational experience in the public schools.

36
EDITED TRANSCRIPTS OF A SERIES OF FOUR UNIVERSITY-COMMUNITY SEMINARS ON
THE RURAL EXPERIENCE: IMPLICATIONS FOR BUILDING EFFECTIVE YOUTH CARE
SERVICES IN RURAL AREAS
Urzi, Mary
St. Paul: University of Minnesota, Center for Youth Development and
Research, August 1976, 95 pp. NTIS/SHR-0002829.

The seminars were part of a short term Training and Curriculum Development
Project conducted under the auspices of the Center for Youth Development
and Research at the University of Minnesota. Seminar topics were rural
youth and rural adults, rural communities and rural youth, special considerations relative to the rural poor and minority groups assessing and
delivering services to rural youth, and education-training for rural
service providers.

37
THE EDUCATION OF MENOMINEE YOUTH IN WISCONSIN
Caspar, Margery G.
Integrated Education, 11(1): 45-51, 1973.

Personal, familial, and cultural factors influencing the failure of
Wisconsin Indian school children are discussed in this article.

38
ESKIMOS, CHICANOS, INDIANS
Coles, Robert
Children in Crisis, Vol. 4.
Boston: Little, Brown, 1978.

In this volume Coles attempts to describe what it is like growing up not only poor, but outside the dominant culture in America, as children in the lower castes as well as the lower classes. He argues that the children of Eskimos, Chicanos, and Indians, even more than other poor children, are discouraged from independence and assertiveness; they learn to hold back their thoughts, not to take issue with outsiders or to make their individual presence felt.

39
ESTABLISHING A RURAL CHILD ABUSE/NEGLECT TREATMENT PROGRAM
Sefcik, Thomas R. and Nancy J. Ormsby
Child Welfare, 57(3): 187-195, 1978.

Project Children is a rural child abuse/neglect program in south central Indiana. This article relates the methods employed in the program to various issues. In an environment with limited resources, one of the most significant factors in program success was learning to work with people, both professional and lay, in a manner nonthreatening to the small community.

40
FAMILY AND COMMUNITY ACTIVITIES OF RURAL NONFARM FAMILIES WITH CHILDREN
Bollman, Stephen R., Virginia M. Moxley, and Nancy C. Elliott
Journal of Leisure Research, 7(1): 53-62, 1975.

Six factors--resource level, stage of family life cycle, presence of a preschool child, family size, geographic mobility, and employment status of the mother--were analyzed in terms of their effect on nonwork activities of families with children.

41
FAMILY INCOME AND STATUS ORIENTATION OF OZARK YOUTH
Oberle, Wayne H., Kevin R. Stowers, and James P. Darby
Youth and Society, 6(1): 91-103, 1974.

This paper examines the relationship between the household income of the family and selected educational and occupational status orientations of youth residing in the Ozarks. Income was found to be positively related to status orientations.

42
A FUTURE FOR INDIAN YOUTH IN RURAL AREAS
Roessel, Robert A., Jr.
In Rural Youth in a Changing Environment. Ruth C. Nash, ed.
Washington, D.C.: National Committee for Children and Youth, 119-120, 1965.

This paper is a brief review of the problems and future of Indian youth in rural areas.

43

GROUP THERAPY FOR BEHAVIOR-PROBLEM CHILDREN IN A RURAL JUNIOR HIGH SCHOOL
Webster, Carole T.
Child Welfare, 53(10): 653-657, 1974.

A group therapy program to aid students with behavioral problems was initiated by an agency social worker, and achieved permanent status by enlisting the cooperation of both the school administration and the teachers.

44

GUIDELINES FOR YOUTH INVOLVEMENT IN LOCAL GOVERNMENT
Saunders, Walter L.
Petersburg: Virginia State University, Cooperative Extension Service, 1974, 18 pp.

Outlines program designed to close the "information gap" between youth and local government. Program provides opportunities for practical learning experiences with classroom instruction.

45

A HAZARD TO MENTAL HEALTH: INDIAN BOARDING SCHOOLS
Beiser, Morton
American Journal of Psychiatry, 131(3): 305-306, 1974.

In this editorial the author argues that in spite of volumes of testimony before Congressional Committees little or no improvement in the conditions of Indian boarding schools has taken place. Even when model programs are successful, they are usually terminated, with the overall system continuing as it did before.

46

HIGH SCHOOL STUDENTS AND THE USE OF ALCOHOL IN A RURAL COMMUNITY: A RESEARCH NOTE
Globetti, Gerald, Majeed Alsikafi, and Richard Morse
Journal of Drug Issues, 8(4): 435-441, 1978.

This study reports on the drinking habits of a sample of white high school students who reside in a rural community that is the prototype of the abstinent tradition.

47

HUMAN SERVICES FOR MEXICAN-AMERICAN CHILDREN
Tijerina, Andres A.
Austin: Texas State Department of Human Resources. ERIC: ED171480.

A compilation of five readings uses the Chicano perspective to analyze the interaction between Mexican American families, their children, and the institutions charged with the Child Welfare concerns of the society. A variety of strategies for policy makers and practitioners charged with serving the needs of Mexican American families and children are suggested.

48
INDIAN CHILD WELFARE: A REVIEW OF THE LITERATURE
Slaughter, Ellen L.
Denver: University of Denver, Center for Social Research and Development,
January 1976.

In addition to the review of the literature, this study entails field
surveys of graduate schools of social work and their American Indian
faculty, students, and graduates.

49
INTERNAL-EXTERNAL CONTROL AND DRUG USE AMONG JUNIOR HIGH SCHOOL STUDENTS
IN A RURAL COMMUNITY
Carman, Roderick S.
The International Journal of the Addictions, 12(1): 53-64, 1977.

Internal-external control and current drug use were assessed among rural
junior high school students.

50
JUVENILE JUSTICE: A RURAL URBAN COMPARISON
Pawlak, Edward J.
In Social Work in Rural Areas: Preparation and Practice. Ronald K.
Green and Stephen A. Webster, eds.
Knoxville: The University of Tennessee, School of Social Work,
303-320, 1978.

A comparison of the handling of juvenile offenders by urban and rural
juvenile courts is presented in this paper.

51
LEGAL PROTECTION FOR FARM CHILDREN
O'Hara, James G.
New Generation, 54(3): 24-28, 1972. ERIC: EJ064665.

A congressman recounts hearings and legislative progress relative to a
house bill which he introduced in 1971 to ban child labor in agriculture
altogether.

52
LOCUS OF CONTROL DIFFERENCES BETWEEN RURAL AMERICAN INDIAN AND WHITE
CHILDREN
Tyler, John D. and David N. Holsinger
The Journal of Social Psychology, Vol. 95, 149-155, 1975.

The data of the study support the hypothesis that culturally disadvantaged children are more externally controlled than white children.

53
MENTAL HEALTH FACTORS IN AN INDIAN BOARDING SCHOOL
Krush, Thaddeus and John Bjork
Mental Health, Vol. 49, 94-103, 1969.

The article describes a mental health project at a boarding school in South
Dakota in which efforts were made to elicit factors pertinent to the mental
health of Indian students by a series of cultural, behavioral and physical
studies.

54
MIGRANT RESPONSE TO INDUSTRIALIZATION IN FOUR RURAL AREAS, 1965-1970
Olsen, Duane A. and John A. Kuehn
Washington, D.C.: U.S. Department of Agriculture, Economic Research
Service, Agricultural Economic Report 270, 1974.

Study of four multi-county areas in Arizona, Mississippi, Central Ozarks,
and Arkansas. Found that 78 percent of jobs created by industrial growth
were filled by the local residents, 22 percent were filled by in-migrants
despite high unemployment rate. Concludes that rural industrialization
programs are likely to experience some leakage of jobs to in-migrants.
However, because in-migrants are younger and better educated, this may
have salutory indirect effects on declining rural areas. Also, new jobs
have slowed the exodus of the young.

55
MIGRANTS, SHARECROPPERS, AND MOUNTAINEERS
Coles, Robert
Children in Crisis, Vol. 2.
Boston: Little, Brown, 1969.

The author begins by describing his clinical research method in the study.
Then he describes the lives of children of migrant pickers, sharecroppers,
and poor whites in Appalachia, using material from interviews with these
children.

56
NEW NEEDS OF NEW RURAL STUDENTS - MISERY IN SMALL TOWN AMERICA?
Turnage, Martha
Community College Review, 2(3): 40-45, 1974.

Due to the shock of social change in rural society, rural community
colleges must adjust toward student rather than institutional needs.
Coping skills are especially needed.

57
PERSONALITY ADJUSTMENT OF RURAL AND URBAN YOUTH: THE FORMATION OF A
RURAL DISADVANTAGE SUBCULTURE
Nelson, Hart and Stuart Storey
Rural Sociology, 34(1): 43-54, 1969.

Numerous adjustment and personality studies concerned with differences between rural and urban youth have been reported in the literature over the past 25 years, but the findings have been inconclusive. In this analysis the authors examine rural-urban differences in youth adjustment and consider the hypotheses that rural youth would be most poorly adjusted, followed by town and city youths.

58
PERSPECTIVES ON RURAL YOUTH SERVICES AND HELPING FAMILY AND COMMUNITY NETWORKS
Libertoff, Ken
In Effective Models for the Delivery of Services in Rural Areas: Implications for Practice and Social Work Education. Barry L. Locke and Roger A. Lohmann, eds.
Morgantown: West Virginia University, 1978.

The central purpose of this paper is to develop a framework for better understanding the ways in which human service providers can better meet the needs of teenagers and families in rural communities.

59
PLANNING AN ADOLESCENT DRUG TREATMENT PROJECT IN A RURAL AREA: THE PATCHWORK APPROACH TO PROGRAM DEVELOPMENT
Jacobs, Claudia
In Social Work in Rural Areas: Preparation and Practice. Ronald K. Green and Stephen A. Webster, eds.
Knoxville: The University of Tennessee, School of Social Work, 266-283, 1978.

This paper discusses six steps to the design and implementation of drug treatment projects in small-town and rural areas, where services to adolescents are sparse.

60
POWERLESSNESS AMONG RURAL APPALACHIAN YOUTH
Polansky, Norman
Rural Sociology, 34(2): 219-222, 1969.

Rather than focus on the felt powerlessness of the urban disadvantaged, this study focused on that of rural disadvantaged. It was found that powerlessness may affect anyone in Appalachia, but it is less likely to be as strong among youngsters who are white, and in more secure life circumstances.

61
PREPARING YOUNG PEOPLE TO PARTICIPATE IN LOCAL GOVERNMENT
Carroll, William and Jerry Rayburn
In Farm Economics
University Park: Pennsylvania State University, February, 1977.

The Pennsylvania State University 4-H program in government and community planning provides an opportunity for the youth of the Commonwealth to reflect their aspirations in the daily decision-making of the community in which they live.

62
A PROGRAM IN ALCOHOL EDUCATION DESIGNED FOR RURAL YOUTH
Fullerton, Madonna
Journal of Alcohol and Drug Education, 24(2): 58-62, 1979.

This article is a description of the Alcohol Education Project in Joy,
Maine. Psychotherapy provided the theoretical base to the program.

63
RACE AND SEX INFLUENCES IN THE SCHOOLING PROCESS OF RURAL AND SMALL
TOWN YOUTH
DeBord, L. W., L. J. Griffin and M. Clark
Sociology of Education, Vol. 42, 85-102, April 1977.

This paper assesses how race and sex act to determine the educational
performance and career aspirations of over 3,000 students enrolled in 23
public schools in Mississippi.

64
REWARD AND PUNISHMENT PATTERNS IN RURAL AND TOWN SCHOOL CHILDREN
Lawson, E. D. and M. F. Slaughter
Child Study Journal, 7(3): 145-158, 1977.

The purpose of this investigation was to use the critical incident technique with reward and punishment to evaluate sex differences, community
differences, and grade level differences.

65
RIO GRANDE YOUTH CARE CENTER FINAL REPORT
Los Lunas, New Mexico: Valencia County Commission, 1974, 14 pp.
NTIS/PB-254 888/1ST.

A counseling and referral center for youths was established in 1972 to
alleviate delinquency problems in the community with special reference
to Chicanos.

66
ROLE MODELS OF BLACK AND WHITE RURAL YOUTH AT TWO STAGES OF ADOLESCENCE
Aberle, Wayne H.
The Journal of Negro Education, 43(2): 234-244, 1974.

The purpose of this paper is to describe the types and occupational status
of the role models which black and white Texas youth selected (during and
after high school).

67
THE RUNAWAY YOUTH ISSUE: IMPLICATIONS FOR RURAL COMMUNITIES
Libertoff, Kenneth
In 2nd Annual Northern Wisconsin Symposium on Human Services in the
Rural Environment Reader. David Bast and Julie Schmidt, eds.
Madison: University of Wisconsin - Extension, Center for Social
Science, 1977.

This paper discusses the runaway youth issue as it relates to rural communities. A primary concern of the author is that rural human service workers will simply replicate urban programs as federal support becomes available.

68

RURAL ADOLESCENTS WITH PROGRAMS IN SEXUALITY
Personnel and Guidance Journal, Vol. 54, 387, March 1976.

Critiques the development and operation of Massachusetts Family Planning Program. Trust building was cited as crucial element in establishing services for rural communities. Other important factors were parent support and careful selection of topic titles. Program serves youth both in and out of the school setting.

69

THE RURAL CHURCH AND RURAL RELIGION: ANALYSIS OF DATA FROM CHILDREN AND YOUTH
Nelson, Hart and Raymond Potvin
In The American Academy of Political and Social Science. F. Clemente, ed.
Vol. 429, 103-114, January 1977.

This study reviews the literature on the rural church and presents data on differences between religious orientations of rural and urban children and adolescents. Speculation on the future of the rural church is also discussed.

70

RURAL JUVENILE DELINQUENCY: PROBLEMS AND NEEDS IN EAST TENNESSEE
Brown, David W. and W. D. Bolton
Knoxville: University of Tennessee, Agricultural Experiment Station, 1978.

An exploratory study of delinquency problems and possibilities for improving juvenile services in 15 nonmetropolitan counties surrounding Knoxville.

71

RURAL PRETRIAL SERVICES: KENTUCKY'S EXPERIENCE
Wheeler, Stephen F.
Human Services in the Rural Environment, 1(2): 6, 1979.

The bail reform movement of the past two decades has been a predominantly urban phenomenon, but it is now starting to spread slowly into rural areas. This article explores one of the unique features of bail reform growth in rural areas, particularly Kencutky.

72

THE RURAL SOCIAL WORKER AND CORRECTIONS
Schultz, LeRoy G.
In Social Work in Rural Communities. Leon H. Ginsberg, ed.
New York: Council on Social Work Education, 87-92, 1976.

Rural crime and delinquency, criminal justice in rural America, and implications for rural social work curriculum are presented in this paper.

73
RURAL, SUBURBAN, AND CENTRAL CITY CHILDREN: SEX-TYPE ROLES IN OCCUPATIONS
Scheresky, Ruth F.
Psychological Reports, 43(2): 407-411, 1978.

Children's views of occupational roles which are traditionally sex-typed by society were explored as differences among the views of children located in rural, suburban, or central city areas.

74
RURAL YOUTH IN A CHANGING ENVIRONMENT
Nash, Ruth Cowan, ed.
Washington, D.C.:   National Committee for Children and Youth, 1965.

This text consists of papers presented to the first National Conference on the Problems of Rural Youth in a Changing Environment.   The purpose of the conference was to generate information to prepare young people growing up in a rural environment to adjust and to compete in a changing society.

75
RURAL YOUTH IN CRISIS: FACTS, MYTHS, AND SOCIAL CHANGE
Burchinal, Lee G., ed.
Washington, D.C.:   U.S. Department of Health, Education and Welfare, Welfare Administration, Office of Juvenile Delinquency and Youth Development, 1965.

This collection of papers and background information prepared for a conference held by the National Committee for Children and Youth in 1963 covers several content areas: rural community backgrounds, rural education, physical and mental health of rural youth, juvenile delinquency, rural youth in urban environments, and strategies for helping socially disadvantaged rural youth.

76
SCREENING EMOTIONALLY DISTURBED CHILDREN IN A RURAL SETTING
Schultz, Edward W., Anne B. Manton and John A. Salvia
Exceptional Children, 39(2): 134-137, 1972.

This study was undertaken to ascertain the efficacy of screening procedures in a two-county rural area in east central Illinois.

77
SECONDARY CREDIT EXCHANGE, ESEA TITLE I MIGRANT: PROGRAM DESCRIPTION
Randall, David W.
1977.   ERIC: ED151493.

The purpose of this report is to describe "how to do it" aspects of setting up a secondary credit exchange program.   This type of program allows migrant students to keep up with their education by attending night classes. The program was successful in reducing the percentage of migrant students who withdrew from this program.

78
SERVICES AND ENVIRONMENTAL ADJUSTMENTS NEEDED FOR RURAL YOUTH WHO MOVE
TO URBAN COMMUNITIES
Ramsey, Ralph J.
Speech presented at the National Outlook Conference on Rural Youth,
October 23-26, 1967, 11 pp. ERIC: ED014361.

This speech was presented at the National Outlook Conference on Rural
Youth, October 23-26, 1967. It oulines the adjustments of rural youth
who migrate to urban settings. Many of the rural-urban migrants have
been Puerto Ricans, Southern whites, Blacks, whites from the Plains,
Mexican Americans from the Southwest, and Native Americans.

79
SOCIAL GROUP WORK WITH YOUNG AMERICAN INDIANS
Edwards, Dan and Marge Edwards
Boulder, Colorado: Western Interstate Commission for Higher Education,
Monograph #9, Faculty Development--Minority Content in Mental Health,
Fall 1974.

This monograph relates group work methods and programming to working with
young American Indians.

80
SOCIAL PSYCHOLOGICAL IMPACT OF GEOGRAPHICAL LOCATION AMONG DISADVANTAGED
RURAL AND URBAN INTERMEDIATE GRADE CHILDREN
Olsen, Henry D. and Donald E. Carter
Child Study Journal, 4(2): 81-91, 1974.

This article reports a study that ascertained differences in perceived
self-concept of academic ability due to residential setting (rural vs.
urban).

81
THE SOCIAL ROLE OF A COUNTY SHERIFF
Esselstyn, T. C.
Criminology and Police Science, Vol. 44, 177-184, August 1953.

The author maintains that open country crime does not conform to general
ideas of crime in urban areas. He also argues that, in part because of
these differences, the social role of the county sheriff is different
in rural areas.

82
SOME ASPECTS OF INCOME DISTRIBUTION: THE EFFECTS OF THE RURAL INCOME
MAINTENANCE EXPERIMENT ON THE SCHOOL PERFORMANCE OF CHILDREN
Maynard, Rebecca A.
American Economic Association, 67(1): 370-375, 1977.

This paper summarizes the findings of an analysis of the effects of the Rural Income Maintenance Experiment on four measures of school performance; attendance, comportment grades, academic grades and standardized achievement test scores.

83
SOME CORRELATES OF DRUG USE AMONG HIGH SCHOOL YOUTH IN A MIDWESTERN RURAL COMMUNITY
Tolone, William L. and Diane Dermott
The International Journal of Addictions, 10(5): 761-777, 1975.

A study of the correlates of drug use (marijuana, LSD, mescaline, speed) among high school students in a rural, midwestern community indicated that peer group factors were the most influential in such behavior. Also, youth from less intact families and whose parents were perceived to use various legal drugs were more prone to drug use.

84
SOME THOUGHTS ON THE FORMATION OF PERSONALITY DISORDER: STUDY OF AN INDIAN BOARDING SCHOOL POPULATION
Krush, Thaddeus, P., et al.
American Journal of Psychiatry, Vol. 122, 868-876, February 1966.

The authors contend that Indian boarding schools promote "psycho-social nomadism" and shifting value systems which lead to confusion and disorganization of the Indian child's personality.

85
THE SPANISH-SPEAKING YOUTH: FROM THE FARM TO THE CITY
Ulibarri, Horacio
In Rural Youth in a Changing Environment. Ruth C. Nash, ed.
Washington, D.C.: National Committee for Children and Youth, 117-119, 1965.

The problems of Mexican-American youth in the rural areas of New Mexico are discussed in this paper.

86
STRATEGIES FOR IMPLEMENTING SEX EDUCATION AND PRE-NATAL CARE FOR RURAL TEENAGERS: ONE COUNTY'S EXPERIENCE
Glosser, Ruth
A paper presented at the Third Annual Northern Wisconsin Symposium on Human Services in the Rural Environment - Meeting the Needs of Rural Youth.
Madison: University of Wisconsin, Cooperative Extension Programs, September 1977.

This paper examines some of the special needs and problems of rural Appalachian teenagers, and describes some of the programs in a county initiated to identify and reach teenagers at risk.

87

A SURVEY OF PSYCHOLOGICAL AND SOCIAL CONCERNS OF RURAL ADOLESCENCE
House, Elizabeth
Adolescence, 14(54): 361-376, 1979.

This paper reports the results of a survey of 1349 secondary school
students in a rural county in northeastern North Carolina. Data are
presented on psychological and social problems, self-concept, utilization of professional and non-professional resources, and family
relationship.

88

THE TOKEN MINORITY: AN ATTITUDINAL COMPARISON OF BLACK, ORIENTAL, AND
ANGLO RURAL YOUTH UTILIZING THE MATCHED-SET ANALYSIS
Cockerham, William C., Peter B. Imrey, and Sidney J. Kronus
Sociological Methods and Research, 6(4): 493-513, 1978.

This paper examines the attitudes of a "token" number of black and
oriental youth who live in a rural and predominantly Anglo setting.

89

UPROOTED CHILDREN: THE EARLY LIFE OF MIGRANT FARMWORKERS
Coles, Robert
Pittsburgh: The University of Pittsburgh Press, 1970.

Coles relates in the words of migrant families with whom he has lived for
seven years, what it means for a child to live a rootless, transitory
existence, always surrounded by hard work and pain, often ridiculed for
being an outsider.

90

VALUES, EXPECTATIONS, AND DRUG USE AMONG HIGH SCHOOL STUDENTS IN A RURAL
COMMUNITY
Carman, Roderick S.
The International Journal of the Addictions, 9(1): 57-80, 1974.

Rotter's Social Learning Theory of Personality was used to investigate
relationships among values for certain goals, expectations for achieving
these goals, and self-reported drug use among rural high school students.

91

WHEN DO THEY LEARN? A STUDY OF DRUG AWARENESS IN CHILDREN IN A RURAL
ELEMENTARY SCHOOL
Freeman, Janice K. and William F. Freeman
Journal of Drug Education, 7(2): 133-140, 1977.

This study is concerned with the age at which a program of drug education
should be offered to children, if it is to be effective.

92

WORKING WITH RURAL YOUTH: SOCIAL PROBLEMS AND SOCIAL POLICY
Brunner, Edmund
New York: Arno Press, 1974.

The book examines an experiment of the American Youth Commission during
the thirties and forties to demonstrate possible ways in which state,
county, and local resources could be marshalled to solve some of the
problems of rural youth.

93

YOUTH IN ACTION IMPROVING THEIR COMMUNITIES
Dyer, Del and Gene McMurty
Blacksburg: Virginia Polytechnic Institute and State University,
Cooperative Extension Service, 1972, 75 pp.

A leader's guide to assist youth in understanding their community and
develop the skills necessary for involvement in local decision making.
Includes ways leaders can initiate discussion leading to making plans
for action.

94

YOUTH AND ADULT ATTITUDES TOWARD YOUTH INVOLVEMENT IN COMMUNITY PLANNING
AND DECISION-MAKING
Rowe, Corinne
Moscow: University of Idaho, No. 31, 1975, 7 pp.

Provides a literature review of publications on beliefs and attitudes of
youth and their involvement in communities.

95

YOUTH DEVELOPMENT PROGRAM MODELS
Washington, D.C.: Project Map, Inc., October 1971, 107 pp.
NTIS/PB-211 066.

This report is designed to share with the reader some of the ways that
local sponsors of youth development projects have chosen to develop programs. Models in rural areas are included in the report.

CHAPTER 9

AGING

General Topics

Adult Foster Care

Death

Housing

Isolation

Networking

Nursing Homes

Older Natural Helpers

Public Policy

Social Services

1
ACTION FOR AGING: HOUSING OPTIONS
College Park: University of Maryland, Cooperative Extension Service,
1977, 117 pp.

Proceedings of Extension Service training workshop. Objectives were to
identify and counsel the elderly on their housing options, identify and
evaluate community resources available to meet the housing needs of the
elderly and to improve and initiate housing programs for the elderly.

2
ADULT FOSTER CARE - AN ALTERNATIVE TO NURSING HOME CARE IN MARATHON COUNTY
Aliven, Walter
In 2nd Annual Northern Wisconsin Symposium on Human Services in the
Rural Environment Reader. David Bast and Julie Schmidt, eds.
Madison: University of Wisconsin-Extension, Center for Social Science,
56-68, 1977.

The author reviews the adult foster care program of Marathon County
Department of Social Services and concludes that adult foster care is a
needed and feasible program for rural areas.

3
AGING: ITS IMPACT ON THE HEALTH OF AMERICAN INDIANS
Okalahoma City: Association of American Indian Physicians, Inc., May 1978.

This document includes technical papers on the physical and mental health
of the aging American Indian. The papers were prepared at the request of
the Indian Health Service.

4
ALTERNATIVES FOR PLANNING A CONTINUUM OF CARE FOR ELDERLY AMERICAN INDIANS
Norman, Oklahoma: American Indian Nurses Association, 231 South Peters,
Norman, Oklahoma 73069.

Provides information for Indian and non-Indian professionals and others
seeking to serve elderly American Indians. Among other things, literature
is reviewed to indicate trends in delivery of care required by the
ambulatory, homebound, and institutionalized persons. Information on
cultural requirements is highlighted as well.

5
AWAKENING OF THE RURAL AGING: AN INTERDISCIPLINARY SOCIAL WORK - RURAL
AGING TRAINING AND PROGRAM DEVELOPMENT PROJECT
Kim, Paul K. H. and John R. Ballantine
In Social Work in Rural Areas: Issues and Opportunities. Joseph Davenport,
III, Judith A. Davenport and James R. Wiebler, eds.
Laramie: The University of Wyoming, Department of Social Work, 69-78, 1980.

The purpose of this project is to increase the manpower available to serve in the field of rural aging, as well as increase the competence of practitioners already working with the rural elderly.

6

COMPREHENSIVE PROGRAM FOR THE ELDERLY IN RURAL AREAS
Chandler, Suzannah
Washington, D.C.: National Council on Aging, March 1972, 38 pp.
NTIS/SHR-000/319.

Ways in which a rural community action program can encourage the participation of the elderly in efforts to eliminate poverty are addressed.

7

DEATH: A RURAL PERSPECTIVE
Barker, Judy T.
In Social Work in Rural Areas: Issues and Opportunities. Joseph Davenport, III, Judith A. Davenport and James R. Wiebler, eds.
Laramie: The University of Wyoming, Department of Social Work, 11-19, 1980.

This study focuses on the death customs of southern rural communities surrounding Chattanooga, Tennessee. Knowledge of these customs can help social workers to deal more effectively and efficiently with rural natural helping systems and organizational helping systems in reducing the number of emotional problems often associated with death.

8

DEVELOPING SOCIAL SERVICES IN RURAL LONG TERM CARE FACILITIES
Munson, Carlton E.
In Effective Models for the Delivery of Services in Rural Areas:
Implications for Practice and Social Work Education. Barry L. Locke and Roger A. Lohmann, eds.
Morgantown: West Virginia University, 1978.

This paper applies a theoretical perspective to conceptualizing development of the role of social workers as consultants for developing social services in long-term care facilities. Role theory is used to organize the reporting of experiences in defining the tasks and functions of the consultant in a non-profit, church related, long-term care facility.

9

DIFFERENTIAL NEEDS OF THE METROPOLITAN, SMALL TOWN AND RURAL ELDERLY:
SERVICE IMPLICATIONS
Welichs, K. W. and P. K. Kim
Gerontologist, 15(5): 96 pp., 1975.

This is a paper presented at the 28th annual meeting of the Gerontological Society, Louisville, Kentucky, October, 1975 which discusses the needs of the elderly persons relative to their residential locality, and the service implications which propose a service modality aimed at alleviating the identified needs.

10
DISCRIMINATORS OF LONELINESS AMONG THE RURAL ELDERLY: IMPLICATIONS
FOR INTERVENTION
Kivett, Vira R.
The Gerontologist, 19(1): 108-115, 1979.

This study examines several physical and social variables as discriminators
of loneliness among the rural elderly. Intervention is suggested in
three overall areas: social activities and relationships, health and
vision, and transportation.

11
ELDERLY NEEDS ASSESSMENT
Frankfort, Kentucky: Kentucky Executive Department for Finance and
Administration, June 1976, 95 pp. NTIS/SHR-0001525.

The methods and the findings of a survey of the needs of the elderly in
six rural counties in the Northern Kentucky Area Development District are
reported. A copy of the survey instrument is appended.

12
THE ELDERLY IN RURAL AREAS: DIFFERENCES IN URBAN AREAS AND IMPLICATIONS
FOR PRACTICE
Auerbach, Arnold J.
In Social Work in Rural Communities. Leon H. Ginsberg, ed.
New York: Council on Social Work Education, 99-107, 1976.

The author presents the findings of a survey of rural elderly. Comparisons
of rural-urban differences are made, and the special problems of minority
aged people are discussed.

13
AN EVALUATION OF CASA PROJECT: COMMUNITY ACTIVITIES FOR SENIOR ARKANSANS
Little Rock: Arkansas Farmers Union. Final Report, 1970, 56 pp.
NTIS/PB-209 090.

The project was based on the assumption that the majority of older persons
would rather stay in their own homes, near their friends, than move to
newer housing designed for older persons. The study is revealing about
the needs of persons living alone.

14
EXPERIENCES IN SYSTEMATIC TRAINING IN A RURAL PROGRAM FOR ELDERLY
MISSISSIPPIANS
Williams, Leola
American Journal of Clinical Nutrition, 26(10): 1138-1142, 1973.

The objective of this research and demonstration program was to plan, or
gauge, and complement a nutritional program for the rural elderly in the
Mississippi Delta area. It was found that program success depended on

volunteer efforts and on the provision of other services, including arts and crafts, social and recreational opportunities, and shopping.

15
FEDERALLY ASSISTED HOUSING PROGRAMS FOR THE ELDERLY IN RURAL AREAS:
PROGRAMS AND PROSPECTS
Washington, D.C.: Housing Assistance Council Inc., 1978, 24 pp.

Describes, analyzes and makes recommendations on federal housing programs which can serve the elderly in rural areas. Includes federal agencies and programs involved.

16
GENERATIONS
Western Gerontological Society, Quarterly Newsletter, 2(3), 1977.

This issue focuses on the rural elderly. The articles first cover a basic overview of the rural aged, followed by articles on policy issues, rural service delivery, research projects, fund raising, and service programs.

17
GROWING OLD IN RURAL AMERICA
Harbert, Anita and Carroll Wilkinson
Aging, Vol. 291, 36-40, January 1979.

This article discusses the lives of the rural elderly including problems of rural areas, tradition, and standards of rural life.

18
THE IMPACT OF SOCIAL CHANGE ON THE SOCIAL-PSYCHOLOGICAL STATE OF OLDER
PERSONS IN LOW-INCOME RURAL AREAS AND ITS IMPLICATION ON HUMAN SERVICE
IN AGING
Kim, Dong I. and Sung L. Boo
In Effective Models for the Delivery of Services in Rural Areas:
Implications for Practice and Social Work Education. Barry L. Locke and
Roger A. Lohmann, eds.
Morgantown: West Virginia University, 1978 .

This study explored the relationship between social change, as indicated by change in the degree of urbanization, and the social-psychological state, namely pessimism, for older people living in low-income areas of the South. The authors' findings indicate that rural people living in lagging areas may welcome change in order to "catch-up" with more advanced areas.

19
INDUSTRIAL DEVELOPMENT AND THE ELDERLY: A LONGITUDINAL ANALYSIS
Clemente, Frank and Gene F. Summers
Journal of Gerontology, 28(4), 479-483, 1973.

Study compares a control and experimental region. Concludes that industrialization caused decay of the relative economic status of the aged.

20
MIGRATION, MOBILITY AND AGING
Osterbind, Carter C.
Gainesville: University Presses of Florida, 1974. NTIS/HRP-0015221/5ST

The proceedings of a conference on gerontology are reported. The role of older people in a mobile society is discussed. Social services for older people in rural areas are considered in terms of needs resources, availability for services, and demand for services as effected by population mobility.

21
NEGLECTED OLDER AMERICAN
Cull, J. G. and R. E. Hardy
Springfield, Illinois: Virginia Commonwealth University,
Richmond Department of Rehabilitation Counseling, 1973.

The needs and concerns of the elderly in the United States are documented in a collection of writings directed to the professional social scientist. The text is intended to develop an awareness and concern among social scientists and other professionals about the untapped reservoir of exper- ienced, mature manpower among elderly Americans.

22
THE OLD ONES OF NEW MEXICO
Coles, Robert
Albuquerque: The University of New Mexico Press, 1973.

This book combines a collection of conversations with photographs of the plight of both Anglo and Chicano elderly in New Mexico.

23
THE OLDER AMERICANS ACT AND THE RURAL ELDERLY
Hearings before the Special Committee of Aging, U.S. Senate, 94th Congress,
First Session, April 28, 1975.
Washington, D.C.: Senate Special Committee on Aging, Congress of the
United States, 119 pp. ERIC: ED116839.

The Older Americans Act of 1965 has not met the needs of the rural elderly and was, consequently, the subject of these hearings which considered pro- posed legislation under Title III of the Act which gives support for demonstration programs to assist older rural people and to improve the delivery systems of rural America.

24
OLDER AMERICANS IN RURAL AND SMALL TOWNS, 1971 WHITE HOUSE CONFERENCE
ON AGING
In Social Work in Rural Communities. Leon H. Ginsberg, Ed.
New York: Council on Social Work Education, 95-98, 1976.

This is reprinted from The Rural Poor and the Poor Elderly (USGPO, 1972). Problems of older rural adults and suggested ways of dealing with these problems are examined.

25
OLDER NATURAL HELPERS: THEIR CHARACTERISTICS AND PATTERNS OF HELPING
Patterson, Shirley L. and Esther E. Twente
Public Welfare, pp. 400-403, Fall 1971.

This paper examines the helping activities of a group of persons 60 years
of age and older in a rural Kansas community. It demonstrates that certain
kinds of help and certain ways of helping are more appropriately extended
by the natural helper.

26
OLDER RURAL AMERICANS: A SOCIOLOGICAL PERSPECTIVE
Youmans, E. Grant, ed.
Lexington: The University of Kentucky Press, 1967.

This collection of articles presents information about older people living
in open country and small towns. While some of the information is out-
dated, much of it is quite useful, particularly articles focusing on work
roles, family relationships and community roles. Also useful are three
articles at the end of the book dealing with older American Indians, older
rural Spanish-speaking people of the Southwest, and older rural blacks.

27
OPEN CARE FOR THE AGED--SWEDISH MODEL
Little, Virginia C.
Social Work, 23(4): 282-287, 1978.

The author explains how the Swedish model of open care for the aged offers
a wide range of services in urban and rural areas as well as multiple points
of access to services. The model supplants both unnecessary institutional-
ization and unorganized family care in rural areas with innovative program-
matic efforts.

28
PLANNING COMMUNITY SERVICES FOR THE RURAL ELDERLY: IMPLICATIONS FROM
RESEARCH
Coward, Raymond T.
The Gerontologist, 19(3): 275-282, 1979.

This paper contains selected research literature on critical areas which
contain practical implications for practitioners and planners concerned
with aged in rural America.

29
THE POLITICS OF AGING AND RURAL SOCIAL SERVICES: AN EXPLORATORY ANALYSIS
Lohmann, Roger
In Effective Models for the Delivery of Services in Rural Areas:
Implications for Practice and Social Work Education. Barry L. Locke and
Roger A. Lohmann, eds.
Morgantown: West Virginia University, 1978

The author presents a descriptive account of political and social service activities by, and in behalf of, old people in rural areas. The author concludes that aging has not yet merged as a significant or powerful political interest in the United States.

30
PRESERVING THE DIGNITY OF THE ELDERLY IN A RURAL AREA
Bohart, Rosemary
In 2nd Annual Northern Wisconsin Sumposium on Human Services in the Rural Environment Reader. David Bast and Julie Schmidt, eds. Madison: University of Wisconsin-Extension, Center for Social Science, 49-55, 1977.

Social workers must be aware of the social, psychological, and physical needs of the rural elderly to enable them to function at their maximum capabilities. Appropriate roles for the rural social worker are discussed.

31
A PROFILE OF INDIAN AGED
Benedict, Robert
Ann Arbor: University of Michigan, Institute of Gerontology, 1971.

The author provides a profile of characteristics of the Indian aged in the United States.

32
A PROFILE OF NEEDS AND RECOMMENDATIONS FOR IMPLEMENTING AGING PROGRAMS ON TEN ARIZONA RESERVATIONS
Allen, Michael
In cooperation with the Gerontological Society and Bureau of Aging, Arizona Department of Economic Security, 1974.

The purpose of this study was to discover the needs of Indian elderly on the reservation, to analyze how appropriate the guidelines of Title III of the Older Americans Act are in effecting programs for aged on reservations, to discuss how appropriate Title VII guidelines are for providing a successful nutrition program and to ask what recommendations are needed on how American legislation may be changed to be more effective in meeting the needs of the reservation elderly.

33
PROJECT RURAL A.L.I.V.E.: AN EVALUATION
Kohles, Mary K., et al.
Walthill, Nebraska: Goldenrod Hills Community Action Council, May 1973, 119 pp. NTIS/PB-243 206/OST.

The purpose of the four year demonstration project was to examine the effects of a planned nutrition and social interaction program on the physical and psychological well-being of citizens in the area.

34
A PROPOSAL FOR A STUDY OF FORMAL AND INFORMAL NETWORK SYSTEMS OF THE
RURAL ELDERLY
Yoelin, Michael and Curtis Krishef
In Social Work in Rural Areas: Issues and Opportunities. Joseph Davenport,
III, Judith A. Davenport and James R. Wiebler, eds.
Laramie: The University of Laramie, Department of Social Work, 80-86, 1980.

Describes a research proposal which will examine the attitudes and values
of older adults in rural areas in relation to formal and informal service
delivery systems for the aged.

35
REACHING OUT TO THE RURAL ELDERLY - SERVICES TO RURAL AMERICA
Means, Gary, Joseph Mann and David Van Dyk
Submitted to Western Gerontological Society Annual Meeting,
Denver, Colorado, 1977
Tempe: Arizona State University, School of Social Work, 1977.

This study examines barriers to the utilization of human services by the
elderly from a rural area of Arizona. Data presented are based on the
survey responses conducted in October to December, 1975 of Pinal and
Gila county residents.

36
RECOMMENDATIONS FOR SOCIAL WORK CURRICULAR BUILDING IN RELATIONSHIP TO
AMERICAN INDIAN AGED
Daines, Geri M.
Salt Lake City: University of Utah, Graduate School of Social Work,
May 1978.

Recommendations resulting from An American Indian Collaborative Workshop
held at the University of Utah on March 29 and 30, 1978. The purpose of
the workshop was to initiate a curriculum building effort for the improvement of educational experiences relative to the needs and potentials of
aging ethnic minorities of color.

37
RELUCTANCE OF THE ELDERLY TO ACCEPT HELP
Moen, Elizabeth
Social Problems, 25(3): 293-303, 1978.

This study focused on two issues: 1) how the needs of the rural elderly
can be measured, and 2) why the rural elderly fail to take advantage of
the programs and services available to them.

38
REPORT OF THE SPECIAL CONCERNS SESSION: THE RURAL AND THE POOR ELDERLY
RECOMMENDATIONS FOR ACTION FROM THE 1971 WHITE HOUSE CONFERENCE ON AGING
Washington, D.C.: U.S. Government Printing Office, 1971.

An abstract of materials on the rural and poor elderly presented at the 1971 White House Conference on Aging.

39
RESEARCH ON THE RURAL AGED: IMPLICATIONS FOR SOCIAL WORK PRACTICE
Lohmann, Nancy L.
In Effective Models for the Delivery of Services in Rural Areas:
Implications for Practice and Social Work Education.   Barry L. Locke and
and Roger A. Lohmann, eds.
Morgantown: West Virginia University, 1978.

This paper reports on four gerontological research areas which are of interest to social work practitioners and educators: demographic research; research on family and other social relationships; research on social services; and research on the quality of life.

40
RESISTANCE TO ISOLATION AMONG ELDERLY WIDOWS
Arling, G.
International Journal of Aging and Human Development, 7(1): 67-86, 1976.

The widow's ability to resist isolation in old age - to either maintain the involvement of earlier years or develop new social networks - may be conditioned by a number of different factors.   Drawing upon a survey of 409 widows, age 65 and older, from the Piedmont region of South Carolina, this study concludes that good health and the availability of economic resources are the primary factors which facilitate involvement with family, friends, and neighbors, and participation in a number and variety of daily activities.

41
THE ROLE OF THE NURSING HOME OMBUDSMAN PROGRAM IN RURAL WISCONSIN
Zitske, Judy
In 2nd Annual Northern Wisconsin Symposium on Human Services in the
Rural Environment Reader.   David Bast and Julie Schmidt, eds.
Madison: University of Wisconsin-Extension, Center for Social Science,
69-79, 1977.

This paper discusses Wisconsin Nursing Home Ombudsman Program which has three tasks: a) to establish effective and viable means for receipt and resolution of nursing home related compliance; b) to document significant problems in the system of long term care; and c) to develop the ombudsman program at the community level.

42
THE RURAL AGED
Youmans, E. Grant
Annals of the American Academy of Political and Social Science, Vol. 429,
81-90, January 1977.

A variety of questions are considered in this article: What are the income levels of the rural aged?   Does industrialization of rural areas

benefit older people? What is the nature of the social life of the rural
elderly? What is the health status of older persons living in rural
areas? How adequate is the subjective life of the rural aged? What are
the implications of the answers to these questions for older rural
Americans?

43
THE RURAL ELDERLY
Washington, D.C.: Rural America, Inc., December 1977, 5 pp. (30¢).

Outlines problems of rural elderly in housing, transportation, health care,
and employment. Recommends measures that will aid rural elderly.

44
RURAL-URBAN DIFFERENCES IN SATISFACTION AMONG THE ELDERLY
Hynson, L. M.
Rural Sociology, 40(1): 64-66, 1975.

The extent of satisfaction that the rural and the urban-elderly have with
their family, their community, themselves, and others is examined. The
rural elderly were more satisfied with their community, expressed greater
general happiness, and had less fear than the urban elderly.

45
RURAL-URBAN DIFFERENCES IN THE STRUCTURE OF SERVICES FOR THE ELDERLY IN
UPSTATE NEW YORK COUNTIES
Taiety, Philip and Sande Milton
Journal of Gerontology, 34(3): 429-437, 1979.

This research examines the impact of federal intervention and local community effort on the development of programs for the elderly.

46
SPECIAL PROBLEMS OF THE RURAL AGING
Washington, D.C.: U.S. House Committee on Government Operation, Report
No. 1, April 1973, 24 pp. NTIS/HRP -0014407/1ST.

The problems facing the rural aging, including low income, unemployment,
poor housing and limited health services, are described in this report to
the U.S. House of Representatives by the Committee on Government Operations.

47
A STATEMENT BY THE INDIAN ADVISORY COUNCIL TO THE SENATE SPECIAL COMMITTEE
ON AGING
Washington, D.C.: U.S. Government Printing Office, U.S. Senate, 1971.

In this working paper the Advisory Council on the Elderly American Indian
raises issues and recommendations on rights to old-age benefits, housing,
nursing homes, nutrition, recreation, transportation, employment, health,
education, and standard of living.

48

SUMMARY REPORT OF THE NATIONAL INDIAN CONFERENCE ON AGING
Phoenix, Arizona: Sponsored by the National Tribal Chairmen's Association,
June 15-17, 1976.

This book is a summary of the recommendations and resolutions submitted into
the conference record. Issues discussed include income, environment
(personal), legal problems, physical well-being, and legislation.

49

URBAN-DESIGNED PROGRAMS FOR THE RURAL ELDERLY: ARE THEY EXPORTABLE?
Lohmann, Nancy and Roger Lohmann
In Social Work in Rural Areas: Preparation and Practice. Stephen Webster
and Ronald Green, eds.
Knoxville: The University of Tennessee, School of Social Work, 284-297, 1978.

The potential usefulness in rural areas of social programs often found in
urbanized areas is examined in this paper.

CHAPTER 10

CURRICULUM MATERIALS FOR RURAL SOCIAL WORK EDUCATION

General Topics

Advocacy

Community Organization
and Development

Continuing Education

Curriculum Development and
Training

Direct Practice Issues

Field Instruction

Generalist vs. Specialist
Practice

History of Social Work in
Rural Areas

Natural Helping Networks

Paraprofessional Workers

Self-Determination

Service Delivery Problems

1

ADDING RURALLY ORIENTED CONTENT TO SOCIAL WORK CURRICULUM: PROCESSES
AND PRODUCTS - A REPORT OF A WORKSHOP
Hookey, Peter, ed.
Annual Program Meeting of the Council on Social Work Education,
New Orleans, Louisiana, February 1978.

This workshop was staffed by seven resource persons and there were four
main presentations into which this report is based on: 1) Rurally-oriented
components of social work curricula; 2) A description of the process of
launching a new rural social work course; 3) Incorporating rural content
into existing curricula in schools of social work; and 4) Implementing
rural social work contents: need is not enough.

2

ALCOHOLISM SERVICES IN RURAL AREAS: IMPLICATIONS FOR SOCIAL WORK EDUCATION
Dinitto, Diana and Santos H. Hernandez
In Social Work in Rural Areas: Issues and Opportunities. Joseph Davenport,
III, Judith A. Davenport and James R. Wiebler, eds.
Laramie: The University of Wyoming, Department of Social Work,
111-121, 1980.

This paper surveys the characteristics of rural communities and how these
impact the delivery of alcoholism services. Since a major factor affecting
the delivery of services has been the lack of professionally trained personnel, particular emphasis is placed upon implications for social work
education.

3

AMERICAN INDIAN SOCIAL WORKER ADVOCATES
Farris, Charles E.
Social Casework, 57(8): 494-503, 1976.

It is contended in this article that the social work profession could help
America resolve the Indian problems, particularly the problems of the
nonreservation Indian, by creating advocacy programs that would directly
implement the social work professional commitment to client advocacy for
the disadvantaged.

4

AND THAT'S THE WAY IT WAS
Mermelstein, Joanne and Paul Sundet
In Human Services in the Rural Environment Reader. David Bast, ed.
Madison: University of Wisconsin-Extension, Center for Social Service,
10-15, June 1976-May 1977.

The authors review briefly the history of rural social work and conclude
that even though the field is rediscovering truths of 50 years ago the
field is moving into new and unchartered areas today.

5
AN ANNOTATED BIBLIOGRAPHY ON RURAL SOCIAL WORK
Schultz, Carol M.
In Social Work in Rural Communities. Leon H. Ginsberg, ed.
New York: Council on Social Work Education, 121-30, 1976.

This annotated bibliography on rural social work was published in 1976.
Citations are separated into the following categories: communication and
helping patterns in communities, community development, projects in rural
areas, rural problems, and social aspects of rural community life.

6
AN APPROPRIATE ROLE FOR SOCIAL WORK: SMALL BUSINESS DEVELOPMENT IN THE
RURAL COMMUNITY
Deaton, Robert and Allen Bjergo
In 2nd National Institute on Social Work in Rural Areas Reader.
Edward B. Buxton, ed.
Madison: University of Wisconsin--Extension, Center for Social Service,
61-67, 1978.

The authors discuss the involvement of social workers in small business
development, an area not traditionally included in social work practice.
Drawing upon experiences in Montana, they demonstrate how rural social
workers can apply their skills in business development, and suggest several
general steps to be considered before establishing an enterprise.

7
BICULTURAL SOCIAL WORK AND ANTHROPOLOGY
Keller, Gordon K.
Social Casework, Vol. 53, 455-465, October 1972.

A field study of Navajos in Utah reveals many changes in their culture,
some direct and some indirect results of Anglo-American social welfare
programs. Social workers often become acculturating agents in their
work with minorities.

8
THE BSW DELIVERS SERVICE TO SMALL TOWN AMERICA
Johnson, Louise C.
In Human Services in the Rural Environment Reader. David Bast, ed.
Madison: University of Wisconsin-Extension, Center for Social Service,
21-27, May 1966 - June 1977.

The BSW is the primary social worker in small town rural America. With
this premise, the author discusses roles that a BSW may be expected to
fill and tasks related to those roles.

9

BUILDING RURAL CONTENT INTO UNDERGRADUATE CURRICULUM
Rasberry, Betty H.
In Social Work in Rural Areas: Preparation and Practice. Stephen Webster
and Ronald K. Green, eds.
Knoxville: The University of Tennessee, School of Social Work,
137-147, 1978.

This paper describes an accredited, undergraduate social work program at
the University of Tennessee at Marten. The program focus is on rural
social services.

10

A CASE FOR THE GENERALIST SOCIAL WORKER: A MODEL FOR SERVICE DELIVERY
IN RURAL AREAS
Hanton, Sharon
In Effective Models for the Delivery of Services in Rural Areas:
Implications for Practice and Social Work Education. Barry L. Locke
and Roger A. Lohmann, eds.
Morgantown: West Virginia University, 1978.

It is the purpose of this paper to focus on the generalist concept of
social work and its application within a rural multi-service agency. Areas
discussed are: the area representative model and its role in rural service
delivery; the generalist model within a rural multi-service center; and a
specific project now operating and using the generalist social worker in
a rural multi-service center.

11

CASEWORK IN AN IGLOO--ADAPTATION OF BASIC CASEWORK PRINCIPLES IN WORK
WITH ESKIMOS
Neville, Floyd J.
In Differential Diagnosis and Treatment in Social Work. F. J. Turner, ed.
New York: Free Press, 515-529, 1968.

Three years of research and practical field experience behind this commentary show why and how basic casework principles can and must be adapted
to the situation of the Eskimo.

12

LA CAUSA CHICANA. THE MOVEMENT FOR JUSTICE
Mangold, Margaret M., ed.
1972. ERIC: ED085133 .

The intent of this book is to present information about Chicanos to social
workers and members of other helping professions. Articles reflect the
perspectives of persons working in various settings, geographical regions,
and disciplines.

13
THE CHALLENGE OF THE COUNTRY AND THE UNDERGRADUATE CURRICULUM
Whitcomb, G. Robert and Augustus Rodgers
In Effective Models for the Delivery of Services in Rural Areas:
Implications for Practice and Social Work Education. Barry L. Locke and
Roger A. Lohmann, eds.
Morgantown: West Virginia University, 1978.

This paper discusses the evaluation of an undergraduate course entitled,
"Human Needs and Services in the Rural Community," offered in the Spring
Semester, 1977, by the University of South Carolina's College of Social
Work.

14
THE CHALLENGE IN RURAL SOCIAL WORK UNDERGRADUATE FIELD INSTRUCTION
Glosser, Ruth
In Social Work in Rural Areas: Preparation and Practice. Ronald K. Green
and Stephen A. Webster, eds.
Knoxville: The University of Tennessee, School of Social Work,
182-196, 1978.

This paper describes the development of an undergraduate field instruction
program at St. Francis College in rural Pennsylvania, analyzes some of the
characteristics which differentiate it from field instruction models serving urban areas, and explicates how the program has met area social
service needs by focusing on multiple and diversified placements.

15
CHANGING SOCIAL CHARACTERISTICS OF RURAL POPULATIONS
Demerath, N. J.
In Social Work in Rural Areas: Preparation and Practice. Ronald K. Green
and Stephen A. Webster, eds.
Knoxville: The University of Tennessee, School of Social Work,
18-23, 1978.

This paper examines some of the social changes in rural America and
briefly discusses the role of social workers in rural development.

16
A CLINICAL MODEL FOR RURAL PRACTICE
Nooe, Roger M.
In Social Work in Rural Areas: Preparation and Practice. Ronald K. Green
and Stephen A. Webster, eds.
Knoxville: The University of Tennessee, School of Social Work,
347-360, 1978.

This paper describes a short-term psychotherapeutic approach which is
applicable in rural settings.

17
COMMUNITY DEVELOPMENT AND SOCIAL WORK PRACTICE
Warren, Roland L.
New York: National Association of Social Workers, 1962.

These proceedings are from a workshop held in 1962 at the Florence Heller
Graduate School for Advanced Studies in Social Welfare, Brandeis University.

18
COMMUNITY ORGANIZATION AND THE OPPRESSED
Shaffer, Anatole
Journal of Education for Social Work, 8(3): 65-75, 1972.

A new approach to teaching community organization methods is developed.
The primary element is the consciousness of the worker and oppressed
sharing the goal of ending oppression.

19
COMMUNITY ORGANIZATION IN RURAL AREAS
Morrison, Jim
In Social Work in Rural Communities. Leon H. Ginsberg, ed.
New York: Council on Social Work Education, 57-67, 1978.

The author suggests particular skills necessary for effective community
organizing in rural areas. He offers some criticisms of radical and
confrontation approaches stemming from Alinsky-type models of practice.

20
COMMUNITY SOCIAL WORK IN A RURAL SETTING
Harmon, Dorothy R.
In Effective Models for the Delivery of Services in Rural Areas:
Implications for Practice and Social Work Education. Barry L. Locke and
Roger A. Lohmann, eds.
Morgantown: West Virginia University, 1978.

The author discusses the use of student field placements in the development
of an adult activity center for mentally retarded citizens in a rural
area. This rural situation offered new and innovative practicum experiences for prospective professionals, and meanwhile provided services to
the local community.

21
CONFIDENTIALITY: ISSUES AND DILEMMAS IN RURAL PRACTICE
Kirkland, Janet and Karen Irey
In 2nd National Institute on Social Work in Rural Areas Reader. Edward B.
Buxton, eds.
Madison: University of Wisconsin -- Extension, Center for Social Service,
142-150, 1978.

The authors propose "A new perspective on confidentiality and some practice
principles which may guide social workers toward . . . new standards,
particularly in a rural setting."

22

CONFIDENTIALITY: WHAT IS PRIVATE IN A RURAL AREA
Sherman, Joanna and Lucy Rowley
In 2nd Annual Northern Wisconsin Symposium on Human Services in the Rural
Environment Reader. David Bast and Julie Schmidt, eds.
Madison: University of Wisconsin-Extension, Center for Social Sci., 10-19, 1977.

The authors suggest redefinition of confidentiality for rural areas and
roles social workers can play to protect individual privacy.

23

CONTEXTUAL DIFFERENCE IN THE RURAL SOCIAL WORK ENVIRONMENT
Webster, Stephen and Paul Campbell
In 2nd Annual Northern Wisconsin Symposium on Human Services in the
Rural Environment Reader. David Bast and Julie Schmidt, eds.
Madison: University of Wisconsin - Extension, Center for Social Science,
2-9, 1977.

This paper reports the results of a survey of social workers who were asked
to identify major differences between urban and rural social work practice
environments.

24

CONTINUING EDUCATION AS PROBLEM-FOCUSED EXTENSION
Lauffler, Armand
Education for Social Work, 40-49, Fall 1972.

Continuing education programs are increasingly becoming problem focused.
Their activities may be as much oriented towards changing the ways in
which services are offered, resources allocated and policies determined,
as in improving practice behavior or upgrading practitioner skills. The
author discusses social work education within this framework.

25

CONTINUING EDUCATION FOR RURAL SOCIAL WORKERS - WISCONSIN STYLE
Bast, David
In Social Work in Rural Areas: Preparation and Practice. Ronald K. Green
and Stephen A. Webster, eds.
Knoxville: The University of Tennessee, School of Social Work.
213-223. 1978.

Wisconsin's approach to continuing education for rural social workers--
emphasizing localized formal and informal instruction, problem-solving
consultation, and practical research--is described.

26

THE COUNTRY MOUSE COMES INTO HER OWN
Davies, Joann F.
In Human Services in the Rural Environment Reader. David Bast, ed.
Madison: University of Wisconsin-Extension, Center for Social Science,
16-24, June 1976 - May 1977.

Some of the more important attributes of the social work professional in rural areas are described in this paper. Emphasis is particularly placed on autonomous practice and on "who you know."

27

COWBOY SOCIAL WORK: UNIQUE FEATURES OF SOCIAL SERVICE NEEDS IN THE RURAL WESTERN STATES
Deaton, Robert and Terry Mohr
Rural Social Work Annual Meeting
New York: Council on Social Work Education, February 27, 1977.

This article discusses features of the Rocky Mountain Region States. Features discussed are: geographic remoteness, energy demands, racial and ethnic features, and the implications for social work practice in the west.

28

THE CRACKER-BARREL CLASSROOM: PROGRAMMING FOR CONTINUING EDUCATION IN RURAL AREAS
Horejsi, Charles R. and Robert L. Deaton
In Social Work in Rural Areas: Preparation and Practice. Ronald K. Green and Stephen A. Webster, eds.
Knoxville: The University of Tennessee, School of Social Work. 197-212, 1978.

This paper describes common problems and issues related to programming for continuing education in a rural state along with efforts to deal with the problems. The "Cracker-Barrel" approach for continuing education, which has been successful in Montana, is discussed.

29

CURRICULUM FOR AREA AND COMMUNITY DEVELOPMENT
Longest, James W.
Paper presented at the Annual Meeting of the Rural Sociological Society. San Francisco, California, 1969.

Four stages of curriculum for area and community development are analyzed and described. These four stages are: 1) determination of educational objectives, 2) screening and selection, 3) organization of learning experience and 4) evaluation of effectiveness of learning experiences. Functions of professionals are discussed.

30

CURRICULUM DEVELOPMENT AND TRAINING IN THE MANAGEMENT OF RURAL YOUTH CARE SERVICES
St. Paul: University of Minnesota, Center for Youth Development and Research, 1976, 40 pp. NTIS/SHR-0002828.

The ultimate goal of the project was to enhance the quality of rural youth care services. Project objectives focused on curriculum development in the management of youth care systems in rural areas; training efforts in youth care for community caretakers; community service providers, parents, volunteers, adults, and youth; and education planning and resource development.

31

EDUCATION FOR SOCIAL WORK PRACTICE WITH AMERICAN FAMILIES. PART 1.
INTRODUCTORY TEXT, PART II. INSTRUCTOR'S MANUAL
Brown, E. F. and Timothy Shaughnessy
Tempe, Arizona: Arizona State University, School of Social Work.
American Indian Projects for Community Development, Training, and
Research, 1977.

The introductory text and instructor's manual serve several purposes in
social work training: 1) provide an introductory knowledge of diverse
lifeways of Southwest Indian tribes to help the practitioner become better
prepared to deal with the social problems of Indian children and families;
2) develop an understanding of Indian extended families, clan systems, and
tribal social networks and their impact upon tribal members' beliefs and
behavior, 3) relate social work practice concepts to serving Indian people;
4) provide an account of the unique federal-tribal relationship and its
significance on the lives of Indian people; and 5) provide information on
child/family welfare services available to Indians.

32

EDUCATION FOR SOCIAL WORK IN RURAL SETTINGS
Ginsberg, Leon
Social Work Education Reporter, 17(3): 28-61, 1969.

This article reviews crucial problems facing rural America, introduces
some generalizations about rural life and the implications for social
work practice, and outlines curriculum proposals for the education of
rural practitioners.

33

EDUCATIONAL ASSUMPTIONS FOR RURAL SOCIAL WORK
Southern Regional Education Board, Manpower Education and Training
Project, Rural Task Force
In Social Work in Rural Communities. Leon H. Ginsberg, ed.
New York: Council on Social Work Education, 41-44, 1976.

Assumptions for and characteristics of effective rural social work are
outlined by this task force.

34

EDUCATORS AND PRACTITIONERS WORK TOGETHER FOR PROFESSIONAL DEVELOPMENT OF
RURAL SOCIAL WORKERS
In 2nd National Institute on Social Work in Rural Areas Reader.
Edward B. Buxton, ed.
Madison: University of Wisconsin--Extension, Center for Social Service,
94-104, 1978.

This paper describes a small undergraduate Social Work program at Mars Hill
College in North Carolina which has begun the initial phase of training
social workers to provide service surrounding rural communities.

35

EFFECTIVE MODELS FOR THE DELIVERY OF SERVICES IN RURAL AREAS: IMPLICATIONS
FOR PRACTICE AND SOCIAL WORK EDUCATION
Locke, Barry L. and Roger Lohmann, eds.
Proceedings of the Third Annual National Institute on Social Work in
Rural Areas. West Virginia University, August 7-10, 1978.

This book contains selected papers presented at the Third National Institute on Social Work in Rural Areas. Subject areas included in the book
are services to rural aged, services to rural communities, correction
services in rural areas, services to rural families, health services in
rural areas, mental health services, and educating for social work
practice in rural areas.

36

ENHANCING SKILLS: ASSESSMENT, GOAL SETTING, AND CASE DOCUMENTATION
Kurtz, Gail and David Kurtz
Knoxville, Tennessee: University of Tennessee, School of Social Work,
Office of Continuing Social Work Education, 1979.

The stated purpose of this trainer's manual is "to assist workers in
enhancing their skills in the assessment and goal-setting phase of
service." The content is generic in that it can be applied to numerous
service settings. It is skill-oriented and provides participants
opportunities to practice and integrate the content in the classroom setting as well as in their agency settings.

37

AN EXAMINATION OF THE RELATIONSHIP OF RURAL SOCIOLOGY/RURAL SOCIAL WORK:
SHOULD A PRACTICE-THEORY COALITION BE CONSIDERED?
Martinez-Brawley, Emilia E.
In Social Work in Rural Areas: Issues and Opportunities.
Joseph Davenport, III, Judith A. Davenport and James R. Wiebler, eds.
Laramie: The University of Wyoming, Department of Social Work, 1980.

This paper examines the interconnections between the developments of rural
sociology and rural social work. The paper concludes with the suggestion
that the two fields should examine the possibilities for cooperative educational programs.

38

EXPECTATIONS OF THE BACCALAUREATE SOCIAL WORKER OF MOREHEAD STATE
UNIVERSITY
Richter, Loren
In Effective Models for the Delivery of Services in Rural Areas:
Implications for Practice and Social Work Education. Barry L. Locke and
Roger A. Lohmann, eds.
Morgantown: West Virginia University, 1978.

This article discusses the social work program of Morehead State University
from its inception to the present. Social Work is considered by
Morehead students to be one of the most demanding fields of study on campus.

39

HISTORY AND REMINISCENCE IN RURAL SOCIAL WORK: LESSONS FOR TRAINING AND
RETRAINING
Martinez-Brawley, Emilia
In Social Work in Rural Areas: Issues and Opportunities. Joseph Davenport,
III, Judith A. Davenport and James R. Wiebler, eds.
Laramie: The University of Wyoming, Department of Social Work, 1980.

This paper reviews periodical literature sources between the years 1929
and 1939 in order to identify and review issues related to rural social
work practice during that period. Many of the questions posed then are
similar to those posed now.

40

HOW PEOPLE GET POWER: ORGANIZING OPPRESSED COMMUNITIES FOR ACTION
Kahn, Si
New York: McGraw-Hill Book Company, 1970.

This book is a practical text written for community organizers working
in rural areas.

41

HUMAN SERVICES IN THE RURAL ENVIRONMENT READER
Bast, David, ed.
Madison: University of Wisconsin-Extension, Center for Social Service,
June 1976 - May 1977.

This text is a collection of readings dealing with social work and the
delivery of human services in rural areas.

42

IDENTIFYING THE STRUCTURE OF COMMUNITY POWER - SOME SUGGESTIONS FOR RURAL
SOCIAL WORKERS
Colliver, Mac
In 2nd National Institute on Social Work in Rural Areas Reader. Edward
B. Buxton, ed.
Madison: University of Wisconsin-Extension, Center for Social Service,
35-53, 1978.

This paper examines three aspects of community power: 1) the need for
community power structure information on the part of rural social workers
based upon the emerging rural social work literature; 2) the different
forms or structures of community power; and 3) information on the different approaches the rural social worker could use to identify those
key community influentials who could provide vital support for the community social delivery system.

43

IDENTIFYING TRAINING NEEDS AND DEVELOPING A TRAINING RESPONSE TO RURAL
SOCIAL WORKERS IN TITLE XX PROVIDER AGENCIES
Edwards, Richard, Gail Kurtz and Nancy S. Dickenson
In Social Work in Rural Areas: Issues and Opportunities. Joseph
Davenport, III, Judith A. Davenport and James R. Wiebler, eds.
Laramie: The University of Wyoming, Department of Social Work, 1980.

Describes a systematic assessment of training needs of Title XX provider agency personnel and the concomitant development of a comprehensive training program aimed at improving service delivery. The training project was carried on by the Office of Continuing Social Work Education at the University of Tennessee School of Social Work.

44
THE IMPROBABLE CHANGE AGENT AND THE PH.B.
Hanson, Mark
In Human Services in the Rural Environment Reader. David Bast, ed.
Madison: University of Wisconsin-Extension, Center for Social Service, 75-83, 1976-1977.

The author reviews a research experience with Native Americans while completing work on his doctoral studies. The unforgettable opportunity of working with impoverished Indians and the ability of one Indian to use bureaucracy rather than be used by it are highlighted in the paper.

45
INDIAN SELF-DETERMINATION: A DILEMMA FOR SOCIAL WORK PRACTICE
Brown, E. F.
In Mental Health Services and Social Work Education with Native Americans.
F. J. Pierce, ed.
Norman, Oklahoma: University of Oklahoma, School of Social Work, 1977.

The goals of several national policies and social service delivery systems often conflict with the goal of Indian self-determination. Schools of social work must train professionals to reflect the perspectives of American Indians with commitment to the self-determination of Indian communities.

46
ISSUES IN CAMPUS-BASED FIELD INSTRUCTION IN RURAL SOCIAL WORK EDUCATION
Mermelstein, Joanne and Paul Sundet
Paper presented at the Roundtable on Rural Social Work Education,
Council on Social Work Education, New Orleans, Louisiana, 1978.

This paper reviews nine issues most significant in the reinstatement of practicum in a practice profession to a role more compatible with the professional values and ideals of social work. The discussion is directed toward the rural educator/practitioner.

47
MAKING WAVES IN A SEA OF PEANUT BUTTER: IMPLICATIONS FOR SOCIAL WORK PRACTICE IN SPARSELY POPULATED, CONSERVATIVE AREAS
Whitaker, William H.
In Social Work in Rural Areas: Issues and Opportunities.
Joseph Davenport, III, Judith A. Davenport and James R. Wiebler, eds.
Laramie: The University of Wyoming, Department of Social Work, 194-204, 1980.

Discusses change related issues that were encountered by a coalition of Wyoming citizens who attempted to bring the Special Supplemental Food Program for Women, Infants and Children to their state.

48
MEETING THE CHALLENGE OF OFF-CAMPUS SOCIAL WORK STUDY PROGRAMS
Granger, Ben P.
In Social Work in Rural Areas: Issues and Opportunities.
Joseph Davenport, III, Judith A. Davenport and James R. Wiebler, eds.
Laramie: The University of Wyoming, Department of Social Work, 1980.

The purpose of this paper is to highlight the problem of extended study
in professional social work education and to present certain assumptions
and considerations that should be taken into account as one considers
this issue.

49
MENTAL HEALTH COURSES AS A FACILITATOR FOR CHANGE IN A RURAL COMMUNITY
Naftulen, Donald H., Frank A. Donnelly, and Patricia B. O'Halloran
Community Mental Health Journal, 10(3): 359-365, 1974.

This article presents the findings of a study of a university effort to
assist a rural community in developing a mental health educational
program for primary interveners within the community.

50
MENTAL HEALTH SERVICES: THE RURAL BSW'S
Myers, John P.
In Effective Models for the Delivery of Services in Rural Areas:
Implications for Practice and Social Work Education. Barry L. Locke and
Roger A. Lohmann, eds.
Morgantown: West Virginia University, 1978.

This paper discusses the use of BSW professionals in rural areas. It is
becoming abundantly clear that not only do BSW's implement the generalist
approach to practice, but their educational preparation and field learning experiences are expanding qualitatively.

51
A MODEL FOR RURAL FIELD INSTRUCTION: THE DELIVERY OF RURAL DEVELOPMENT
AND PREVENTIVE MENTAL HEALTH SERVICES THROUGH THE COOPERATIVE EXTENSION
SERVICE IN WEST VIRGINIA
Heady, Hilda and Jane Riffe
In Effective Models for the Delivery of Services in Rural Areas:
Implications for Practice and Social Work Education. Barry L. Locke and
Roger A. Lohmann, eds.
Morgantown: West Virginia University, 1978.

This paper describes a model of rural social work field instruction which
has developed as a result of faculty leadership and student resourceful-
ness and dedication and can be seen as a translation of the resource
capability within the WVU School of Social Work.

52

MSW AND BSW STUDENT PLACEMENTS IN RURAL COMMUNITIES
Victor, Polly N.
In Social Work in Rural Areas: Preparation and Practice. Ronald K. Green
and Stephen A. Webster, eds.
Knoxville: The University of Tennessee, School of Social Work,
175-181, 1978.

MSW and BSW generalists are being trained by the School of Social Work in
California, State University in Fresno. Models of rural field instruction
are discussed in this paper.

53

A MULTI-DISCIPLINARY SKILL DEVELOPMENT STRATEGY FOR RURAL AREAS
Clark, Frank
In 2nd National Institute on Social Work in Rural Areas Reader.
Edward B. Buxton, ed.
Madison: University of Wisconsin--Extension, Center for Social Service.
132-140, 1978.

The acquisition of functional skills and the use of interdisciplinary
collaboration have proven to be successful education strategies for
effective rural social work practice in service delivery.

54

NATIVE AMERICAN NON-INTERFERENCE
Goodtracks, Jimm G.
Social Work, 18(6): 30-34, November 1973.

The Native American principle of noninterference with others creates an
obstacle for social workers trying to practice 'intervention', but much
patience and respect for the principle can enable workers to be effective
in Indian communities.

55

NATIVE INDIAN ALCOHOLICS: ECOLOGICAL PERSPECTIVE AND LIFE MODEL OF PRACTICE
Suseelan, Madhan
In Effective Models for the Delivery of Services in Rural Areas:
Implications for Practice and Social Work Education. Barry L. Locke and
Roger A. Lohmann, eds.
Morgantown: West Virginia University, 1978.

The Native American could very well be the most deprived identifiable
group of American citizens. The author discusses prevalent concepts and
theories of alcoholism, practice models, and a life model.

56

A NEW EMPHASIS IN RURAL WELFARE
Neely, Carolyn
Social Work, 24(4): 335-337, 1979.

This article describes some experiences of a group of social work students
who spent several months working in the public welfare agency of one of
Georgia's poorest counties.

57
THE 1970'S AND CHANGING DIMENSIONS IN RURAL LIFE - IS A NEW PRACTICE MODEL
NEEDED?
Webster, Stephen A. and Paul M. Campbell
In Social Work in Rural Areas: Preparation and Practice. Ronald K. Green
and Stephen A. Webster, eds.
Knoxville: The University of Tennessee, School of Social Work, 75-94, 1978.

The authors review problems in rural areas and changes in local patterns
of service delivery and suggest a new practice model--the administration
and planning specialist--for the rural human service delivery system.

58
ONE EARTH, A CHANGING WORLD: GLOBAL PERSPECTIVES ON SOCIAL WORK EDUCATION
FOR RURAL PRACTICE
Zeglinski, Joan
In 2nd National Institute on Social Work in Rural Areas Reader
Edward B. Buxton, ed.
Madison: University of Wisconsin--Extension, Center for Social Service,
1-9, 1978.

The author examines how social work has addressed the problems of rural
areas. Special emphasis is placed upon the effectiveness and appropriate-
ness of social work education for rural practice in the past, present, and
future.

59
ORAL HISTORY AND SOCIAL WORK: A TIMELY MIX
Martinez-Brawley, Emilia
Human Services in the Rural Environment, 5(1): 21-22, 1980.

Training to apply oral history techniques in rural social work is recommended
in this article.

60
PERSPECTIVES ON THE MENTAL HEALTH OF RURAL BLACKS RELATED TO SOCIAL WORK
EDUCATION
Icard, Larry
Paper presented at the Council on Social Work Education, Annual Program
Meeting, Boston, Massachusetts, March 1979.

This paper attempts to describe selected sociocultural and sociostructural
conditions evidencing being endemic to rural Blacks. The selected conditions
are addressed as being significant for the mental health, and possible
mental health care needs of this sub-group.

61

PIONEER EFFORTS IN RURAL SOCIAL WELFARE: FIRSTHAND VIEWS SINCE 1908
Martinez-Brawley, Emilia E., ed.
University Park: Pennsylvania State University Press, 1979.

This collection of articles on the history of rural social work demonstrates
that the issues in organizing and delivering social services in rural
areas are not very new. The problems and service needs of rural people
and the nature, methods and training for rural practice are often quite
similar to those considered today.

62

PREPARING SOCIAL WORK STUDENTS IN OCCUPATIONAL HEALTH: ORGANIZING AROUND
BROWN LUNG
Jankovic, Joanne and David Dotson
In Effective Models for the Delivery of Services in Rural Areas:
Implications for Practice and Social Work Education. Barry L. Locke and
Roger A. Lohmann, eds.
Morgantown: West Virginia University, 1978.

During the past several years, there has been a small but stirring interest
within the helping professions in regard to problems of occupational
health and safety. Social workers, by and large, have not been involved
with efforts to intervene in these problems of the work place.

63

PREPARING SOCIAL WORKERS FOR PRACTICE IN RURAL SOCIAL SYSTEMS
Weber, Gwen K.
Journal of Education for Social Work, 12(3): 108-115, 1976.

This paper reviews the basic character of rural areas, the need for
systematic intervention and program development to alter social problems,
and the setting and concepts for rural social work practice.

64

PROFESSIONAL COMPETENCY, AUTONOMY, AND JOB SATISFACTION AMONG SOCIAL WORKERS
IN AN APPALACHIAN RURAL AREA
Boo, Sung L., Dong I. Kim and Alban Wheeler
In Effective Models for the Delivery of Services in Rural Areas:
Implications for Practice and Social Work Education. Barry L. Locke and
Roger A. Lohmann, eds.
Morgantown: West Virginia University, 1978.

The purpose of this paper is to explore the levels and sources of job satisfaction among social service workers in an Appalachian rural area. The
second and major research question in the study is addressed to the problem
of "What are the factors associated with social worker's job satisfaction?"

65
PROFESSIONAL RURAL SOCIAL WORK IN AMERICA
Swanson, Merwin
Agricultural History, 46(4): 515-526, 1972.

This paper presents a general description of the movement of rural social
work from 1900 to 1940. The author discusses rural problems and social
work's appraisal of them.

66
PROVIDING PUBLIC SOCIAL SERVICES IN NONMETROPOLITAN AREAS: EVALUATION
OF A NONTRADITIONAL MODEL
Daley, John Michael, Dennis L. Poole, and Riley Price
Paper Presented at the Fifth National Institute on Social Work in Rural
Areas. Burlington, Vermont, July 27-30, 1980.

This paper provides the first systematic evaluation of a three year,
federally funded demonstration project in southeastern Arizona, known as
the Satellite Diagnostic Social Service Centers Project. The evaluation
team is testing the concept of SDSSC as a mechanism to serve at a reasonable cost previously underserved or unserved rural communities.

67
REFLECTIONS ON FORTY YEARS WITH THE RURAL CHURCH MOVEMENT
Greene, Shirley
In Social Work in Rural Areas: Issues and Opportunities. Joseph
Davenport, III, Judith A. Davenport and James R. Wiebler, eds.
Laramie: The University of Wyoming, Department of Social Work, 173-180, 1980.

Presents some personal reflections on the history of the Rural Church
Movement, its problems and successes.

68
RURAL DEVELOPMENT AT THE SCHOOL OF SOCIAL DEVELOPMENT, UNIVERSITY OF
MINNESOTA - DULUTH
Musick, John
In 2nd Annual Northern Wisconsin Symposium on Human Services in the
Rural Environment Reader. David Bast and Julie Schmidt, eds.
Madison: University of Wisconsin - Extension, Center for Social Science,
147-151, 1977.

The model of rural development practiced by the School advocates that human
service professionals should attempt to develop new institutional potenti-
alities for human service delivery systems rather than merely perpetuating
the delivery of residual programs and services.

69
RURAL HEALTH CARE AND THE PARAPROFESSIONAL WORKER: IMPLICATIONS FOR
SOCIAL WORK EDUCATION
Gregg, Robin and Billy D. Horton
In Effective Models for the Delivery of Services in Rural Areas:
Implications for Practice and Social Work Education. Barry L. Locke and
Roger A. Lohmann, eds.
Morgantown: West Virginia University, 1978.

The authors discuss the background and rationale for the use of paraprofessionals, the use and abuse of paraprofessionals, the cult of profes-
sionalism, and the implications for social work education.

70
RURAL POVERTY IN THE UNITED STATES. A REPORT BY THE PRESDIENT'S NATIONAL
ADVISORY COMMISSION ON RURAL POVERTY
Wilber, George L. and C. E. Bishop, eds.
Washington, D.C.: U.S. Government Printing Office, May 1968. ERIC: ED078985.

Major topics covered in this report include: the structural changes taking
place in rural areas and the inter-relationship between rural and urban
American occupational mobility and migration; health care and family planning;
the developmental nature of agriculture and other natural resources; the
economics of poverty; and policies and programs to alter income distribution.

71
RURAL PRACTICE MODELS: COMMUNITY DEVELOPMENT
Omer, Salema
In Social Work in Rural Areas: Preparation and Practice. Ronald K. Green
and Stephen Webster, eds.
Knoxville: The University of Tennessee, School of Social Work, 107-137, 1978.

This paper discusses community development as a rural practice model for the
development of human resources. The author traces the history of community
development and relates theoretical concepts to the rural practice model.

72
RURAL SOCIAL WORK
Ginsberg, Leon
Encyclopedia of Social Work, Vol. 2, 1138-1144, 1971.

The author presents a generalist perspective on rural social work. Included are discussions of rural minority groups, rural social services,
and distinctive features of rural areas.

73
SCREENING EMOTIONALLY DISTURBED CHILDREN IN A RURAL SETTING
Schultz, Edward W., Anne B. Manton, and John A. Salvia
Exceptional Children, 39(2): 134-137, 1972.

This study was undertaken to ascertain the efficacy of screening procedures
in a two-county rural area in east central Illinois.

74
2ND ANNUAL NORTHERN WISCONSIN SYMPOSIUM ON HUMAN SERVICES IN THE RURAL
ENVIRONMENT READER
Bast, David and Julie Schmidt, eds.
Madison: University of Wisconsin-Extension, Center for Social Science, 1977.

These proceedings contain papers on rural issues including human services,
youth, aged, health, and service delivery.

75

SECOND NATIONAL INSTITUTE ON SOCIAL WORK IN RURAL AREAS READER
Buxton, Edward B.
Madison: University of Wisconsin -- Extension, Center for Social Service,
1978.

This selection of papers from the rural social work institute covers such
diverse topics as education for rural practice, homemaker services,
community development, business development, and the history of rural
social work.

76

SERVICE DELIVERY FOR MEXICAN-AMERICAN CHILDREN: COURSEBOOK
Tijerina, Andres A.
Austin: Texas State Department of Human Resources, 1978. ERIC: ED171448 .

A special curriculum to be used in training sessions on Mexican American
culture was developed to assist the Texas Department of Human Resources
personnel with service delivery for Mexican American children. The
curriculum is designed to heighten awareness in caseworkers and other
personnel on the cultural variables affecting their relationship with
Mexican American clients.

77

THE SILENT LANGUAGE
Hall, Edward T.
Greenwich, Connecticut: Fawcett Premier Books, 1959.

This text is an excellent source for workers in new or culturally different settings. The author discusses the components of culture and offers
suggestions on how to deal with cross-cultural differences.

78

SOCIAL DEVELOPMENT IN NONMETROPOLITAN AREAS
Johnson, Louise C.
In Social Work In Rural Areas: Preparation and Practice. Ronald K. Green
and Stephen Webster, eds.
Knoxville: The University of Tennessee, School of Social Work.
224-232, 1978.

Three modes of practice, including the settlement house, social goals, and
locality development, are synthesized into one model, and some implications for rural social work practice are discussed.

79

SOCIAL WORK CONTINUING EDUCATION FOR RURAL AREAS: BEGINNING WHERE
GENERALIST PREPARATION ENDS
Deaton, Robert
Roundtable Discussion Paper Presented at the Council on Social Work
Education, Annual Program Meeting, February 26, 1978.

The author uses prevailing ideas of generalist social work and briefly
applies them to continuing education efforts for rural practice.

80
SOCIAL WORK EDUCATION FOR AMERICAN INDIANS
Compton, John H.
Denver: University of Denver, Center for Social Research and Development,
September 1976.

This document surveys social work education as it pertains to American
Indians. Special emphasis is given to relating Indian Child Welfare to
social work education for American Indians.

81
SOCIAL WORK EDUCATION FOR PRACTICE IN RURAL AREAS: DIRECTIONS FOR THE
FUTURE
Nooe, Roger and Joanne Jankovic
Unpublished paper presented at the Council on Social Work Education,
Annual Program Meeting, Boston, March 1979.

In this paper the authors demonstrate how social work education can be
instrumental in developing opportunities for rural social work manpower
and rural services for: innovative deinstitutionalization programs,
health services, legal assistance programs, and social service programs
funded by unions and other labor-advocacy organizations.

82
SOCIAL WORK EDUCATION FOR RURAL PROGRAM DEVELOPMENT
Mermelstein, Joanne and Paul Sundet
In Social Work in Rural Communities. Leon H. Ginsberg, ed.
New York: Council on Social Work Education, 15-27, 1976.

The authors describe social work education for rural program development,
stemming mostly from their experiences in rural Missouri. They discuss
the generalist model and its application to classroom content and field
instruction in rural social work education.

83
SOCIAL WORK WITH NATIVE AMERICANS
Lewis, Ronald and Man K. Ho
Social Work, 20(5): 379-382, 1975.

Describes how social work techniques, to be effective, must vary with the
distinctive characteristics of Native Americans.

84
SOCIAL WORK IN RURAL AREAS: ISSUES AND OPPORTUNITIES
Davenport, Joseph, III, Judith A. Davenport and James R. Wiebler, eds.
Laramie: The University of Wyoming, Department of Social Work, 1980.

Proceedings from the Fourth National Institute on Social Work in Rural Areas
held in Laramie, Wyoming from July 29 to August 1, 1979. Content areas
include rural culture, boom towns, health, aging, mental health, education
and training and service delivery.

85
SOCIAL WORK IN RURAL AREAS: PREPARATION AND PRACTICE
Green, Ronald K. and Stephen A. Webster, eds.
Knoxville: The University of Tennessee, School of Social Work, 1978.

This document consists of papers presented at the First National Institute
on "Social Work in Rural Areas," at the University of Tennessee School of
Social Work, Knoxville, Tennessee, July 13-16, 1976. The document reflects
the most comprehensive package of materials for training in rural social
work preparation and practice.

86
THE SOCIAL WORKER IN THE RURAL COMMUNITY MENTAL HEALTH CENTER
Wagenfeld, Morton O. and Stanley S. Robin
In Social Work in Rural Communities. Leon H. Ginsberg, ed.
New York: Council on Social Work Education, 69-83, 1976.

The themes in this paper include: rural mental health and social problems,
characteristics of rural community mental health centers (CMHCs),
characteristics of social workers, social workers as community mental
health workers, and social workers in rural CMHCs.

87
A SPECIALIST-GENERALIST MODEL OF SOCIAL WORK PRACTICE FOR CONTEMPORARY
RURAL AMERICA
Gruss, Ann, et al.
In Social Work in Rural Areas: Preparation and Practice. Ronald K. Green
and Stephen A. Webster, eds.
Knoxville: The University of Tennessee, School of Social Work, 95-106, 1978.

A discussion of the specialized generalist model for the training of rural
social workers is presented. The need for an integrated model of practice
for working with individuals and families, delivering services, and
effecting social policies is argued by the authors of this paper.

88
STUDY OF EDUCATIONAL NEEDS: SOCIAL WORK TRAINING FOR INDIANS IN ARIZONA
Hill, Bernard and G. Donald Polenz
Tempe: Arizona State University, School of Social Work, 1971.

This exploratory study is based on data gathered from persons involved in
planning, directing and carrying out welfare services to the Navajo
people. The findings have relevance to the format and method of social
work insturction.

89
A SYSTEMS APPROACH TO RURAL COMMUNITIES
Oates, Janice
In Human Services In the Rural Environment Reader. David Bast, ed.
Madison: University of Wisconsin-Extension, Center for Social Service,
67-74, 1976-1977.

This paper discusses the systems approach and demonstrates that it is applicable to social workers who have roles in rural areas.

90
A TEACHING MODEL FOR RURAL FIELD INSTRUCTION
Mermelstein, Joanne and Pual Sundet
In Social Work in Rural Areas: Preparation and Practice. Ronald K. Green and Stephen A. Webster, eds.
Knoxville: The University of Tennessee, School of Social Work, 161-174, 1978.

In the rural context there lies a variety of educational experiences ranging from individual social treatment to program planning and organizational development. The authors examine specific field education models which are suited for this range of experience.

91
TOWARD A CONCEPTUALIZATION OF NATURAL HELPING
Patterson, Shirley L.
ARETE, 4(2): 1977.

This research study demonstrates that informal, unorganized networks exist in small towns and rural communities. These networks cannot be duplicated; they should be nurtured and extended, rather than supplanted by professional practice.

92
TRAINING HELPERS IN RURAL MENTAL HEALTH DELIVERY
Kelley, Verne R., et al.
Social Work, 22(3): 229-232, 1977.

Two training programs in rural Iowa demonstrated that community helpers can be trained to function effectively in rural mental health service delivery. These programs are described in this article.

93
TRAINING FOR RURAL SOCIAL WORK
Smick, A. A.
Sociology and Social Research, Vol. 32, 538-544, 1973.

This article highlights the short distance traveled in the development of rural social work programs since the writing of the article in 1937

94
TRIBAL SOCIAL WORKER--A CHALLENGE TO CREATIVITY
Lewis, Ronald
In Mental Health Services and Social Work Education with Native Americans, F. J. Pierce, ed.
Norman: University of Oklahoma, School of Social Work, 1977.

The author examines whether it is possible for a social worker, who is normally bound by a code of ethics, formalism and rigid bureaucratic rules, to fulfill the role of "helper," "facilitator" and "advocate" in Indian communities. The social worker must work within the framework of Indian self-determination, and function within tribal expectations of the social worker role.

95
THE USE OF CLUSTERS AND PRECEPTORS IN THE ORGANIZATION AND DEVELOPMENT OF A STATEWIDE PRACTICUM PROGRAM
Tolliver, Lennie-Marie P.
In 2nd National Institute on Social Work in Rural Areas Reader.
Edward B. Buxton, ed.
Madison: University of Wisconsin--Extension, Center for Social Service, 54-60, 1978.

The use of clusters, cluster coordinators and preceptors in the organization and development of a social work practicum program in the predominantly rural state of Oklahoma are described.

96
USING THE BSW TO DELIVER HEALTH RELATED SOCIAL SERVICES IN RURAL AREAS
Davenport, Joseph and Judith Ann Davenport
Paper presented at the Second National Institute on Social Work in Rural Areas, Madison, Wisconsin, July 19, 1977, 16 pp. NTIS/PB-279 842/9ST.

The effective delivery of health-related social services in rural areas by persons with a bachelor's degree in social work is explored. The social work program at Mississippi State University is discussed. It is concluded that its model for delivering health-related social services is viable for any rural area.

97
USING EDUCATION FOR SOCIAL CHANGE WITH RESERVATION INDIANS
Askerooth, Gary and Barbara King
In Social Work in Rural Areas: Issues and Opportunities.
Joseph Davenport, III, Judith A. Davenport and James R. Wiebler, eds.
Laramie: The University of Wyoming, 1980.

Discusses how the School of Social Development at the University of Minnesota - Duluth implemented a change-oriented education to deal with political issues in Reservation communities. An assessment of the program's success is also given.

98
UTILIZATION OF SCHOOL SOCIAL WORK STUDENTS AS RISK-TAKING CHANGE AGENTS
Jankovic, Joanne and Richard Anderson
In 2nd National Institute on Social Work in Rural Areas Reader.
Edward B. Buxton, ed.
Madison: University of Wisconsin--Extension, Center for Social Service, 76-82, 1978.

An educational program at the University of Georgia School of Social Work is described. The model utilized by the program is unique in that students work within their home school districts and are educated as innovative, risk-taking change agents.

99
WHITE WORKER-MINORITY CLIENT
Mizio, Emelicia
Social Work, 17(3): 82-86, 1972.

The social work profession must increase its efforts to eliminate the blocks to effective interaction between the white worker and minority client if its professed goal of serving all clients effectively is to be taken seriously.

100
WORKING WITH PEOPLE IN COMMUNITY ACTION, AN INTERNATIONAL CASEBOOK FOR TRAINED COMMUNITY WORKERS AND VOLUNTEER COMMUNITY LEADERS
King, Clarence
New York: The Association Press, 190 pp.

This casebook stresses cooperation with community workers and leaders. Separate sections deal with means of developing rapport with host communities, assessing felt needs, initiating community action, planning and conducting committees, organizing and using community and neighborhood councils, providing field work and discussion-oriented training for new community workers, and meeting various psychological and sociocultural problems in community action.

101
YESTERDAY'S PEOPLE
Weller, Jack E.
Lexington: University of Kentucky Press, 1965.

Based on thirteen years experience as a missionary in southern Appalachia, the author describes the life of the mountaineer. The book is particularly useful to social workers by aiding them in their understanding of the mountaineers' family and social life.

INDEX OF AUTHORS*

*In this Index references are cited only once, even though some appear several times in the body of the text.

About the Author

DENNIS L. POOLE is Assistant Professor at the School of Social
Work, Arizona State University, where he serves as Chair of
the Social Policy and Services Curriculum Sequence. He is
also the Director of the Multi-Cultural Rural Mental Health
Prevention Project, and Coordinator of the Rural Social Work
Specialization.

Dr. Poole specializes in research on the social problems and
service needs of rural families and communities. He has forth-
coming articles in RURAL SOCIOLOGY and HUMAN ORGANIZATION.

Dr. Poole holds a B.A. from St. Anselm's College, an M.S.W.
from West Virginia University, and a Ph.D. from Brandeis
University.